The American Evangelicals, 1800-1900

The American Evangelicals, 1800 - 1900

An Anthology

edited by

William G. McLoughlin

GLOUCESTER, MASS.

PETER SMITH

1976

THE AMERICAN EVANGELICALS, 1800–1900

Introduction, editorial notes, and compilation
copyright © 1968 by William G. McLoughlin.

First HARPER TORCHBOOK edition published 1968 by
Harper & Row, Publishers, Incorporated,

Library of Congress Catalog Card Number: 68-26894.

Reprinted 1976, by Permission of
Harper and Row, Publishers, Inc.

ISBN 0-8446-0793-2

Contents

Introduction
The American Evangelicals: 1800–1900

William G. McLoughlin

The story of American Evangelicalism is the story of America itself in the years 1800 to 1900, for it was Evangelical religion which made Americans the most religious people in the world, molded them into a unified, pietistic-perfectionist nation, and spurred them on to those heights of social reform, missionary endeavor, and imperialistic expansionism which constitute the moving forces of our history in that century. Both as motivation and as rationale evangelical religion lay behind the concept of rugged individualism in business enterprise, laissez faire in economic theory, constitutional democracy in political thought, the Protestant ethic in morality, and the millennial hope in the manifest destiny of white, Anglo-Saxon, Protestant America to lead the world to its latter-day glory. The national anthem of the evangelical movement was "The Battle Hymn of the Republic," whose words, now empty symbols, once surged with the emotional fervor of three whole generations of pious Americans.

The history of Evangelicalism in America must be told on three levels: first as philosophy, second as theology, and third as social history. As philosophy it is the story of the permeation of nineteenth-century thought with the ideas and system of the Scottish Common Sense School. As theology it is the story of the decline of Calvinism, the Protestant Counter Reformation against deism, and the emergence of a new theological consensus on Arminian principles which prevailed between the Second Great Awakening and the rise of Modernism. As social history it is the story of the final triumph of voluntarism over establishmentarianism and the rise of a new revivalistic religion which was as interdenominational in its pattern as the moral reform crusades and benevolent associations which it spawned to purify the nation and redeem the world.

That Evangelicalism was the pervasive system behind American philosophic thought in the nineteenth century can be demonstrated by examining the principal textbooks of moral philosophy, moral science, and political economy used in the colleges and written by the leading college presidents from the days of John Witherspoon at Princeton to Noah Porter at Yale. The course in moral philosophy was the capstone of every college student's career and its principles stemmed directly from the writings of Francis Hutcheson, Thomas Reid, Dugald Stewart, Thomas Brown, and James Beattie who had, since 1750, been busily at work in Scotland creating what came to be known as the Scottish School of Realism. Its prime purpose was to counter the skepticism, atheism, and infidelity of the Age of Reason by redefining the sensational philosophy of John Locke in terms which were just as reasonable but eminently more Christian than anything concocted by the deistic and rationalistic writers of that century.

The American college presidents, most of them ordained evangelical ministers, who taught these compulsory courses of Moral Philosophy found the Scottish philosophers useful because they provided irrefutable proof of the existence of God against the claims of skeptics and because in answering these skeptics they provided equally sound evidence for the truths of evangelical religion as found in Scripture. Reacting against the empirical psychology and epistemology of Locke, the Scottish philosophers derived proof of God's moral laws not only from the design of Nature but also from man's consciousness or common sense of his own frailty, immorality, and spiritual necessities. It was from their emphasis upon "common sense" in refuting Berkeleyan idealism and Humean skepticism that these philosophers acquired their name.

The Scottish School of Common Sense Realism held that from his own innate common sense man could "intuitively" derive, beyond the shadow of a doubt, the validity of such abstract ideas as immortality, the existence of the soul, and the concept of rewards and punishments after death. The Scottish philosophers claimed to be using an empirical or inductive method of deriving the truth of these moral laws because they were scientifically observing men's inner consciousness (the working of the faculties of the mind) just as astronomers or biologists scientifically observed the external world. Newtonian science had demonstrated the architectural design of the Universe, thereby making the existence of a Great Architect or Creator "self-evident." His benevolence toward His creation and creatures, particularly man, could logically be deduced not only from "the natural order of things" which provided man with food, shelter and other creature comforts for his survival and advancing civilization, but also by His having imbedded in man certain instinctive affections or feelings. But to the Scottish philosophers the three most important of God's gifts to man were the social affections, which made men want and need to live in groups, the moral faculty or "moral sense," commonly called conscience, by which man derived his feelings of right and wrong, guilt and remorse, and the power of reasoning by which man could, on the basis of experience and consciousness, intuit God's omniscience, justice, mercy and deduce His natural laws regarding economics, sociology, psychology, and political science.

Underlying all Scottish thinking was the conviction that God had implanted in man a sense of self-love or the capacity for pleasure and pain by which man learned to pursue happiness and avoid misery. Moral Philosophy thus defined itself in American textbooks as the science by which men learned to pursue happiness or moral well-being by learning those fundamental laws of duty to which they must conform in their personal life, their family, their occupations, and their government. Or, as Francis Wayland put it in his famous textbook, The Elements of Moral Science (1835), "Moral Philosophy or Ethics is the science which clarifies and illustrates moral law" just as physics illustrates the physical laws of the universe. If it turned out, as of course it did, that these moral laws which men derived from experience and common sense, were in conformity with the moral and spiritual laws revealed in the Bible, this merely proved how high a stage of scientific development mankind had at last reached in the Anglo-Saxon Protestant nations of Britain and America. And since it also turned out that these nations, by virtue of their dedication to evangelical religion, had in fact created a set of social and political institutions which were almost perfectly in accord with God's laws of moral philosophy, this could only mean that the Anglo-Saxons were somehow chosen of God.

Inasmuch as moral philosophy, as Francis Hutcheson said, was "to direct men to that course of action which tends most effectually to promote their greatest happiness and perfection as far as it can be done by observation and conclusions discoverable from the constitution of Nature without the aids of supernatural religion," the courses in Moral Philosophy did not inculcate any particular religious doctrines, dogmas, or creeds. Even a deist like Thomas Jefferson, or a Unitarian like William Ellery Channing could and did accept the teachings of the Scottish School in regard to moral duty and political economy. Defenders of the predominant Calvinistic Christian orthodoxy in America in the early years of the nineteenth century consequently emphasized those premises of this school which substantiated their tenets against the onslaughts of infidelity. By 1830 they had succeeded so well that deism was virtually extinct in America and rational Christianity (as Unitarianism described itself), which Jefferson fondly expected to be the religion of the new republic, was thoroughly on the defensive where it remained for the rest of the century. Given the choice between deistic rationalism and common sense piety, the Americans chose the latter and America was saved for Evangelicalism. But it was not an easy victory.

In winning this battle the Calvinists had to make considerable concessions to the rationalists' arguments. They had, for example, to concede that God was benevolent and not wrathful, merciful not stern, reasonable not mysterious; that he worked by means and not by miracles, that man was active not passive in his salvation, that grace was not arbitrarily or capriciously dispensed like the royal prerogative of a sovereign but offered freely to all men as the gift of a loving Father to his children; that God wants men to help themselves not to wait on Him, and that He is a God of love not a God to be feared. In short, the clergy of America virtually had to abandon the Calvinistic conception of God's relationship to man, which had dominated American thought through the Colonial era, and to supplant it with an Arminian conception. The stormy period of reorientation is known to historians as the Second Great Awakening. It lasted from 1800 to 1835, and its chief engineers were

Nathaniel W. Taylor, Lyman Beecher, Albert Barnes, and Charles Grandison Finney.

In the process of reinterpreting Calvinism the modifiers had to fight on two fronts. On one side they faced the rationalists and infidels; on the other the neo-Edwardsean hyper-Calvinists and Presbyterian die-hards who saw every doctrinal revision as heresy. In this process of theological reorientation many drastic revisions in theology and church practice occurred which were indeed heretical even by evangelical Calvinist standards: the followers of Alexander Campbell and Barton W. Stone on the southwestern frontier broke off from the Presbyterian Church to form the radical new sects called the Christians and the Disciples; the Baptists were riven by the schism of the "Freewillers," and many others in their ranks followed Elhanan Winchester, one of their chief spokesmen, into the Universalist camp; the Congregationalists were divided by the Unitarian movement, and the rising tide of Methodism, based frankly on the Arminian doctrines of John Wesley, made great inroads into all the older denominations and particularly into the Episcopal Church in the South.

By 1835, however, Calvinism had been modified so much that the distinction between Calvinism and Arminianism was minimal. The famous Presbyterian schism of 1837 dramatized but could not stem this trend. By 1843 the Rev. Robert F. Baird, an eminent Presbyterian spokesman, calmly classified all American denominations under the two headings, "Evangelical" and "Unevangelical," merely noting that the former were divided on a historical basis between Evangelical Calvinists and Evangelical Arminians. Other ostensible Calvinists, like Albert Barnes, preferred to divide them into "hierarchical" and "evangelical" denominations, noting that "There is a spirit in this land which requires that the gospel shall depend for its success" not upon the nonessentials of church liturgy or polity "but on solemn appeals to the reason, the conscience, the immortal hopes and fears of men attended by the holy influences of the Spirit of God." Evangelical religion, despite its increasing fragmentation into denominations during the nineteenth century, prided itself on its interdenominational fraternalism. Which was another way of saying that after 1800 America ceased to have any systematic theology or creedalism which could be defined as orthodoxy in any denomination. Lyman Beecher's famous statement of "The Faith Once Delivered to the Saints" (1823) may be taken as the essence of the Evangelical creed so far as it had one: Belief on faith alone in "the great Christian fundamentals" of the miraculous birth, death, and resurrection of Jesus to save men from damnation was the only essential element in Evangelical theology.

The theological controversies in the rise of Evangelicalism involved a redefinition of all the famous five points of Calvinism, but the arguments chiefly centered upon the atonement and the freedom of the will. The problem was to overcome the criticism of deists like Thomas Paine and Ethan Allen that God as defined in Calvinist theology was a cruel, merciless tyrant who enjoyed condemning innocent children to hellfire; who angrily dangled sinners over the pit of hell like loathsome spiders; who condemned millions to eternal torment and admitted to Heaven only a pitiful few called "the predestined elect"; who commanded men to live up to His moral laws but left them so totally depraved since Adam's fall that they never could do so without His help, and who sent His innocent Son to death to pay the debt of sinful men.

One means by which the Calvinists in New England countered these criticisms was to evolve a new theory of the atonement, called "the moral government theory," which declared that Jesus' death was a proof of the justice and morality of God's government not of its cruel injustice. Since God could not leave sin unpunished or reward sinners in rebellion against his government with salvation and still maintain the moral order of the universe, Christ's offer of atonement was necessary to satisfy the claims of moral order. The atonement, properly construed, said Nathaniel W. Taylor in the lectures on moral government which he delivered to a generation of divinity students at Yale, was an act of justice by "a perfect moral governor"; and justice in this case "is a benevolent disposition to maintain his authority as the necessary means of the highest good of his kingdom." The atonement was thus an act of benevolence for it enabled God to pardon sinners who accepted Christ's sacrifice on faith, thereby maintaining the justice and highest good of divine government even though sinners themselves were incapable of paying the just penalty for their transgressions.

But Taylor's most important contribution to the evolution of Evangelicalism was his use of the Scottish common sense philosophy in order to redefine Jonathan Edwards' theory of the freedom of the will. Edwards and his disciples, the neo-Edwardseans or Hopkinsians, followed a strict Lockean theory of psychology which described the will of man as motivated by the understanding and the understanding as motivated directly by external perceptions. Edwards accepted Locke's view that man seeks to gain pleasure and avoid pain, but according to Edwards man's understanding of pleasure and pain is extremely short-sighted and selfish. Even apparent altruism is generally, if not always, motivated by our selfish desire to gain our way to Heaven out of fear of Hell. True virtue or holiness, said Edwards, means to act out of "disinterested benevolence toward Being in general." But according to Edwards no man was capable of acting upon motives of disinterested benevolence until God transformed his will by returning to his soul that taste or sensibility for divine things which the human race lost with Adam's original sin. Since Edwards and his followers implied that the will was motivated upon a virtual stimulus-response basis to carnal self-gratification, the rationalists maintained that Calvinism made God, not man, the author of sin. In addition, they said, the doctrine of predestination which instructed men to wait passively upon God's foreordained grace produced a fatalistic view of life contradictory to the Biblical commands to "strive to enter in at the gate" and to "make yourselves a new heart and a new spirit for why will ye die."

Taylor, following the Scottish philosophers, redefined Edwards' Lockean philosophy in terms of man's self-love. "On the authority of Dugald Stewart," he said, "we use the term self-love to denote the simple desire of happiness." Self-love is "an essential attribute of a rational and even a sensitive nature." It is not simply selfishness, as the neo-Edwardseans implied, but rather a sensitivity in human nature which leaves man open to moral appeals; it is a propensity or inclination imbedded in the will or heart which yearns, however faintly, for otherworldly pleasures as well as for carnal pleasures. This human propensity, though feeble, can be addressed by the preacher seeking to persuade men to save their souls. Without this propensity man would not be a morally responsible or free agent. God therefore endowed man with self-love in order to make him susceptible to His Word. Assuming, as the rationalists and Scottish philosophers both did, that God is benevolent, He must have devised some means by which He could communicate with his creatures and hold them responsible for their sins if they failed to heed Him.

Or, to put it another way, since God is the moral governor of the universe, men live under a system of moral influence. God seeks by all possible means to lead us into righteousness. He desires our happiness as part of the ultimate goodness and happiness of His kingdom. All men share a common sense or consciousness of their freedom to choose, and it is this feeling that we are free which constitutes our sense of moral responsibility. To this common consciousness of our freedom and to this moral sense of our guilt in not acting rightly, the preacher or revivalist may address his pleas for repentance and conversion expecting that we will be capable of responding to them. Taylor believed and preached that it was the sinner's duty to make himself a new heart. His sermon on "Immediate Repentance Practicable" stated that "the sinner is authorized to regard immediate compliance with the terms of salvation practicable." It was absurd, contrary to common sense, for anyone to argue that God commanded men to do what they were unable to do: "To talk of a work [conversion] which God only performs, as my duty, is out of the question." As a free moral agent man "has power to perform every duty which God requires."

Far from creating a fatalistic system God has ordained a carefully constructed system of means and ends commensurate with moral government and moral responsibility. An effective, capable minister learns how to work within the means which God has provided. His appeals to the moral sensibilities of his congregation will succeed if he operates according to God's spiritual laws of salvation. The world is not therefore a vale of tears where most are predestined to hellfire, but a valley of hope in which men have the freedom to work out their own salvation.

To a certain extent man's feelings, or propensities, or inclinations toward virtue can be strengthened by training in moral philosophy. Through the study of moral science we come to know the moral laws of our duty just as through reading the Bible we know God's revealed moral law. The purpose of government and social institutions is to compel us to act in conformity with these laws of duty even when we may not wish to. That is why God ordained government. The rationalists pushed this matter too far, however. They believed that moral training and the habits of morality inculcated by education and laws would enable men to develop sufficient self-discipline to overcome their selfish propensities. Or as the Unitarians put it, man being a reasonable animal, desiring his own ultimate happiness, and knowing the reasonableness of God's law could cultivate sufficient strength of character through education and training to assure his own salvation without any miraculous help from God. To them it seemed unreasonable that God would design the moral laws of his universe so carefully and yet, in the crucial matter of conversion, require the supernatural injection of His power into the natural world in order to save a man's soul.

This graceless theory of salvation the Evangelicals called Pelagianism and fought as the worst of heresies. The Bible teaches that all men are sinners who fall short of the glory of God and no amount of education, or mere intellectual knowledge or moral training, can ever overcome man's natural inclination to choose the short-range selfish pleasures of this world whenever he is faced with a choice. The human will was too weak, as a result of original sin, ever to control its bad impulses. Men keep smoking and drinking even when they know it might kill them, just as they give way to their worst impulses of lust, anger, power, and pride despite the still, small voice of conscience which tells them such acts are sinful. And being thus in bondage to Satan, they do not readily heed the minister's warnings to repent and seek salvation. As Taylor put it, men themselves had the *power* to act rightly but it is a *certainty* that until they underwent a miraculous change of heart they would never use that power to act virtuously. We are physically able but morally unable to obey God. Hence we may be said to be totally depraved even though we have free will.

Despite his modifications of Edwardsean theology Taylor thus seemed to be maintaining the doctrines of Calvinism which he professed to adhere to. But his departure from them became evident when he discussed the act of conversion and how it would be achieved. For having admitted that men were so constituted that their self-love can be appealed to and that their inclination to act rightly is subject to moral suasion by the preacher, Taylor had also to admit that the role of the preacher was to press the Word of God and the glory of God so forcefully upon the moral sensibilities of the sinner that he would understand the superior happiness to be obtained by following God's laws and would repent of his sins. The power of God's Word applied energetically and unremittingly to the human heart can make it *see* and *feel* a *sense* of divine reality. A well-preached sermon can touch the heart, break down the sinful will, and lay the sinner prostrate before God's mercy. Thus revivalism became the key to the new Evangelical message. Lyman Beecher and Charles Grandison Finney took Taylor's theory and put it into practice. And the proof of this theory of moral suasion was found in the results of their revivalism.

Of course Evangelical Christianity insisted that conversion was ultimately the work of God not of man. But man can become the proximate cause of his own salvation. He can begin the process which will lead directly to it. He can repent, believe, throw himself upon God's mercy and ask God to help him. Repentance does not compel God to save a man, but, said Taylor, we have "ample warrant" through the promises in the gospel, to believe that our "compliance with the terms of salvation" will induce God's compliance. The process of conversion thus became a shared act, a complementary relationship. Man striving and yearning; God benevolent and eager to save; the sinner stretching out his hands to receive the gift of grace held out by a loving God. This belief in man's free will or his partial power to effect his own salvation had in earlier Calvinist days been condemned as the heresy of Arminianism. For this reason most nineteenth-century ministers preferred to call themselves Evangelicals. They avoided creeds, doctrines, and dogmas and concentrated upon the practical aspects of soul saving. Evangelicalism was in its way a very pragmatic theology.

The inevitable result of this Arminianized Calvinism was a new emphasis upon revival preaching. Finney's contribution to the evolution of Evangelicalism lay in his outlining more starkly and scientifically than Taylor, Barnes, or Beecher, the divine laws by which God operated in revivals. He also developed new measures or techniques (called by the rationalists "revival machinery") which laid the basis of modern revivalism. Indirectly he was responsible for the development of a corps of professional evangelists especially gifted and experienced in these techniques who traveled around helping less gifted preachers to add new members to their churches and to revive the fervor of old ones, a practice which continues to this day in the work of men like Billy Graham.

Rationalists had ridiculed revivals ever since Edwards' day as mere emotional displays, the work of religious demagogues who stirred up the "animal affections" of their auditors and pretended that the resulting hysteria was a divine manifestation of the Spirit. Edwards had tried to answer these criticisms but his Calvinistic rationale for revivalism had been unconvincing. Finney, however, relying upon the concessions which Evangelicalism had made to natural law, convinced most Americans that "new measures" and "protracted meetings" were "the divinely appointed means" by which God chose to transform the souls of Americans en masse. Far from being miraculous "showers of blessing" sent mysteriously by God at His whim, revivals could be "promoted" by anyone acquainted with the spiritual laws governing them. The laws of psychology, human and divine, were now so clearly understood, Finney said, that ministers no longer had to "pray down" a revival but could "work one up" whenever they chose.

Finney, though originally a Presbyterian, also helped to bring into American Evangelicalism the doctrine of perfectionism which he found so appealing in Wesleyan Methodism. As professor of theology at Oberlin after 1835, Finney told his students that men could grow in grace until they reached a state of virtual sinlessness. Somehow the power of conversion no longer seemed sufficient to produce the exalted state of Christian life demanded by Evangelical pietism. This doctrine of sanctification or holiness as a kind of second conversion or "higher blessing" which the Holy Spirit granted to the more devout saints never became central to Evangelicalism but the principle of growing in grace or aspiring to "likeness to God" was merely a more respectable version of it. Like his open rejection of the Westminster Confession of faith, Finney's perfectionism indicated how thin the line had become between Evangelical Calvinists and Evangelical Arminians by 1835.

Another aspect of this perfectionist impulse within Evangelicalism was the conviction that God's revelation was progressive and that Christianity was the religion of progress. "We take the Christian religion as we find it," President Noah Porter of Yale told his classes in Moral Science, "and compare it with the other theories which preceded and followed it," and we find that "it is the only system that provides for progress. . . . Whatever can be discovered by science concerning man's relations, whether public or private, will and must be used in its service." In the heyday of Evangelical religion there was no significant conflict between religion and science, for all scientific discoveries ultimately testified to the glory of God, unveiling new aspects of his architectural skill and benevolent intent. Every scientist sought to harmonize his findings with Evangelical truth because the truth of his discovery lay in its harmony with the known laws of moral philosophy and of revelation. It would be a mistake to think of Evangelicalism as either anti-scientific or anti-intellectual. The best philosophers, professors, and scientists in all fields accepted it as the unquestionable expression of divine revelation and hence of the natural and supernatural laws of the universe.

Finney's revivalism and perfectionism were matched by his millennial faith and his interest in benevolent reform. These too were basic attributes of the Evangelical temper. Finney stated that the spirit of every true Christian "is necessarily that of the reformer. To the universal reformation of the world they stand committed." His converts, like Theodore Dwight Weld, Henry B. Stanton, and the Tappan brothers became leading members of the multifarious benevolent reform associations of the day. Finney believed, like almost all Evangelicals, however, that the social and moral reformation of the world must begin with the individual, and in this he was a true exponent of the conservative nature of Evangelicalism. For example, while he firmly opposed slavery and considered it a sin against which all Christians must testify, he nevertheless tried to dissuade his students at Oberlin from engaging in antislavery activities. Antislavery reform, he told them, must remain "an appendage of a general revival." Unless the souls of the slaveholders were converted, the antislavery agitation of men like Weld and Garrison could only "role a wave of blood over the land," he predicted. But if all Christians devoted their energies primarily to saving souls, then abolition would spread peacefully across "the whole land in two years." In this respect Finney resembled both the frontier Methodist circuit rider, Peter Cartwright, and the New England Baptist leader, Francis Wayland, who equally detested slavery but who insisted that it was a moral question to be solved by moral means and not by political agitation. For the Evangelicals the road to the millennium lay through God's reformation of the human heart. All man-made efforts of social reform, as the French Revolution demonstrated so forcefully, were sheer folly.

Hence all of the reform agencies to which the Evangelicals devoted so much of their time, energy, and money—helping the drunkard, the prostitute, the opium addict, the widows and orphans, the deaf, the dumb, and the blind, the criminals in jail and the tramps in the streets—were primarily missionary endeavors. Their purpose was to save the souls of these unfortunates and then they would no longer be a social problem. If, through God's will, they remained maimed in body, they would nevertheless be whole in spirit and would accept uncomplainingly the role which Providence had allotted to them on earth, meanwhile keeping their thoughts fixed upon the glorious world they would enter after death. For most of these "unfortunates," however, those known as "the deserving poor," conversion would immediately implant in them the virtues of true Protestantism—industry, sobriety, thrift and piety. And having these, they could not help but rise in the world. "It is a wonderful fact," said Dwight L. Moody, the foremost Evangelical revivalist of the post-Civil War era, "that men and women saved by the blood of Jesus rarely remain subjects of charity, but rise at once to comfort and respectability." The famous novels of the Rev. Horatio Alger, another prominent Evangelical spokesman, captured perfectly the fundamental social principles of Evangelical self-help and made "the success myth" seem a reality within the grasp of all Christian men. "Christianity is your character and character is your capital," was the essence of this myth and it was believed by everyone from office boys to J. P. Morgan and John D. Rockefeller.

The unquenchably optimistic faith in the free individual in the free market was perfectly adapted to the entrepreneurial climate of American laissez-faire capitalism and Jacksonian democracy. Yet the Evangelicals had to acknowledge as the century advanced that despite the rapid increase of conversion, church membership, church wealth, charitable giving, and revivals, the great mass of Americans were still lost souls. And even the converted were sorely tempted by the greedy scramble for fame, wealth, and political power which permeated the system. The ambivalence of Americans toward their society and of the Evangelicals' awareness that "a Christian must be

in this world but not of this world," produced a subtle shift in
Evangelical thinking and preaching in the middle years of the
century.

If Evangelicalism of the first third of the century was dominated
by the common sense philosophy of the Scottish Realists, that of the
middle third of the century was dominated by an increasingly
Romantic strain which owed much to subtle infiltrations of post-
Kantian idealism. The most extreme manifestation of idealistic
philosophy in America was of course that of Emersonian Transcendentalism. There were a few otherwise orthodox ministers who
tried consciously to amalgamate Transcendentalism and Christianity
in the 1830's and 1840's, but by and large the impact of this new
philosophy upon the predominant Evangelicalism was to romanti-
cize or sentimentalize it rather than to overturn its basic premises.
Evangelicalism remained firmly wedded to the dualistic schism between the natural and supernatural worlds. The rejection of miracles
by Emerson and Theodore Parker shocked the Evangelicals even
more than the Unitarian rational Christians.

Romantic Evangelicalism in its most significant aspects can best
be seen in the works of Horace Bushnell and Henry Ward Beecher,
two of the leading Evangelical ministers of the middle years, one
acknowledged to be the most eminent American theologian between Edwards and Walter Rauschenbusch, the other the most
eloquent preacher between George Whitefield and Harry Emerson
Fosdick. Like the earlier Evangelicals who engineered the modifications of Calvinism, these Romantic modifiers of common sense
Evangelicalism were accused of heresy. Both of them also developed
attitudes which merged with the third and final stage of American
Evangelicalism when it began to give way to Liberal Protestantism
or Modernism after 1875.

The three essential features of Romantic Evangelicalism were its
emphases upon the intuitive perception of truth through the feelings
or emotions of the heart, upon a Christocentric theology in which
"the personality of Jesus" became more important than the moral
order of God, and upon a concomitant sentimental idealization of
women, children, and parenthood as the most perfect embodiments
if not the most efficient means of grace. Horace Bushnell more than
once acknowledged his debt to Samuel Taylor Coleridge's *Aids to*

Reflection (published in America in 1829) the crucial nexus between Kantian idealism and American Transcendentalism and a central document in the whole Romantic movement. The essence of Coleridgean philosophy was that the empirical system of Locke and the Scottish Realists had overrated the Understanding or reasoning powers of man and grossly underrated or ignored his intuitive powers. The Understanding being based upon sense perception could never attain more than an indirect knowledge of God. But the Intuition, that innate feeling in all men that they are partly divine, or partake of divinity, must mean that men are capable of responding directly to the emanations of God's presence in all things and through all things. Coleridge called the seat or agency of these innate feelings the Reason, but the Romantics called it the Heart. The Understanding, the powers of reasoning, ratiocination, quantification and measurement by which men carefully and prudently weighed their experiences in terms of pleasure and pain was for Coleridge a dull, feeble, and ineffective means of comprehending truth just as the dry analogies of Paley and Butler were totally inadequate evidences of divinity. Since ultimate truth or divine truth is invisible, insubstantial, and ethereal then God must have given man some more certain way of ascertaining it than by mere reasoning from sense experience or common sense. As one Christian Transcendentalist put it, "There are more things in heaven and earth than are dreamed of in the sensuous and empirical philosophy of the day." Man was more than a reasoning animal and Nature more than a world of inanimate objects. God had implanted in man an inner consciousness or intuitive sense of the divine which, properly aroused and alert, was able to perceive supernatural truth directly. The Reason was the power by which man received his real knowledge of the moral law emanating through Nature from the core of the universe. The experience of directly perceiving God in Nature through the inner eye of the soul awakened such intimations of immortality and sublimity as to be in themselves the highest form of spiritual communion between God and man. From such intuitive experiences man learned more about moral duty, worship, and true holiness than he could ever learn from the most intricate speculations and deductions of Scottish metaphysics.

The ramifications of this idealistic subjectivism for the Evangelical movement in general were indirect, for few Evangelicals were ready to abandon their dualistic and objective view of Nature and the supernatural for transcendental monism and mysticism. Arminian they might be but not Antinomian. Nevertheless after 1835 there was an increasing tendency in Evangelical religion to rely more upon appeals to the heart, to the feelings, the imagination, and emotions, than to reason and conscience. Without going all the way with Emerson in trusting implicitly to the promptings of the heart the Evangelicals showed increasing willingness to believe that the sentiments of the heart, the higher and more refined impulses of the soul, were at least as trustworthy and important as the deductions of the head. Bushnell's theology and Beecher's rhetoric marked the most radical but also the most highly acclaimed departures from earlier common sense Evangelicalism.

Bushnell's most obvious use of Coleridgean Transcendentalism can be found in his famous "Dissertation on the Nature of Language as Related to Thought and Spirit" which he prefixed to his controversial and, to some, heretical book, *God in Christ* (1849). While ostensibly a plea for an end to dogmatism and pedantic creedalism among Evangelicals, the essay is also an eloquent, if tortured, plea for regarding the Bible as a book of poetry rather than "mere dialectics." Frankly preferring the romantic idealism of Frederick Schlegel to the dry realism of Locke's "precise theory of language," Bushnell offered this Coleridgean description of man's relationship to God in Nature:

> And if the outer world is the best dictionary and grammar of thought we speak of, then it is also itself an organ throughout of intelligence. Whose intelligence? By this question we are set directly confronting God, the Universal Author, no more to hunt for him by curious arguments and subtle deductions, if haply we may find him; but he stands EXPRESSED everywhere, so that turn whichsoever way we please, we behold the outlooking of his intelligence.

In conclusion, he declared that "Man is designed, in his very nature, to be a partially mystic being; the world to be looked upon as a mystic world. Christ himself revealed a decidedly mystic element in his teachings." Truth, he said, "in its highest and freest forms is not of the natural understanding."

A certain Romanticism was also implicit in the title of his volume *Nature and Supernatural Together Constituting the One System of God* (1858), but here he backed away from some of his earlier mysticism and merely cautioned his Common Sense brethren to beware of falling into the error of naturalism. "In ourselves we discover a tier of existences that are above nature, and in all their most ordinary actions are doing their will upon it. The very idea of our personality is that of a being not under the law of cause and effect, a being supernatural." An attack upon the monistic idealism of Transcendentalism as well as upon the naturalistic monism of the scientific determinist, the book placed Bushnell well within the Evangelical camp despite the claims of later disciples who thought they read in him the doctrine of divine immanence.

One reason for claiming that Bushnell was a herald of Liberal Protestantism lay in the implications of his most notorious book *Christian Nurture* (first published in 1847), an essay designed to offer a more comprehensive or better balanced conception of Christianity than the prevailing overemphasis upon revivalism and crisis conversion. In their effort to convert as many Americans as possible as rapidly as possible, professional evangelists, pastors, and parents were placing increasing pressure upon children to save their souls. The Sunday school movement, essentially a device to institutionalize the conversion of children, added to this pressure. In this book Bushnell frankly said that God did not always work through miraculous conversions and that in a Christian home it was entirely possible for a child "to grow up a Christian and never know himself as being otherwise." While this assertion of the importance of Christian environment and the organic development of Christian faith was attacked by many, Bushnell's doctrine of "familial grace" was not far from the Romantic image of the family which pervaded all Evangelical thought in the Victorian era.

It is difficult to find a collection of Evangelical sermons in this period which does not devote at least one sermon to "The Christian Home" and another to "Motherhood." It was the Evangelicals who made home and hearth the central features of American sentimentalism. Almost as though in reaction from the horrible features of infant damnation which appalled so many parents in the early part of the century, the Romantic Evangelicals went out of their way to praise the innocence and spiritual purity of childhood. And no doubt also out of an ambivalent feeling toward the aggressive masculine world of business and politics, Americans suddenly began after 1835 to eulogize the saintliness and virtue of womanhood. No doubt the Romantic mood which made Wordsworth write about the intimations of immortality in childhood contributed much to this Victorian fantasy. For a variety of reasons the bourgeoisie, seeking gentility and culture, found it convenient to make the female the repository of those higher qualities of artistic and spiritual appreciation which were thought to refine manners and morals. The businessman, engaged in the rough and tumble of worldly affairs, lacked those finer sensibilities so vital to a nation devoted to moral uplift and the cultivation of the higher sentiments of the Genteel Tradition. Similarly Evangelical Christianity began to define itself as "the cultivation of the soul."

"Woman," said Henry Ward Beecher, the prime exponent of Romantic Evangelicalism, "is ordained to perform many things much better than man, on account of her superior delicacy of organization and keenness of perception. Woman is a better instructor, from her very make and education, and as the molder and trainer of children in the household is by far man's superior." The relationship of the Victorian father to his children was like that of God to His children, benevolent but firmly disciplinarian. The relationship of the mother to her children was like that of Christ toward erring man, ready to sacrifice herself wholly to the child; she leads him in love and tenderness into paths of righteousness; she mediates between his misdeeds and the justice of a stern father; she is a softening influence upon the father and on society. Home thus became a model of heaven and the mother the image of Christ. "When I see what mothers do for their children, what anguish they endure," said Beecher, and "when I see the wonder of mother-love, devoting itself to the child that is helpless and useless. . . . I frame such a sense of the real, ever-living Christ, that when I go to my people I go to them with as much certainty as ever John had" of the divinity of Jesus.

It is not surprising that most Evangelicals were opposed to woman suffrage and insisted that woman's place was in the home. To allow her to enter the brutal world outside would be to harden

if not to crush her tender nature. The sanctified Christian home
became a refuge from the care and strife of the world of business
and politics, a refuge essential to the cultivation of both the souls
of children and of fathers. One result of this sentimentalism was to
give Evangelicalism a decidedly effeminate cast by the end of the
century. Theodore Roosevelt's masculine Christianity and Billy
Sunday's militant revivalism were clearly reactions to this—and
woman suffrage triumphed in their day.

The abandonment of common sense religion for "heart religion"
after 1835 led also to a re-evaluation of the moral government
theory of the atonement. Both Bushnell and Beecher disliked its
emphasis upon a God of justice rather than a God of love. Romantic
Christianity placed its emphasis upon "the personality of Jesus"
and upon His sacrificial love. Revival preaching after 1835 constantly stressed the theme that "Christ suffered and died for you,"
can you not give up your worldly sins for Him? "I apprehend,"
said Beecher, "that more men have been converted by the simple
presentation of Christ as a Person than by the presentation of the
Atonement as a doctrine."

> If you preach the Lord Jesus Christ as One who came into the
> world to pity, to spare, to uphold, and to save man, you will be more
> apprehensible, and you will come nearer and more quickly to men's
> consciousness, than if you go a long way around and undertake to
> explain the problem of the moral government of God. . . .

The emphasis upon "the Cross," "the blood of the Lamb," "the
suffering of the crucifixion," provided endless possibilities for touching the sensibilities of churchgoers and endless variations for Evangelical hymn writers. The whole quality of hymnody was revised
by Romantic Christianity, for it was recognized that through songs
and poetry it was possible to reach many hearts not touched by
sermons. Beecher was convinced that men's hearts could be opened
most easily to spiritual appeals by touching the artistic or esthetic
side of their nature, and he blamed his father for failing to understand this:

> I find a great many persons who say, "I do not much enjoy going
> to church, but if I am permitted to wander out into the fields, along

the fringes of the forests, and to hear the birds sing, to watch the cattle, and to look at the shadows on the hills, I am sure it makes me a better man." Some others, like my dear old father, would say, "That is all moonshine; there is nothing in it, no thought, no truth, and no doctrine of edification." But there *is* truth in it.

Henry Ward Beecher knew there was truth in it because he had experienced just the same kind of spiritual exaltation when he first visited a great art gallery in Europe: "The sense of exhilaration was so transcendent that I felt as if I could not stay in my body. I was filled with that supersensitiveness of supernal feeling which is true of worship; and I never seemed to myself so near the gate of heaven. I never felt capable of so nearly understanding my Master." Beecher claimed to be an Evangelical Calvinist but he said that Calvin had "an inordinate share of intellect" and too small a "share of heart" to really understand how to reach people. For Beecher the true minister was an artist or a poet and "the most important of all the elements that go to make the preacher" is *"Imagination."* His definition of Imagination was not far from that of Coleridge: "Imagination is the true germ of faith; it is the power of conceiving as definite the things which are invisible to the sense —of giving them distinct shape. And this not merely in your own thoughts but with the power of presenting the things which experience cannot primarily teach to other people's minds so that they shall be just as obvious as though seen with the bodily eye." The conversion experience in this theory of Romantic Evangelicalism was to be "made sensitive in every part," to "have the power to transfuse Jesus Christ into your whole life" so that "there is something in the morning dawn that brings you the thought of Him, in the hush of the evening, at noon-time, in the budding and spring of the trees, in the singing of the birds. . . ." For Beecher "Faith is only a modification of the imagination." Preaching of this kind was a far cry from the rough and ready wit of Peter Cartwright, the subtle logic of Nathaniel W. Taylor, and the browbeating argumentation of Lyman Beecher and Charles Grandison Finney.

But with the increase in gentility and sentiment, Evangelicalism also developed an increasing class consciousness. Beecher and Bushnell were ardent defenders of the Protestant ethic who found in their well-to-do parishioners the superiority of self-reliant individualism and esthetic refinement. Only in a genteel Christian home could children grow up in that state of cleanliness, self-discipline, and cultivated feeling which would assure them of grace. The children of the poor were unfortunately doomed to a harsher existence and their tender souls were soon brutalized in the rough and tumble of life in unsanctified homes. "The community is perpetually stratifying itself," said Beecher, "and there is no harm in this provided the upper classes are perpetually a drawing-up force to the lower." The note of charity was paternalistic and increasingly complacent. After the Civil War the well-to-do Evangelicals, fearful of the increasing swarms of unrefined immigrants and ignorant poor in the city slums, moved out to the suburbs and hired professional evangelists like Dwight L. Moody and Sam P. Jones to reach the toughened or un-assimilated hearts of the lower classes. Moody and Jones preached in a crude vernacular style suited to the more common tastes of their audiences, and their revivals employed more flamboyant tech-niques to reach more callous hearts.

It is significant that for most Evangelicals the Civil War repre-sented not a break with the past but a reaffirmation of America's manifest destiny. Even the Southern Evangelicals could not resist the strong patriotic nationalism and optimism which interpreted the war as the ultimate sanctification in blood of the divine mission of the United States. Horace Bushnell's famous sermon, "Our Obli-gations to the Dead," evoked the essentially romantic spiritualization of the great trauma. Central to his praise for the dead is the Evan-gelical theme of a bloody sacrifice, an atonement for national sin parallel to that of Christ for universal sin. Bushnell said in prose what Julia Ward Howe had put into poetry. The war was the final stage in the national drama of self-purification and dedication in preparation for the millennium. Henceforth to be a good Christian was to be a good patriot and vice versa.

Nevertheless, if the war itself proved to be a bridge to the future some of the problems which arose in the years after the war posed serious problems for the Evangelical faith. Most notable among these were Darwinian science, Comtean Positivism, and the higher criticism of the Bible. Even Beecher's optimism quailed a bit at the threat posed by science: "I have been under the penumbra of doubt," he said in 1872; "I look upon the progress of physical science and see the undermining influences that are going on." Yet in the next paragraph he said reassuringly, "There is one fact that is not going to be overturned by science; and that is the necessity of human development, and the capability there is in man of being opened up and improved. . . . Men walk from the fleshly to the spiritual."

What Beecher implied was what Evangelicals had always believed, that God had plans for the spiritual improvement and ultimate redemption of the human race. But like many other Romantic Evangelicals he was able to blend his theory of spiritual improvement with the new evolutionary concept of physical improvement without losing his Evangelical equilibrium for more than a moment. Evangelical class consciousness was already implicitly environmentalist. The third and final phase of the Evangelical movement, therefore, may be called Evangelical Liberalism. That is, it accepted the concepts of evolution and the higher criticism upon its own Romantic Evangelical terms. Either consciously or unconsciously it ignored, or distorted, those aspects of both these concepts which it did not find compatible.

The Romantic view of the Bible as literature or poetry proved a convenient way to rationalize much of the higher criticism. The belief in man's spiritual growth seemed sufficient to support some vague idea of evolutionary progress. But the Darwinian view that Nature was amoral, that the laws of Nature were "red in tooth and claw," that there was perhaps a First Cause or Great Unknowable at the origin of the universe but no perceivable purpose or end in view, and that man derived from the primordial slime through a missing link among the hairy quadrupeds—these views were either hotly denied or quietly ignored. Charles Hodge, the aging lion of Presbyterian Calvinism at Princeton Theological Seminary, frankly declared in 1874 that Darwinism was atheism. But James McCosh, equally devoted to Evangelicalism as president of Princeton College, had taken a more benign view of the possible truths imbedded in Darwin's hypothesis three years earlier. Beecher declared himself "a cordial Christian evolutionist" in 1885 without conceiving any contradiction in the terms.

Phillips Brooks, spokesman for the Evangelical Episcopalians of Boston's upper-class Trinity Church, took a stand very similar to

Beecher's. In his sermon "The Law of Growth" (1877) he declared that the parable of the talents in Matthew 25:15–29 was "a sort of 'survival of the fittest'" doctrine expounded by Jesus himself. The diligent businessman grows richer and the slothful more poor. "When a man reaches a certain point of wealth, his money reduplicates itself almost without his efforts, even drawing into itself the hard-earned profits of the toil of poorer men." But having reconciled social Darwinism and the Protestant ethic, Brooks preferred to lift the problem to the higher plane of Evangelical thought and concluded this sermon by urging that the deeper meaning of Matthew 25:29 was that all men should grow in spiritual diligence. It is not being rich in wealth that is important but being rich in spirit. Romantic Evangelicalism of this variety was too amorphous to be threatened by Darwin or the higher critics. It simply enveloped them in clouds of spiritual complacency and sentiment.

Josiah Strong, on the other hand, found the new problems made to order for his new brand of militant Evangelicalism. A secretary of the Home Mission Society of the Congregational Church, he wrote his best-selling volume, *Our Country* (1885), to raise funds to evangelize the destitute towns of the West. Though he was later to move on into the Social Gospel movement, he spoke at this time for the Evangelical Liberals. The country, he acknowledged, was faced with a multitude of grave problems. Demonstrating the new scientific penchant for statistical analysis, he offered a panoply of facts and figures, charts and graphs, to document each of the perils which threatened the nation. Some of them were old but increasingly dangerous—like intemperance, Romanism, Mormonism, and socialism. Some of them were newer but equally perilous, like urbanism, the exhaustion of the public lands, and the threatened loss of Anglo-Saxon racial supremacy. Like a true middle-class Evangelical he feared both the perils of greater concentration in wealth and the perils of embittered poverty. And like them he found the primary solution for these perils in more revivalism, more home missionaries, more dedicated Christian paternalism in the form of self-help charity. His concept of stewardship parallels that of the agnostic Andrew Carnegie's "Gospel of Wealth" while his doctrine of "Christian service" looked forward to the Social Gospel and Social Welfare era of American Liberalism. Still, for Strong the

only way to reform society was to convert the sinners in it, and this
was the work of God and his missionaries not of political, economic,
or social reformers. Strong had yet some distance to go before he
caught the new vision of the Social Gospel.

Strong's ambivalent note of optimism tinged with fear and danger
was typical of much of the preaching of this final phase of Evangelicalism. Those Evangelicals who failed to take the optimistic
leap forward into Liberal Protestantism, as Strong eventually did,
ultimately found themselves classed among the Old Lights of
America's Third Great Awakening. In the twentieth century they
accepted the name Fundamentalists.

Dwight L. Moody, the pre-eminent revivalist of the post-Civil
War period, found the times so fearful that he dropped the old post-
millennial outlook of Evangelicalism for a pre-millennial one.
Looking literally at the words of Scripture he concluded, "I don't
find any place where God says the world is to grow better and
better, and that Christ is to have a spiritual reign on earth of a
thousand years. I find that the earth is to grow worse and worse...."
Noting the increasing difficulties of American society—the domi-
nance of the big cities, the problems of unassimilated Roman Cath-
olic immigrants, the rise of socialist labor agitators, the widespread
corruption in business and government, increasing immorality
among the idle rich, increasing drunkenness and wickedness among
the poor—all of these seemed to him proof that the day of Judgment was approaching and that only the Second Coming of Christ
could set the world right. "I look upon this world as a wrecked
vessel," he said. "God has given me a lifeboat and said to me,
'Moody, save all you can.'"

At the same time, Moody was such a success as an urban revivalist
(at least among the rural born), he received such wholehearted
support from the leading businessmen of his day, he saw such
clear evidence of the success of the pious and industrious, that he
was astonished when workingmen complained of unemployment
and hard times: "I do not believe we would have these hard times
if it had not been for sin and iniquity. Look at the money that is
drank up! The money that is spent for tobacco! That is ruining
men...." As far as he could see "We live in a land flowing with
milk and honey" in which every man could become rich if he were

just sensible enough to "follow Christ." Hence it might just be possible that sufficiently successful evangelism might yet avert the day of doom and usher in a bright new era of peace and prosperity for all.

Moody's Southern counterpart, the Methodist revivalist Sam P. Jones, preached essentially the same message in the cities of the South in these years. Jones, though the son of a Confederate veteran, was imbued with the spirit of the New South, the South that would be raised to new heights by industrialization. He held no bitterness toward the North nor toward the poor "darkies" who sat in the Jim Crow seats of his tents and tabernacles. Riding the crest of the South's temperance movement, Jones could see that God had great plans for the future of the republic. But only if it steered clear of the dangers of Darwinism, socialism, and the higher criticism.

Moody, who died in 1899, was the last of the great Evangelical revivalists capable of winning the wholehearted support of all denominations and all classes of people (including Phillips Brooks and Henry Ward Beecher) for his revival campaigns. His successors faced a divided Evangelicalism and virtually all of them took the side of the Fundamentalists in the Awakening which brought the rise of Modernism as a new consensus in America theology. Moody dodged the issue of the higher criticism: "What is the use of talking about two Isaiahs when most people don't know there's one?" He even managed to remain on friendly terms with Christian evolutionists like Henry Drummond. But after 1900 no such neutrality was possible.

Some historians have seen in the development of American Evangelicalism a conscious effort to achieve a national self-identity, to mold the unity of the young nation into a new kind of covenant with God, to purge the republic of its sins and to create the millennial Kingdom of God on its soil. Others have seen it as the rationale for America's intensely individualistic, competitive, energetic system of private property, free trade, and free enterprise which every textbook of moral philosophy and political economy expounded as the moral law of God. In some respects Evangelicalism was a radical, reform-oriented movement demonstrating the perennial clash of Christ and culture. Here the antislavery impulse is a prime example. Yet many reformers, like William Lloyd Garrison, finding

the Evangelical churches to be among the most entrenched opponents of change, saw Evangelicalism as an escapist, pie-in-the-sky
movement representing a complacent subservience of Christ to
culture.

Evangelicalism was not consistent either in its theology or in its
social theory. It was neither Calvinistic nor Arminian and often
it verged on Pelagianism. It advocated an individualistic conception
of conversion which it promoted by mass revivalistic machinery. Its
doctrine of manifest Christian destiny was an ill-defined amalgam
of conservative fears and radical perfectionist hopes. Even its avowed
belief in voluntarism was belied by its readiness to use the power
of the state to enforce its Christian principles of morality upon
unbelievers. In 1811 Chancellor James Kent ruled from the bench
that despite its technical commitment to separation of Church and
State America was and should remain "a Christian nation." Lord
Bryce, writing in 1885, confirmed the truth of this voluntaristic
establishment in Evangelical America: "Christianity is in fact understood to be, though not the legally established religion, yet the national religion."

The history of American Evangelicalism is then more than the
history of a religious movement. To understand it is to understand
the whole temper of American life in the nineteenth century.

Note

The quotations and interpretations in this Introduction (except
where titles are noted in the text) have been drawn largely from
the following works to which any student of American Evangelicalism should refer for further reading:

Herbert W. Schneider, *A History of American Philosophy* (New
York, 1946); W. H. Werkmeister, *A History of Philosophical Ideas
in America* (New York, 1949); George P. Schmidt, *The Old Time
College President* (New York, 1930); Wilson Smith, *Professors
and Public Ethics: Studies of Northern Moral Philosophers Before
the Civil War* (Ithaca, 1956); Frank H. Foster, *A Genetic History
of the New England Theology* (Chicago, 1907); Sidney E. Mead,
Nathaniel William Taylor: 1786–1858 (Chicago, 1942); Barbara
M. Cross, *Horace Bushnell* (Chicago, 1958); Whitney R. Cross,

The Burned-Over District (New York, 1950); Gilbert H. Barnes, *The Anti-slavery Impulse* (New York, 1933); Clifford S. Griffin, *Their Brothers' Keepers* (New Brunswick, 1960); T. L. Smith *Revivalism and Social Reform* (New York, 1957); Charles C. Cole, Jr., *The Social Ideas of the Northern Evangelists* (New York, 1954); William R. Hutchinson, *The Transcendentalist Ministers* (New Haven, 1959); Ronald V. Wells, *Three Christian Transcendentalists* (New York, 1943); H. Richard Niebuhr and Daniel D. Williams, *The Ministry in Historical Perspectives* (New York, 1956); W. G. McLoughlin, *Modern Revivalism* (New York, 1959); Winthrop S. Hudson, *Religion in America* (New York, 1965); Perry Miller, *The Life of the Mind in America* (New York, 1965); H. Shelton Smith, Robert T. Handy, and Lefferts A. Loetscher, *American Christianity* (New York, 1963); Charles I. Foster, *An Errand of Mercy* (Chapel Hill, N.C., 1960); Sydney E. Ahlstrom, "The Scottish Philosophy and American Theology," *Church History* (September, 1955) XXIV, 257–272.

1.

Julia Ward Howe

"The Battle Hymn of the Republic"
(1861)

Written on November 8, 1861, by Julia Ward Howe (the wife of the famous reformer and doctor, Samuel Gridley Howe), *The Battle Hymn of the Republic* is one of the classic documents of the American spirit. It is still sung today at civil rights rallies, patriotic occasions, and times of national mourning. It is a quintessential expression of the Evangelical moral fervor of the nineteenth century. Though Mrs. Howe was a Northerner and a Unitarian, and though she wrote this to the tune of "John Brown's Body" (itself based upon a pre-Civil War Sunday school hymn), she captured in its words the religious temper of the whole nation. Soon after the war Southerners as well as Northerners were singing it. Its message is one of millennial faith and optimistic conviction that God has chosen the *United* States of America to lead the way to the redemption of the world for Christian freedom. [The text printed here is from the original version of the poem as it first appeared in *The Atlantic Monthly*, February, 1862.]

Mine eyes have seen the glory of the coming of the Lord:
He is trampling out the vintage where the grapes of wrath are stored;
He hath loosed the fateful lightning of His terrible swift sword:
His truth is marching on.

I have seen Him in the watch-fires of a hundred circling camps;
They have builded Him an altar in the evening dews and damps;
I can read His righteous sentence by the dim and flaring lamps:
His day is marching on.

I have read a fiery gospel writ in burnished rows of steel:
"As ye deal with my contemners, so with you my grace shall deal;
Let the Hero, born of woman, crush the serpent with his heel,
Since God is marching on."

He has sounded forth the trumpet that shall never call retreat;
He is sifting out the hearts of men before His judgment-seat:
Oh, be swift, my soul, to answer Him! be jubilant, my feet!
Our God is marching on.

In the beauty of the lilies Christ was born across the sea,
With a glory in his bosom that transfigures you and me:
As he died to make men holy, let us die to make men free,
While God is marching on.

2.

Robert Baird

Religion In America
(1844)

The Rev. Robert Baird was an American Presbyterian who spent eight years in Europe and the British Isles (1835 to 1843) on various religious and philanthropic activities. While there he found that Europeans were puzzled by the religious situation in the United States and dubious as to the hold of Christianity on the young republic. They found the doctrine of separation of Church and State suspect; they were appalled at the multiplicity of American sects; they could not comprehend the new revival system. Just as James Fenimore Cooper felt called upon in these same years to defend his country's political system in France, so Baird came to the defense of its religious system in Germany. The European edition in 1843 was so popular that upon his return to America Baird arranged for its publication in the United States. The selections here are taken from his chapters defending the multiplicity of denominations, a defense based upon the over-arching principles of Evangelicalism which transcend denominational boundaries and serve as a vital, unifying force; they were fast making America the most religious nation in the world, much to the dismay of European churchmen.
[The selections here are from pages 219–220, 264–270 of the first edition.]

BOOK VI. THE EVANGELICAL CHURCHES IN AMERICA

Chapter I. Preliminary Remarks in Reference to This Subject

This part of our work we propose to devote to a brief notice of the doctrines, organization, and history of each of the evangelical denominations in the United States, nothing beyond a sketch of these being consistent with our limits. We shall endeavour, of course, to confine ourselves as much as possible to what is important, omitting what is least essential or necessary.

We begin with the five most numerous evangelical denominations in the United States. These, in the order of their rise, are the Episcopalians, the Congregationalists, the Baptists, the Presbyterians, and the Methodists, and in that order we shall proceed to notice them. We shall then consider as briefly as possible the smaller orthodox denominations, such as the Moravians, the Lutherans, the German Reformed, and other German sects, the Reformed Dutch Church, the Cumberland Presbyterians, the Protestant or Reformed Methodists, the Reformed Presbyterians or Covenanters, the Associate Church, the Associate Reformed, the Quakers, &c.

Numerous as are the evangelical denominations in the United States, yet when grouped in reference to doctrine on the one hand, or church government on the other, it is surprising into how small a number they may be reduced. In doctrine we have but two great divisions—the Calvinistic and the Arminian schools; the former, with its various peculiarities, comprehending the Presbyterians, usually so called, the evangelical Baptists, the Episcopalians (though they generally consider themselves as intermediate between the two), the Congregationalists, the German Reformed, the Dutch Reformed, the Covenanters, the Associate, and the Associate Reformed Churches; the latter, with its variations, comprehending the Methodists of all branches, the Lutherans, the Cumberland Presbyterians, the United Brethren or Moravians, and some other small bodies.

Considered in reference to their forms of church government, they all range themselves in three great families. The *Episcopal*, comprehending the Protestant Episcopal Church, the Methodist Episcopal, and the Moravians; the *Presbyterian*, including the Presbyterians usually so called, the Dutch Reformed, the German Reformed, the Lutherans, the Cumberland Presbyterians, the Protestant Methodists, the Covenanters, the Associate, and the Associate Reformed; the *Congregational* (or Independent, as it is more commonly called in England), embracing the Congregationalists and the Baptists.

But when viewed in relation to the great doctrines which are universally conceded by Protestants to be fundamental and necessary to salvation, then they all form but one body, recognising Christ as their common Head. They then resemble the different parts of a great temple, all constituting but one whole; or the various corps of an army, which, though ranged in various divisions, and each division having an organization perfect in itself, yet form but one great host, and are under the command of one chief.

This suggests the observation that on no one point are all these churches more completely united, or more firmly established, than on the doctrine of the supremacy of Christ in His Church, and the unlawfulness of any interference with its doctrine, discipline, and government, on the part of the civil magistrate. There is not a single evangelical church in the United States that does not assert and maintain the glorious doctrine of the Headship of Christ in His Church, and that from Him alone comes all just and lawful authority in the same. . . .

. . . to assist the reader in taking a general view of the whole, we shall place them before his eye at once in a tabular form. In doing this, we shall first arrange them in the order in which we have already passed them under our review, that of their successive appearance in America. We shall then rearrange them under various heads, such as Episcopal, Congregational, &c.

I. EPISCOPAL	Churches	Ministers	Communicants	Population
Protestant Episcopalians	1,200	1,176	100,000	800,000
Moravians	23	27	3,000	12,000
Total	1,223	1,203	103,000	812,000
II. CONGREGATIONAL				
Orthodox Churches	1,500	1,350	180,000	1,000,000
III. BAPTIST				
Regular Baptists	8,482	4,036	637,477	
Free-Will Baptists	1,165	771	61,372	
Seventh Day Baptists	59	46	6,077	4,000,000
Disciples of Christ, or Campbellites				
Winebrennarians				
Total	9,706	4,853	704,926	4,000,000

IV. PRESBYTERIAN

Regular Presbyterians—

Old and New Schools	3,584	2,672	279,782	
Cumberland Presbyterians	550	550	75,000	
Dutch Reformed Church	267	259	29,322	
Associate Synod	200	100	15,000	
Associate Reformed	300	165	26,000	4,500,000
Reformed Presbyterians	94	57	10,500	
Lutherans	1,371	423	146,303	
German Reformed	600	180	100,000	
Total	6,966	4,406	681,897	4,500,000

V. METHODIST	Churches or other places of worship	Preachers	Communicants	Population
Methodist Episcopal Church	25,109[2]	3,988 T. M.[1] 7,730 L. M.[3]	1,068,525	4,500,000
Protestant Methodists	2,000	500 T. M. 700 L. M.	60,000	300,000
Welsh Calvinistic Methodists	20	20	2,500	12,500
United Brethren in Christ	2,000	250 T. M. 350 L. M.	50,000	200,000
Evangelical Association	900	112 T. M. 200 L. M.	14,000	40,000
Total	30,029	4,870 T. M. 8,980 L. M.	1,195,025	5,052,500
MENNONISTS	200			
ORTHODOX QUAKERS	300			

By uniting the Congregationalists with the Presbyterians, which, as they are in all important respects the same, is perfectly proper, we reduce the evangelical denominations in the United States to four great families, and, thus arranged, they present the following summary:

	Churches	Ministers	Commun.	Population
Episcopalians	1,223	1,203	103,000	812,000
Presbyterians	8,466	5,756	861,897	5,500,000
Baptists	9,706	4,853	704,926	4,000,000
Methodists	30,029	4,870[4]	1,195,025	5,052,500
Total	49,424	16,682	2,864,848	15,364,000

[1] Travelling ministers.

[2] I am indebted for the above estimate of the probable number of places, including churches, schoolhouses, and private houses, in which the Methodist itinerant and local ministers preach, to my friend President Durbin. It has been made with much care, and, I doubt not, is considerably within the truth. President Durbin has a wide and accurate acquaintance with the country, as well as with the entire economy of the church to which he belongs.

[3] Local ministers.   [4] Travelling ministers.

This sypnosis suggests a few observations.

1. We have left out the Campbellites, both because we have no correct information as to their statistics, and because though some of them are, no doubt, sound on all essential points, yet, not knowing how many, we cannot place them with entire confidence among the evangelical denominations. Neither have we included the Mennonists, the German United Brethren, the Winebrennarians, the Orthodox Friends, nor some of the smaller secessions from the Methodist Episcopal Church. Had all these been included, the number of churches, ministers, and members, together with the amount of the general population under the moral influence of the churches included in this category, would have been much greater.

2. It is impossible to state the number of churches or congregations, properly so called. Those of the Episcopalians, Presbyterians, and Baptists, taken together, amount to 19,395. But those belonging to the different Methodist communions it is impossible to ascertain, no return of them having been made. There can be no doubt that, of the places of worship which I have given on President Durbin's authority, more than 10,000 are churches properly so called. This, then, would make the entire number of the churches of the evangelical denominations, without counting the Campbellites, Mennonists, &c., exceed 29,000; and supposing these to contain upon an average 500 people each, they would accommodate more than 14,500,000 of the 18,500,000 of inhabitants. But if we take in all the places, whether churches or not, at which the Gospel is preached, in most cases once a week at least, and in others once a fortnight, seldom less often, these will be found to amount to 49,424. And even to these there ought to be added a part, at least, of the Campbellite, Mennonist, and Winebrennarian places of worship, and those of some of the smaller Methodist sects, before we can arrive at a full enumeration of all the churches and other places in which salvation by a crucified Saviour is proclaimed to sinners.

3. The summary gives 16,682 as the number of ministers who devote themselves entirely to the work. Adding the 8980 Methodist local preachers, we have 25,662 as the number of actual preachers of the Gospel. Even this is exclusive of those of the omitted denominations, and of the licentiates in the Baptist and Presbyterian churches, who cannot well be estimated at less than 1300, and who

may fairly be set against the deduction to be made on account of ordained ministers employed as professors and missionaries. But taking the above 16,682 as the number, all things considered, of ministers that are evangelical on all the saving doctrines of the Gospel, and divide the population of the United States, which, in the beginning of the year 1844, was about 18,500,000, by this number, the result will be one such minister for less than 1110 souls. Now, although figures cannot express moral influences, such calculations are nevertheless not without their use. A country which has an evangelical preacher on an average for every 1110 souls, may be considered as pretty well supplied, if they be well distributed and faithful. A perfect distribution is, indeed, altogether impossible with a population rapidly diffusing itself over immense, half-cultivated regions, yet much is done to obviate the disadvantages of such a state of things. The aid rendered by the Methodist local preachers must be regarded as an important auxiliary to the more regular ministry. The general faithfulness of this ministry has already been fully discussed.

4. The members in full communion with the churches enumerated exceed 2,864,848 in number. Now, although it be very certain that all these do not live up to their profession, yet as they belong for the most part to churches that endeavour to maintain discipline, we may fairly presume that they comprehend at least as large a proportion of consistent Christians as any equal number of professors in other parts of Christendom.

5. The last column of the summary assumes 15,364,000 of the whole population as more or less under the influence of the evangelical denominations. Accuracy in such a calculation is hardly to be expected, but I have taken the best data I could find, and doubt not that the estimate I have made is not much wide of the truth. Including all the denominations that claim to be evangelical, this estimate would exceed 15,500,000.

Chapter XVIII. Number of Evangelical Sects

Much has been said in Europe about the multiplicity of sects in the United States, and many seem of opinion that the religious liberty enjoyed there has led to the almost indefinite creation of different religious communions. This requires a little examination.

No doubt absolute religious liberty will ever be attended with a considerable subdivision of the religious world into sects. Men will ever differ in their views respecting doctrine and church order, and it is to be expected that such differences will result in the formation of distinct ecclesiastical communions. In the absence of religious liberty matters may be much otherwise, but how far for the better a little consideration will show. People in that case may be constrained to acquiesce, ostensibly at least, in one certain ecclesiastical organization, and in certain modes of faith and worship sanctioned and established by law. But such acquiescence, it is well known, instead of being real and cordial, is often merely external and constrained; and if so, its worthlessness is certain and palpable.

But as respects the evangelical communions in the United States, it must have struck the reader that this multiplicity has mainly arisen, not so much from the abuse of religious liberty by the indulgence of a capricious and sectarian spirit, as from the various quarters from which the country has been colonized. Coming in large numbers, and sometimes in compact bodies, from different parts of the Old World, nothing was more natural than the desire of establishing for themselves and their posterity the same religious formularies and modes of worship, church government, and discipline which they had cherished in the lands that had given them birth, and persecution for their adherence to which had led, in many instances, to their having emigrated. Hence we find, in the United States, counterparts not only to the Episcopalian, Congregational, Baptist, and Methodist churches of England, and to the Presbyterian churches of Scotland, Ireland, and Wales, but likewise to the Dutch and German Reformed churches, the German Lutheran Church, the Moravians, Mennonists, &c. Indeed, there is scarcely an evangelical communion in America which is not the mere extension by immigration of a similar body in Europe. The exceptions hardly can be reckoned such, for they consist for the most part of separations from the larger bodies, not because of differences with regard to essential doctrines and forms of church government, but on points of such inferior consequence that they can scarcely be regarded as new sects at all.

In fact, if we take all the evangelical communions that have fallen under review, and contemplate the confessedly fundamental doctrines maintained by each, it is surprising to observe how nearly they are agreed. It may, we believe, be demonstrated that among the evangelical communions in the United States, numerous as they are, there is as much real harmony of doctrine, if not of church economy, as could be found in the evangelical churches of the first three centuries.

Indeed, as we before remarked, by grouping the former in families, according to their great distinctive features, we at once reduce them to four, or at most five. Thus the Presbyterians, commonly so called, of the Old and New Schools, the Congregationalists, the Dutch and German Reformed, the Scotch Secession churches,[1] and, we may add, the Lutherans and Cumberland Presbyterians, form but one great Presbyterian family, composed of elder and younger members, all of them essentially Presbyterian in church polity, and very nearly coinciding, at bottom, in their doctrinal views. Between several of these communions there subsists a most intimate fraternal intercourse, and the ministers of one find no difficulty in entering the service of another without being reordained.

Again, between the different evangelical Baptist sects there is no really essential or important difference; and the same may be said of the Methodists. Indeed, the evangelical Christians of the United States exhibit a most remarkable coincidence of views on all important points. On all doctrines necessary to salvation—the sum of which is "repentance towards God," and "faith towards our Lord Jesus Christ"— there is really no diversity of opinion at all. Of this I may now give a most decisive proof.

I have already spoken of the American Sunday-school Union. Among the laymen who compose its Board of Directors, are to be found members of all the main branches of the evangelical Protestant Church—Episcopalians, Congregationalists, Baptists, Presbyterians, Lutherans, Dutch and German Reformed, Methodists, Quakers, and Moravians. It publishes a great many books for

---

[1] An effort is now making, which promises to be successful, to unite all the Scottish Secession churches in one body. This coalescence of churches holding similar doctrines and maintaining similar organizations may be expected to occur often.

Sunday-school libraries every year, none, of course, being admitted the contents of which are likely to give offence to any member of the Board, or repugnant to the peculiarities of any of the religious bodies represented at it. In the summer of 1841 the Rev. Dr. Hodge, a professor in the Princeton theological seminary, was requested by its committee of publications to write a book exhibiting the great doctrines of the Gospel as held by all evangelical Christians. This he did to the entire satisfaction, not only of the Board, but I believe I may say of all evangelical Christians throughout the land that have read his work. It is appropriately entitled "The Way of Life;" the subjects are the Scriptures; sin; justification; faith; repentance; profession of religion and holy living under which several heads the fundamental doctrines of the Gospel are presented in an able and yet most simple and familiar manner. It is a work, in short, which none can read without surprise and delight at observing the vast extent and fulness of the system of Truth, in which all evangelical communions are agreed.

These communions, as they exist in the United States, ought to be viewed as branches of one great body, even the entire visible Church of Christ in this land. Whatever may have been the circumstances out of which they arose, they are but constituent parts of one great whole—divisions of one vast army—though each brigade, and even each regiment, may have its own banner, and its own part of the field to occupy. And although to the inexperienced eye such an army as it moves onward against the enemy may have a confused appearance, the different divisions of infantry being arranged separately, the artillery interspersed, and the cavalry sometimes in the front, sometimes in the rear, and sometimes between the columns, yet all are in their proper places and to the mind of him who assigns them their places, and directs their movements, all is systematic order where the uninitiated sees nothing but confusion. Momentary collisions, it is true, may sometimes happen—there may be jostling and irritation occasionally—yet they all fulfil their appointed parts and discharge their appropriate duties. So is it with the "sacramental host of God's elect."

No doubt this multiplication of sects is attended with serious evils, especially in the new and thinly-peopled settlements. It often renders the churches small and feeble. But this is an evil that diminishes with the increase of the population. With a zealous and capable ministry the truth gains ground, the people are gathered into churches, congregations increase in numbers and consistency, and though weak ones are occasionally dissolved, the persons who composed them either going into other evangelical churches, or emigrating to other parts of the country, such as maintain their ground become only the stronger; and it often happens, particularly in the rural districts, that the number of sects diminishes while the population increases.

Great, however, as may be the disadvantages resulting from this multiplicity of different communions, were they all reduced to one or two, we apprehend still worse evils would follow. Diversity on non-essential points among the churches and ministers of a neighborhood often gives opportunity to those who reside in it to attend the services and ministrations which each finds most edifying, instead of being reduced to the sad alternative of either joining in forms of worship which they conscientiously disapprove, and of listening to a minister whom they find unedifying, or of abstaining from public worship altogether. Rather than this, it is surely far better to bear the expense of having two or three churches in a community, for which, looking only at the mere amount of population, one might suffice. . . .

BOOK VII. UNEVANGELICAL DENOMINATIONS IN AMERICA

Chapter I. Introductory Remarks

Having thus reviewed, as far as the compass of our work will permit, the Evangelical Churches or Denominations in the United States of America, we come now to speak of those that are considered as *unevangelical* by Orthodox Protestants; and under this head we shall, for convenience' sake, range all those sects that either renounce, or fail faithfully to exhibit, the fundamental and saving truths of the Gospel. Here, however, let us not be misunderstood. When we put Roman Catholics in the same category with Unitarians, we would not for a moment be supposed as placing them on the same footing. The former, doubtless, as a Church, hold those doctrines on which true believers in all ages have placed their hopes for

eternal life, yet these have been so buried amid the rubbish of multiplied human traditions and inventions, as to remain hid from the
great mass of the people. Still, as in their doctrinal formularies they
have not denied "the Lord that bought them," however much they
may have multiplied other "saviours," they must not be confounded
with those who have openly rejected that "sure foundation which is
laid in Zion." While, therefore, we must deplore "their holding
the truth in unrighteousness," and instead of presenting through
their numerous priesthood the simple and fundamental doctrines of
the Gospel, their supplanting these, in a great measure, by introducing "another Gospel," we would not say that an enlightened mind
may not find in their church the way of life, obstructed though it
be by innumerable obstacles.

Neither would we be thought to put the Unitarians on the same
footing with the Universalists. The moral influence of the preaching
of the former, and their standing in society, make them far more
valuable than the latter as a component part of the general population. Nor would we put the Jews, or even the more serious part
of the Universalists, on the same level with "Socialists," "Shakers,"
and "Mormons."

All that we mean by putting these various bodies in one category
is, that they can none of them be associated with the evangelical
Protestant Churches—with churches whose religion is the Bible,
the whole Bible, and nothing but the Bible—nor, indeed, do we
suppose that, however much they may dislike being all reviewed in
one and the same section of this work, they would any of them
choose to be associated with the evangelical Protestant communions,
or challenge for themselves that appellation. . . .

3.

Peter Cartwright

Autobiography

(1856)

At the beginning of the nineteenth century the Methodist Episcopal Church in America was one of the smaller and less influential denominations, having only recently (1784) broken away from the Protestant Episcopal Church. By the middle of the nineteenth century it had become the largest and fastest growing denomination in the nation. It remains the largest Protestant denomination to this day. In part this was the result of its Arminian doctrines which were so perfectly in tune with the mood of nineteenth-century individualism and optimism. Much was also due to the carefully organized and directed circuit-riding system which proved so effective on the rapidly expanding frontier. And finally the Methodists proved to be thoroughly attuned to the revivalistic spirit of Evangelicalism. Methodism, in fact, is generally given the credit for originating the camp-meeting revivalism which began in Kentucky and Tennessee in the 1790's, continued westward until the frontier closed, and can still be found in many parts of the South and West today.

The autobiography of Peter Cartwright, first published in 1856, ranks with the journals of Francis Asbury as the most colorful first-hand account of Methodist Evangelicalism in its early stages. By the standards of the older, more conservative Calvinistic denominations which had previously dominated American religious life, Cartwright seemed ignorant, crude, and heretical. But as Cartwright's autobiography indicates, the Methodists preached a doctrine that the people of the West wanted to hear and preached it far more effectively than the college-educated, seminary-trained ministers of the Presbyterian and Congregational churches. Only by gradually adopting many of the Methodist views and methods did the more staid Calvinists manage to hold their own in the Northeast; but in the South and West they never did catch up with the Methodists.

[These selections, covering the years 1801 to 1828 in Cartwright's career are taken from an edition published in 1956 by the Abingdon Press.]

CHAPTER IV. CONVERSION

In 1801, when I was in my sixteenth year, my father, my eldest half brother, and myself, attended a wedding about five miles from home, where there was a great deal of drinking and dancing, which was very common at marriages in those days. I drank little or nothing; my delight was in dancing. After a late hour in the night, we mounted our horses and started for home. I was riding my race-horse.

A few minutes after we had put up the horses, and were sitting by the fire, I began to reflect on the manner in which I had spent the day and evening. I felt guilty and condemned. I rose and walked the floor. My mother was in bed. It seemed to me, all of a sudden, my blood rushed to my head, my heart palpitated, in a few minutes I turned blind; an awful impression rested on my mind that death had come and I was unprepared to die. I fell on my knees and began to ask God to have mercy on me.

My mother sprang from her bed, and was soon on her knees by my side, praying for me, and exhorting me to look to Christ for mercy, and then and there I promised the Lord that if he would spare me, I would seek and serve him; and I never fully broke that promise. My mother prayed for me a long time. At length we lay down, but there was little sleep for me. Next morning I rose, feeling wretched beyond expression. I tried to read in the Testament, and retired many times to secret prayer through the day, but found no relief. I gave up my race-horse to my father, and requested him to sell him. I went and brought my pack of cards, and gave them to mother, who threw them into the fire, and they were consumed. I fasted, watched, and prayed, and engaged in regular reading of the Testament. I was so distressed and miserable, that I was incapable of any regular business.

My father was greatly distressed on my account, thinking I must die, and he would lose his only son. He bade me retire altogether from business, and take care of myself.

Soon it was noised abroad that I was distracted, and many of my associates in wickedness came to see me, to try and divert my mind from those gloomy thoughts of my wretchedness; but all in vain. I exhorted them to desist from the course of wickedness which we had been guilty of together. The class-leader and local preacher were sent for. They tried to point me to the bleeding Lamb, they prayed for me most fervently. Still I found no comfort, and although I had never believed in the doctrine of unconditional election and reprobation, I was sorely tempted to believe I was a reprobate, and doomed, and lost eternally, without any chance of salvation.

At length one day I retired to the horse-lot, and was walking and wringing my hands in great anguish, trying to pray, on the borders of utter despair. It appeared to me that I heard a voice from heaven, saying, "Peter, look at me." A feeling of relief flashed over me as quick as an electric shock. It gave me hopeful feelings, and some encouragement to seek mercy, but still my load of guilt remained. I repaired to the house, and told my mother what had happened to me in the horse-lot. Instantly she seemed to understand it, and told me the Lord had done this to encourage me to hope for mercy, and exhorted me to take encouragement, and seek on, and God would bless me with the pardon of my sins at another time.

Some days after this, I retired to a cave on my father's farm to pray in secret. My soul was in an agony; I wept, I prayed, and said, "Now, Lord, if there is mercy for me, let me find it," and it really seemed to me that I could almost lay hold of the Saviour, and realize a reconciled God. All of a sudden, such a fear of the devil fell upon me that it really appeared to me that he was surely personally there, to seize and drag me down to hell, soul and body, and such a horror fell on me that I sprang to my feet and ran to my mother at the house. My mother told me this was a device of Satan to prevent me from finding the blessing then. Three months rolled away, and still I did not find the blessing of the pardon of my sins.

This year, 1801, the Western Conference existed, and I think there was but one presiding elder's district in it, called the Kentucky District. William M'Kendree (afterward bishop) was appointed to the Kentucky District. Cumberland Circuit, which, perhaps, was six hundred miles round, and lying partly in Kentucky and partly in

Tennessee, was one of the circuits of this district. John Page and Thomas Wilkerson were appointed to this circuit.

In the spring of this year, Mr. M'Grady, a minister of the Presbyterian Church, who had a congregation and meeting-house, as we then called them, about three miles north of my father's house, appointed a sacramental meeting in this congregation, and invited the Methodist preachers to attend with them, and especially John Page, who was a powerful Gospel minister, and was very popular among the Presbyterians. Accordingly he came, and preached with great power and success.

There were no camp-meetings in regular form at this time, but as there was a great waking up among the Churches, from the revival that had broken out at Cane Ridge, before mentioned, many flocked to those sacramental meetings. The church would not hold the tenth part of the congregation. Accordingly, the officers of the Church erected a stand in a contiguous shady grove, and prepared seats for a large congregation.

The people crowded to this meeting from far and near. They came in their large wagons, with victuals mostly prepared. The women slept in the wagons, and the men under them. Many stayed on the ground night and day for a number of nights and days together. Others were provided for among the neighbors around. The power of God was wonderfully displayed; scores of sinners fell under the preaching, like men slain in mighty battle; Christians shouted aloud for joy.

To this meeting I repaired, a guilty, wretched sinner. On the Saturday evening of said meeting, I went, with weeping multitudes, and bowed before the stand, and earnestly prayed for mercy. In the midst of a solemn struggle of soul, an impression was made on my mind, as though a voice said to me, "Thy sins are all forgiven thee." Divine light flashed all round me, unspeakable joy sprung up in my soul. I rose to my feet, opened my eyes, and it really seemed as if I was in heaven; the trees, the leaves on them, and everything seemed, and I really thought were, praising God. My mother raised the shout, my Christian friends crowded around me and joined me in praising God; and though I have been since then, in many instances, unfaithful, yet I have never, for one moment, doubted that the Lord did, then and there, forgive my sins and give me religion.

Our meeting lasted without intermission all night, and it was believed by those who had a very good right to know, that over eighty souls were converted to God during its continuance. I went on my way rejoicing for many days. This meeting was in the month of May. In June our preacher, John Page, attended at our little church, *Ebenezer*, and there in June, 1801, I joined the Methodist Episcopal Church, which I have never for one moment regretted. I have never for a moment been tempted to leave the Methodist Episcopal Church, and if they were to turn me out, I would knock at the door till taken in again. I suppose, from the year 1786 Methodist preachers had been sent to the West, and we find among these very early pioneers, F. Poythress, presiding elder, T. Williamson, I. Brooks, Wilson Lee, James Haw, P. Massie, B. M'Henry, B. Snelling, J. Hartley, J. Talman, J. Lillard, Kobler, and others.

Perhaps the first conference holden in the West was held in Kentucky, in April, 1789, and then at different points till 1800, when the Western Conference was regularly organized, and reached from Redstone and Greenbrier to Natchez, covering almost the entire Mississippi Valley. I can find at this time a record of but ninety members in 1787, and five traveling preachers. From 1787 up to 1800, Bishop Asbury visited the Western world, called together the preachers in conferences, changed them from time to time, regulated the affairs of the infant Church in the wilderness as best he could.

Several times the Western preachers had to arm themselves in crossing the mountains to the East, and guard Bishop Asbury through the wilderness, which was infested with bloody, hostile savages, at the imminent risk of all their lives. Notwithstanding the great hazard of life, that eminent apostle of American Methodism, Bishop Asbury, showed that he did not count his life dear, so that he could provide for the sheep in the wilderness of the West.

At the time I joined the Church in 1801, according to the best accounts that I can gather, there were in the entire bounds of the Western Conference, of members, probationers, colored and all, two thousand, four hundred and eighty-four, and about fifteen traveling preachers. In the United States and territories, East and West, North and South, and Canada, seventy-two thousand, eight hundred and seventy-four. Total, in Europe and America, one hundred and ninety-six thousand, five hundred and two. The number of traveling preachers this year, for all America and Canada, was three hundred and seven; and during the same year there were eight thousand members added to the Methodist Episcopal Church.

I believe, to say nothing of some local preachers who emigrated to the West at a very early day, that James Haw and Benjamin Ogden were the first two regular itinerant preachers sent out in 1786. After traveling and preaching for several years, they both became disaffected to the Methodist Episcopal Church and withdrew, with the secession of James O'Kelly, elsewhere named in my sketches. O'Kelly left the Church in 1792. He was a popular and powerful preacher, and drew off many preachers and thousands of members with him. He formed what he called the Republican Methodist Church, flourished for a few years, and then divisions and subdivisions entered among his followers. Some of his preachers turned Arians, some Universalists, and some joined the so-called New Lights, and some returned to the Methodist Episcopal Church, and the last authentic account I had of O'Kelly he was left alone in his old age, and desired to return to the Methodist Episcopal Church again; but whether he was ever received I am not informed. And here was an end of the first grand secession from our beloved Church.

James Haw and Benjamin Ogden, we have said, became disaffected and left the Church with O'Kelly's party. They soon found that they could not succeed to any considerable extent in these Western wilds. Haw veered about and joined the Presbyterians, became a pastor in one of their congregations with a fixed salary, but lived and died in comparative obscurity.

Ogden backslid, quit preaching, kept a groggery, and became wicked, and raised his family to hate the Methodists. In the year 1813, when I was on the Wabash District, Tennessee Conference, Breckenridge Circuit, at a camp-meeting in said circuit, B. Ogden attended. There was a glorious revival of religion, and Ogden got under strong conviction, and professed to be reclaimed, joined the Church again, was licensed to preach, was soon recommended and received into the traveling connection again, and lived and died a good Methodist preacher. He was saved by mercy, as all seceders from the Methodist Episcopal Church will be, if saved at all. . . .

CHAPTER V. THE GREAT REVIVAL

From 1801 for years a blessed revival of religion spread through almost the entire inhabited parts of the West, Kentucky, Tennessee, the Carolinas, and many other parts, especially through the Cumberland country, which was so called from the Cumberland River, which headed and mounted in Kentucky, but in its great bend circled south through Tennessee, near Nashville. The Presbyterians and Methodists in a great measure united in this work, met together, prayed together, and preached together.

In this revival originated our camp-meetings, and in both these denominations they were held every year, and, indeed, have been ever since, more or less. They would erect their camps with logs or frame them, and cover them with clapboards or shingles. They would also erect a shed, sufficiently large to protect five thousand people from wind and rain, and cover it with boards or shingles; build a large stand, seat the shed, and here they would collect together from forty to fifty miles around, sometimes further than that. Ten, twenty, and sometimes thirty ministers, of different denominations, would come together and preach night and day, four or five days together; and, indeed, I have known these camp-meetings to last three or four weeks, and great good resulted from them. I have seen more than a hundred sinners fall like dead men under one powerful sermon, and I have seen and heard more than five hundred Christians all shouting aloud the high praises of God at once; and I will venture to assert that many happy thousands were awakened and converted to God at these camp-meetings. Some sinners mocked, some of the old dry professors opposed, some of the old starched Presbyterian preachers preached against these exercises, but still the work went on and spread almost in every direction, gathering additional force, until our country seemed all coming home to God.

In this great revival the Methodists kept moderately balanced; for we had excellent preachers to steer the ship or guide the flock. But some of our members ran wild, and indulged in some extravagancies that were hard to control.

The Presbyterian preachers and members, not being accustomed to much noise or shouting, when they yielded to it went into great extremes and downright wilderness, to the great injury of the cause of God. Their old preachers licensed a great many young men to preach, contrary to their Confession of Faith. That Confession of Faith required their ministers to believe in unconditional election and reprobation, and the unconditional and final perseverance of the saints. But in this revival they, almost to a man, gave up these points of high Calvinism, and preached a free salvation to all mankind. The Westminster Confession required every man, before he could be licensed to preach, to have a liberal education; but this qualification was dispensed with, and a great many fine men were licensed to preach without this literary qualification or subscribing to those high-toned doctrines of Calvinism.

This state of things produced great dissatisfaction in the Synod of Kentucky, and messenger after messenger was sent to wait on the Presbytery to get them to desist from their erratic course, but without success. Finally they were cited to trial before the constituted authorities of the Church. Some were censured, some were suspended, some retraced their steps, while others surrendered their credentials of ordination, and the rest were cut off from the Church.

While in this amputated condition, they called a general meeting of all their licentiates. They met our presiding elder, J. Page, and a number of Methodist ministers at a quarterly meeting in Logan County, and proposed to join the Methodist Episcopal Church as a body; but our aged ministers declined this offer, and persuaded them to rise up and embody themselves together, and constitute a Church. They reluctantly yielded to this advice, and, in due time and form, constituted what they denominated the "Cumberland Presbyterian Church;" and in their confession of faith split, as they supposed, the difference between the Predestinarians and the Methodists, rejecting a partial atonement or special election and reprobation, but retaining the doctrine of the final unconditional perseverance of the saints.

What an absurdity! While a man remains a sinner he may come, as a free agent, to Christ, if he will, and if he does not come his damnation will be just, because he refused offered mercy; but as soon as he gets converted his free agency is destroyed, the best boon of Heaven is then lost, and although he may backslide, wander away from Christ, yet he *shall* be brought in. He cannot finally be lost if he has ever been really converted to God.

They make a very sorry show in their attempt to support this left foot of Calvinism. But be it spoken to their credit, they do not often preach this doctrine. They generally preach Methodist doctrine, and have been the means of doing a great deal of good, and would have done much more if they had left this relic of John Calvin behind.

In this revival, usually termed in the West the Cumberland revival, many joined the different Churches, especially the Methodist and Cumberland Presbyterians. The Baptists also came in for a share of the converts, but not to any great extent. Infidelity quailed before the mighty power of God, which was displayed among the people. Universalism was almost driven from the land. The Predestinarians of almost all sorts put forth a mighty effort to stop the work of God.

Just in the midst of our controversies on the subject of the powerful exercises among the people under preaching, a new exercise broke out among us, called the *jerks*, which was overwhelming in its effects upon the bodies and minds of the people. No matter whether they were saints or sinners, they would be taken under a warm song or sermon, and seized with a convulsive jerking all over, which they could not by any possibility avoid, and the more they resisted the more they jerked. If they would not strive against it and pray in good earnest, the jerking would usually abate. I have seen more than five hundred persons jerking at one time in my large congregations. Most usually persons taken with the jerks, to obtain relief, as they said, would rise up and dance. Some would run, but could not get away. Some would resist; on such the jerks were generally very severe.

To see those proud young gentlemen and young ladies, dressed in their silks, jewelry, and prunella, from top to toe, take the *jerks*, would often excite my risibilities. The first jerk or so, you would see their fine bonnets, caps, and combs fly; and so sudden would be the jerking of the head that their long loose hair would crack almost as loud as a wagoner's whip.

At one of my appointments in 1804 there was a very large congregation turned out to hear the Kentucky boy, as they called me. Among the rest there were two very finely-dressed, fashionable young ladies, attended by two brothers with loaded horsewhips. Although the house was large; it was crowded. The two young

ladies, coming in late, took their seats near where I stood, and their
two brothers stood in the door. I was a little unwell, and I had a
phial of peppermint in my pocket. Before I commenced preaching
I took out my phial and swallowed a little of the peppermint.
While I was preaching, the congregation was melted into tears.
The two young gentlemen moved off to the yard fence, and both
the young ladies took the jerks, and they were greatly mortified
about it. There was a great stir in the congregation. Some wept,
some shouted, and before our meeting closed several were converted.

As I dismissed the assembly a man stepped up to me, and warned
me to be on my guard, for he had heard the two brothers swear they
would horsewhip me when meeting was out, for giving their sisters
the jerks. "Well," said I, "I'll see to that."

I went out and said to the young men that I understood they
intended to horsewhip me for giving their sisters the jerks. One
replied that he did. I undertook to expostulate with him on the
absurdity of the charge against me, but he swore I need not deny
it; for he had seen me take out a phial, in which I carried some
truck that gave his sisters the jerks. As quick as thought it came
into my mind how I would get clear of my whipping, and, jerking
out the peppermint phial, said I, "Yes; if I give your sisters the
jerks I'll give them to you." In a moment I saw he was scared. I
moved toward him, he backed, I advanced, and he wheeled and
ran, warning me not to come near him, or he would kill me. It
raised the laugh on him, and I escaped my whipping. I had the
pleasure, before the year was out, of seeing all four soundly converted to God, and I took them into the Church.

While I am on this subject I will relate a very serious circumstance which I knew to take place with a man who had the jerks
at a camp-meeting, on what was called the Ridge, in William
Magee's congregation. There was a great work of religion in the
encampment. The jerks were very prevalent. There was a company
of drunken rowdies who came to interrupt the meeting. These
rowdies were headed by a very large drinking man. They came with
their bottles of whiskey in their pockets. This large man cursed the
jerks, and all religion. Shortly afterward he took the jerks, and he
started to run, but he jerked so powerfully he could not get away.
He halted among some saplings, and, although he was violently

agitated, he took out his bottle of whiskey, and swore he would drink the damned jerks to death; but he jerked at such a rate he could not get the bottle to his mouth, though he tried hard. At length he fetched a sudden jerk, and the bottle struck a sapling and was broken to pieces, and spilled his whiskey on the ground. There was a great crowd gathered round him, and when he lost his whiskey he became very much enraged, and cursed and swore very profanely, his jerks still increasing. At length he fetched a very violent jerk, snapped his neck, fell, and soon expired, with his mouth full of cursing and bitterness.

I always looked upon the jerks as a judgment sent from God, first, to bring sinners to repentance; and, secondly, to show professors that God could work with or without means, and that he could work over and above means, and do whatsoever seemeth him good, to the glory of his grace and the salvation of the world.

There is no doubt in my mind that, with weak-minded, ignorant, and superstitious persons, there was a great deal of sympathetic feeling with a man that claimed to be under the influence of this jerking exercise; and yet, with many, it was perfectly involuntary. It was, on all occasions, my practice to recommend fervent prayer as a remedy, and it almost universally proved an effectual antidote.

There were many other strange and wild exercises into which the subjects of this revival fell; such, for instance, as what was called the running, jumping, barking exercise. The Methodist preachers generally preached against this extravagant wildness. I did it uniformly in my little ministrations, and sometimes gave great offense; but I feared no consequences when I felt my awful responsibilities to God. From these wild exercises, another great evil arose from the heated and wild imaginations of some. They professed to fall into trances and see visions; they would fall at meetings and sometimes at home, and lay apparently powerless and motionless for days, sometimes for a week at a time, without food or drink; and when they came to, they professed to have seen heaven and hell, to have seen God, angels, the devil and the damned; they would prophesy, and, under the pretense of Divine inspiration, predict the time of the end of the world, and the ushering in of the great millennium.

This was the most troublesome delusion of all; it made such an appeal to the ignorance, superstition, and credulity of all the people, even saint as well as sinner. I watched this matter with a vigilant eye. If I opposed it, I would have to meet the clamor of the multitude; and if any one opposed it, these very visionists would single him out, and denounce the dreadful judgments of God against him. They would even set the very day that God was to burn the world, like the self-deceived modern Millerites. They would prophesy, that if any one did oppose them, God would send fire down from heaven and consume him, like the blasphemous Shakers. They would proclaim that they could heal all manner of diseases, and raise the dead, just like the diabolical Mormons. They professed to have converse with spirits of the dead in heaven and hell, like the modern spirit rappers. Such a state of things I never saw before, and I hope in God I shall never see again.

I pondered well the whole matter in view of my responsibilities, searched the Bible for the true fulfillment of promise and prophecy, prayed to God for light and Divine aid, and proclaimed open war against these delusions. In the midst of them along came the Shakers, and Mr. Rankin, one of the Presbyterian revival preachers, joined them; Mr. G. Wall, a visionary local preacher among the Methodists, joined them; all the country was in commotion.

I made public appointments and drew multitudes together, and openly showed from the Scriptures that these delusions were false. Some of these visionary men and women prophesied that God would kill me. The Shakers soon pretended to seal my damnation. But nothing daunted, for I knew Him in whom I had believed, I threw my appointments in the midst of them, and proclaimed to listening thousands the more sure word of prophecy. This mode of attack threw a damper on these visionary, self-deluded, false prophets, sobered some, reclaimed others, and stayed the fearful tide of delusion that was sweeping over the country.

I will here state a case which occurred at an early day in the State of Indiana, in a settlement called Busroe. Many of the early emigrants to that settlement were Methodists, Baptists, and Cumberland Presbyterians. The Shaker priests, all apostates from the Baptist and the Cumberland Presbyterians, went over among them. Many of them I was personally acquainted with, and had given them letters when they moved from Kentucky to that new country. There were then no Methodist circuit preachers in that region.

There was an old Brother Collins, a local preacher, who with-stood these Shakers, and in private combat he was a full match for any of them, but he was not eloquent in public debate, and hence the Shaker priests overcame my old brother, and by scores swept members of different Churches away from their steadfastness into the muddy pool of Shakerism.

The few who remained steadfast sent to Kentucky for me, pray-ing me to come and help them. I sent an appointment, with an invitation to meet any or all of the Shaker priests in public debate; but instead of meeting me, they appointed a meeting in opposition, and warned the believers, as they called them, to keep away from my meeting; but from our former acquaintance and intimate friend-ship, many of them came to hear me. I preached to a vast crowd for about three hours, and I verily believe God helped me. The very foundations of every Shaker present were shaken from under him. They then besought me to go to the Shaker meeting that night. I went, and when I got there we had a great crowd. I proposed to them to have a debate, and they dared not refuse. The terms were these: A local preacher I had with me was to open the debate; then one or all of their preachers, if they chose, were to follow, and I was to bring up the rear. My preacher opened the debate by merely stating the points of difference. Mr. Brayelton followed, and, instead of argument, he turned everything into abuse and insulting slander. Then he closed, and Mr. Gill rose, but, instead of argument, he uttered a few words of personal abuse, and then called on all the Shakers to meet him a few minutes in the yard, talk a little, and then disperse.

Our debate was out in the open air, at the end of a cabin. I rose, called them to order, and stated that it was fairly agreed by these Shaker priests that I should bring up the rear, or close the argument. I stated that it was cowardly to run; that if I was the devil himself, and they were right, I could not hurt them. I got the most of them to take their seats and hear me. Mr. Gill gathered a little band, and he and they left. They had told the people in the day that if I continued to oppose them, God would make an example of me, and send fire from heaven and consume me. When I rose to reply I felt a Divine sense of the approbation of God, and that he would give me success.

I addressed the multitude about three hours, and when I closed

my argument I opened the door of the Church, and invited all that
would renounce Shakerism to come and give me their hand. Forty-
seven came forward, and then and there openly renounced the
dreadful delusion. The next day I followed those that fled; and the
next day I went from cabin to cabin, taking the names of those
that returned to the solid foundation of truth, and my number rose
to eighty-seven. I then organized them into a regular society, and
the next fall had a preacher sent to them. And perhaps this victory
may be considered among the first-fruits of Methodism in that part
of this new country. This was in 1808.

At this meeting I collected, as well as I could, the names and
places where it was supposed they wanted Methodist preaching. I
made out and returned a kind of plan for a circuit, carried it to
Conference, and they were temporarily supplied by the presiding
elder in 1809 and 1810. In 1811 the circuit was called St. Vincennes, and was attached to the Cumberland District, and Thomas
Stilwell appointed the preacher in charge.

CHAPTER VI. EXHORTING AND FIRST PREACHING

I will now resume my personal narrative. I went on enjoying
great comfort and peace. I attended several camp-meetings among
the Methodists and Presbyterians. At all of them there were many
souls converted to God. At one of these camp-meetings something
like the following incident occurred.

There was a great stir of religion in the crowded congregation
that attended. Many opposed the work and among the rest a Mr.
D——, who called himself a Jew. He was tolerably smart, and
seemed to take great delight in opposing the Christian religion. In
the intermissions, the young men and boys of us, who professed
religion, would retire to the woods and hold prayer-meetings; and
if we knew of any boys that were seeking religion, we would take
them along and pray for them. Many of them obtained religion in
these praying circles, and raised loud shouts of praise to God, in
which those of us that were religious would join.

One evening a large company of us retired for prayer. In the
midst of our little meeting this Jew appeared, and he desired to

know what we were about. Well, I told him. He said it was all wrong, that it was idolatry to pray to Jesus Christ, and that God did not nor would he answer such prayers. I soon saw his object was to get us into debate and break up our prayer-meeting. I asked him, "Do you really believe there is a God?"

"Yes, I do," said he.

"Do you believe that God will hear your prayers?"

"Yes," said he.

"Do you really believe that this work among us is wrong?"

He answered, "Yes."

"Well now, my dear sir," said I, "let us test this matter. If you are in earnest, get down here and pray to God to stop this work, and if it is wrong he will answer your petition and stop it; if it is not wrong, all hell cannot stop it."

The rest of our company seeing me so bold took courage. The Jew hesitated. I said, "Get down instantly and pray, for if we are wrong we want to know it." After still lingering and showing unmistakable signs of his unwillingness, I rallied him again. Slowly he kneeled, cleared his throat, and coughed. I said, "Now, boys, pray with all your might that God may answer by fire."

Our Jew began and said, trembling, "O Lord God Almighty," and coughed again, cleared his throat, and started again, repeating the same words. We saw his evident confusion, and we simultaneously prayed out aloud at the top of our voices. The Jew leaped up and started off, and we raised the shout and had a glorious time. Several of our mourners were converted, and we all rose and started into camp at the top of our speed, shouting, having, as we firmly believed, obtained a signal victory over the devil and the Jew.

In 1802 William M'Kendree was presiding elder of Kentucky District. John Page and Thomas Wilkerson were appointed to the Cumberland Circuit. The Conference this fall was held at Strother's Meeting-house, Tennessee. This was the first time I saw Bishop Asbury, that great, devoted man of God. Here the Cumberland District was formed, and John Page appointed presiding elder. The name of Cumberland Circuit was changed into Red River Circuit, and Jesse Walker was appointed to ride it. This was the circuit on which I lived.

The membership of the Western Conference this year numbered

seven thousand two hundred and one, the traveling preachers numbered twenty-seven, probationers and all.

At a quarterly meeting held in the spring of this year, 1802, Jesse Walker, our preacher in charge, came to me and handed me a small slip of paper, with these words written on it:

> Peter Cartwright is hereby permitted to exercise his gifts as an exhorter in the Methodist Episcopal Church, so long as his practice is agreeable to the Gospel. Signed in behalf of the society at Ebenezer.
>   JESSE WALKER, A. P.
> May, 1802

I was very much surprised. I had not been talked to by the preacher, nor had I formally attempted to exhort. It is true, in class and other meetings, when my soul was filled with the love of God, I would mount a bench and exhort with all the power I had; and it is also true that my mind had been deeply exercised about exhorting and preaching too. I told Brother Walker I did not want license to exhort; that if I did not feel happy I could not exhort, but if my soul got happy I felt that I had license enough. He urged me to keep the license, alleging that it was the more orderly way, and I yielded to his advice.

To show how matters were done up in those early days of Methodism, I will here state that this permit to exhort was all the license I ever received from the Church to preach until I received my parchment of ordination.

The fall of this year my father moved from Logan County down toward the mouth of the Cumberland River, into what was called Lewiston County. This was a new country, and at least eighty miles from any circuit. There was no regular circuit, and no organized classes; but there were a good many scattering members of the Methodist Episcopal Church through that region of country. I applied to Brother Page, our presiding elder, for a letter for myself, my mother, and one sister, which he gave us. On examination I found that mine contained a "Benjamin's mess." It not only stated my membership and authority to exhort, but it gave me authority to travel through all that destitute region, hold meetings, organize classes, and, in a word, to form a circuit, and meet him the next fall at the fourth quarterly meeting of the Red River Circuit, with a plan of a new circuit, number of members, names of preachers, if any, exhorters, class-leaders, &c., &c., &c. I am sorry I did not preserve the document; for surely, all things considered, it would be a curiosity to educated and refined Methodists at this day.

I felt bad on the reception of this paper, and told Brother Page I did not want to take it, for I saw through the solemn responsibilities it rolled upon me. I told him just to give me a simple letter of membership; that, although I did think at times that it was my duty to preach, I had little education, and that it was my intention to go to school the next year. He then told me that this was the very best school or college that I could find between heaven and earth, but advised me, when my father got settled down there, if I could find a good moral school with a good teacher, to go to it through the winter; then, in the spring and summer, form the circuit and do the best I could. . . .

I had much opposition in some places, but in others was kindly received. We had some very powerful displays of Divine grace, a goodly number obtained religion, and I received about seventy into society, appointed leaders, met classes, sung, prayed, and exhorted, and, under the circumstances, did the best I knew how.

Here I found the celebrated James Axley, and took him into the Church. Peace to his memory. He was in after years favorably known as a powerful and successful traveling preacher. He was a great and good man of God. He married, located, and long since went to his reward.

In the fall of this year, 1803, I met Brothers Page and Walker, reported my success, and the plan of the circuit. It was called Livingston Circuit, and Jesse Walker was appointed to it, and traveled it in 1804 and 1805. The increase of members this year was over nine thousand throughout the connection. In the Western Conference the increase was fifteen hundred. The number of traveling preachers was about thirty-five. There were four presiding-elder districts in the Western Conference: Holston, Cumberland, Kentucky, and Ohio. Brother Page located, and Lewis Garrett succeeded him on the Cumberland District. The Red River Circuit, in this district, was a very large one. It had but one preacher appointed to it, namely, Ralph Lotspeich.

Brother Garrett, the new elder, called on me at my father's, and urged me to go on this circuit with Brother Lotspeich. My father was unwilling, but my mother urged me to go, and finally prevailed. This was in October, 1803, when I was a little over eighteen years of age. I had a hard struggle to give my consent, and although I thought it my duty to preach, yet I thought I could do this and not throw myself into the ranks as a circuit preacher, when I was liable to be sent from Greenbrier to Natchez; no members hardly to support a preacher, the discipline only allowing a single man eighty dollars, and in nine cases out of ten he could not get half of that amount. These were times that tried men's souls and bodies too.

At last I literally gave up the world, and started, bidding farewell to father and mother, brothers and sisters, and met Brother Lotspeich at an appointment in Logan County. He told me I must preach that night. This I had never done; mine was an exhorter's dispensation. I tried to beg off, but he urged me to make the effort. I went out and prayed fervently for aid from heaven. All at once it seemed to me as if I could never preach at all, but I struggled in prayer. At length I asked God, if he had called me to preach, to give me aid that night, and give me one soul, that is, convert one soul under my preaching, as evidence that I was called to this work.

I went into the house, took my stand, gave out a hymn, sang, and prayed. I then rose, gave them for a text Isaiah xxvi, 4: "Trust ye in the Lord forever: for in the Lord Jehovah is everlasting strength." The Lord gave light, liberty, and power; the congregation was melted into tears. There was present a professed infidel. The word reached his heart by the Eternal Spirit. He was powerfully convicted, and, as I believe, soundly converted to God that night, and joined the Church, and afterward became a useful member of the same.

I traveled on this circuit one quarter, took twenty-five into the Church, and at the end of three months received six dollars. The health of Brother Crutchfield, who was on the Waynesville Circuit, having failed, he retired from labor, and Brother Garrett placed me on that circuit in his place, and put on the circuit with me Thomas Lasley, a fine young man, the son of an old local preacher who lived in Green County.

Our circuit was very large, reaching from the north of Green River to the Cumberland River, and south of said river into the

State of Tennessee. Here was a vast field to work in; our rides were long, our appointments few and far between. There were a great many Baptists in the bounds of the circuit, and among them were over thirty preachers, some of whom were said to be very talented. In the four weeks that it took us to go round the circuit, we had but two days' rest, and often we preached every day and every night, and although in my nineteenth year, I was nearly beardless, and cut two of my back jaw teeth this year. Hence they called me the boy preacher, and a great many flocked out to hear the boy. A revival broke out in many neighborhoods, and scores of souls were converted to God and joined the Methodist Episcopal Church; but there was also considerable persecution.

We had a preaching place in what, at that early day, was called Stockton Valley. There were several members of the Methodist Episcopal Church scattered around in the neighborhood, but no organized class. The Baptists, some years before, had a society here, and had built a log meeting-house, which was very common at an early day in the West. It was covered with boards. The Baptists flourished here for a considerable time, and they had enjoyed regular monthly preaching; but the society had nearly died out, and the preaching had been withdrawn for several years. The house was old and out of repair. As I passed round my circuit, I was re-quested to preach a funeral sermon at this old church. Accordingly, I felt an appointment on a Sabbath. When I came there was a very large congregation. While I was preaching, the power of God fell on the assembly, and there was an awful shaking among the dry bones. Several fell to the floor and cried for mercy.

The people besought me to preach again at night. I gave out an appointment accordingly, and having several days' rest, owing to a new arrangement in the circuit, I kept up the meeting night and day for some time, and at every coming together we had a gracious work. Many obtained religion, and great was the joy of the people. There were twenty-three very clear and sound conversions. As a matter of course they felt a great love for me, whom they all claimed as the instrument, in the hand of God, of their conversion. I was young and inexperienced in doctrine, and especially was I unacquainted with the proselyting tricks of those that held to exclu-sive immersion as the mode, and the only mode, of baptism. I believe if I had opened the doors of the Church then, all of them would have joined the Methodist Church, but I thought I would give them time to inform themselves. Accordingly, I told them that when I came again, I would explain our rules and open the doors of the Church, and then they could join us if they liked our rules and doctrines. In the meantime I left them some copies of our Discipline to read.

After doing this I started on my circuit round, and although the Baptist preachers had left this place, without preaching in it for years, yet, in a few days after I was gone, there were sent on appointments for the next Sabbath three of the Baptist preachers, and they came on, and all three preached as their custom was, and they all opened with the cry of "Water, water; you must follow your Lord down into the water." They then appointed what they called a union meeting there, to commence the next Friday and hold over Sabbath, and although I have lived long and studied hard, I have never to this day found out what a Baptist means by a union meeting. But to return. The few scattered Methodists in the neighborhood took the alarm, for fear these preachers would run my converts into the water before I would come round, and they dispatched an old exhorter after me, saying I must come immediately, or my converts would all be ducked. I had appointments out ahead, and I told the old exhorter if I went, he must go on and fill my appointments, to which he readily agreed. So back I came on Friday to the commencement of their union meeting. Two of them preached, but they paid no attention to me at all. As they had no meeting at night, I gave out an appointment for night at S——'s, Esq. He and his wife were two of my converts, and kind of leaders in the neighborhood. The people flocked out, and we had a good meeting and two conversions.

Next day we repaired to the old log meeting-house, and heard two more water sermons. When they were done preaching, they opened the way for persons to join the Church by giving in their experience. One old lady rose, and gave in something for an experience that had happened about ten years before. Then an old man rose, and told a remarkable dream he had in North Carolina twenty years before. They were both accordingly received by giving them the right hand of fellowship. There was then a seeming pause.

The preachers urged the people to come forward and give in their experience. O, how I felt! I was afraid that some one of my young converts would break the way, and the rest would then follow, and so I would lose all my converts. At length one of those young converts rose, and gave in his experience, claiming me, under God, as the instrument of his conviction and conversion; then another and another, till twenty-three of them told their experience; every one of them claiming me, under God, as the instrument of their salvation.

Their experiences were pronounced good, and the right hand of fellowship was freely given, and there was great joy in the camp, but it was death in the pot to me. I thought I could not bear up under it. I was sitting thinking what I would do. I am bereft of my children, and what have I left? Just behind me sat a very intelligent lady, who had long been a member of the Methodist Episcopal Church. About the time they were done giving the right hand of fellowship and rejoicing over my stolen children, a thought struck my mind very forcibly to give in my experience, and act as though I intended to join the Baptist Church. It may be that I can yet save them. I rose up, and gave in my experience; they gave me the right hand of fellowship, and then there was great rejoicing over the Methodist preaching boy.

Just as I sat down I felt some one touch me on the shoulder. I turned and as I looked round I met the eyes of my intelligent Methodist sister, and the large tears were coursing down her cheeks and dropping off her chin.

"O, brother," said she, in a subdued tone, "are you going to leave us?"

I replied to her, "Dear sister, fear not; I know what I am about. Pray hard. I hope to retake my children yet." And though she did not understand my plan, yet my reply seemed to quiet her fears.

There was a fine creek running near the old church. The preachers directed us all to appear next morning at nine o'clock, with a change of apparel, to be baptized.

I held meeting again that night, and had a good time. My situation was a critical one. I had no one to advise with. I dared not tell any one what I was going to do, for fear my plan would out and my object be defeated. I rose early next morning, retired to the woods, and if ever I asked God in good earnest for help it was then.

Brother and Sister S——, with whom I stayed, prepared a change of apparel, in order to baptism. At the appointed hour we all met at the creek, but I took no change of apparel. I had been baptized, and I did not intend to abjure my baptism. But I kept this all to myself. There was a great crowd out to see us immersed. My twenty-three young converts and the two old, dry dreamers that first gave in their experience, were all dressed and ready for the performance of what they considered to be their Christian duty. The preachers appeared. One of them sang and prayed, then gave us an exhortation, and bade us come forward. I knew all the time that it was all important to my success that I should present myself first. Accordingly I stepped forward, and said, "Brother M——" —who was the preacher and administrator—"I wish to join the Baptist Church if I can come in with a good conscience. I have been baptized, and my conscience is perfectly satisfied with it, and I cannot submit to be rebaptized. Can I come into your Church on these terms?"

The position I occupied startled the preacher.

"When were you baptized?" he asked.

"Years gone by," I replied.

"But how was it done? Who baptized you?" was the next inquiry.

"One of the best preachers the Lord ever made."

"Was it done by sprinkling?"

"Yes, sir."

"That is no baptism at all."

I replied, "The Scriptures say that baptism is not the putting away the filth of the flesh, but the answer of a good conscience, and my conscience is perfectly satisfied with my baptism, and your conscience has nothing to do with it."

"Well," said he, "it is contrary to our faith and order to let you come into the Baptist Church in that way. We cannot do it."

"Brother M——," said I, "your faith and order must be wrong. The Church has heard my experience, and pronounced it good; and you believe that I am a Christian, and cannot fall away so as to be finally lost. What am I to do? Are you going to keep me out of the Church, bleating round the walls like a lost sheep in a gang by myself? Brother M——, you must receive me into the Church.

I have fully made up my mind to join you on these terms; now, will you let me into the Church?"

Our preacher by this time had evidently lost his patience, and he very sharply bid me stand away, and not detain others. It was an intensely thrilling moment with me. I cast a look around on the crowd, and saw they were enlisted in my favor. I cast a wistful eye on the young converts; their eyes met mine most sympathetically, and many of them were weeping, they were so deeply affected. They all involuntarily seemed to move toward me, and their looks plainly spoke in my favor. It was an awful moment. O, how I felt! who can describe my feelings?

I stepped aside. Brother S—— stood next to the preacher, dressed ready for baptism; his wife was also dressed, and leaning on her husband's arm. Brother S—— said:

"Brother M——, are you going to reject Brother Cartwright, and not receive him into the Church?"

"I cannot receive him," said Brother M——.

"Well," said Brother S——, "if Brother Cartwright, who has been the means, in the hand of God, of my conversion, and the saving of so many precious souls, cannot come into the Church, I cannot and will not join it." "Nor I," said his wife; "Nor I," "Nor I;" and thus it went round, until every one of my twenty-three young converts filed off, and gathered around me. "That's right brethren," said I, "stand by me, and don't leave me; the Lord will bring all right!"

Well, the two old dreamers were baptized, and then the preachers urged the rest to come; but all in vain. Now, my dear reader, just imagine if you can, how I felt. I had a great mind to shout right out, and should have done so, but forbearance, at that time at least, was a virtue.

From the creek we repaired to the old log-church. Three of their ministers preached; and you may depend on it, I got a large share of abuse. They compared me to the Pharisees of old, for they said I would not go in myself, and those that would go in I had prevented; but I bore it as best I could. They stated that in all probability these souls that I had hindered would be lost, and if so, their damnation would be laid to me; but this did not alarm me much, for they had pronounced us all Christians good and true, and had often in their sermons there said that if a person were really converted, he never could lose his religion. How, then, could we be lost? and what was there to alarm us? The congregation saw the absurdity, and more and more were interested in my favor.

Next came on their communion. There were some loose planks laid across the benches, and all the members of their particular faith, that had been immersed, were invited to seat themselves on these planks. I was determined to give them another downward tilt, so I took my seat with the communicants; and some of the young converts, seeing me do so, seated themselves there also. But when the deacons came with the bread and wine, they passed us by. When they had got round, I rose and asked for the bread and wine for myself and the young converts. This threw a difficulty in the way of the deacons; however, they asked the preacher if they might give us the elements. The preachers peremptorily forbade it.

I then said, "My brethren, you, after hearing our experience, pronounced us Christians; and you say a Christian never can be lost; and our Saviour pronounced a solemn woe on those that offend one of his little ones; now do, therefore, give us the bread and wine!"

One of the preachers gave me a sharp reproof, and told me to be silent. This treatment enlisted the sympathies of almost the entire assembly, and they cried out, "Shame! shame!" Just as the preacher was about to dismiss the congregation, I rose, and asked of them the privilege of speaking to the people fifteen or twenty minutes, to explain myself. This they refused. I said, "Very well; I am in a free country, and know my rights." He then dismissed them, and I sprang on a bench, and said to the people that if they would meet me a few rods from the church, and hear me, I would make my defense.

The people flocked out; I mounted an old log, and the crowd gathered around me. I showed them the inconsistency of the Baptist preachers, and laid it to them as well as my inexperience would permit; and closed by saying that, as I and my children in the Gospel could not, in any consistent way, be admitted into the Baptist Church, I was now determined to organize a Methodist Church. I explained our rules, and invited all that were willing to join us, to come forward, and give me their hands and names. Twenty-seven came forward; all of my twenty-three young converts, and four others; and before the year ended, we took into the Church there seventy-seven members, but my Baptist friends blowed almost entirely out. I was greatly encouraged to go on, and do the best I could. . . .

CHAPTER XI. SLAVERY IN THE CHURCH

In the fall of 1812, our Tennessee Conference was holden at Fountain Head, State of Tennessee, on the first of November. At this first session of the Tennessee Conference the Illinois District was organized, and J. Walker appointed presiding elder. The Illinois Circuit, as a mission, was formed in 1804, and Benjamin Young appointed to it. It was attached to the Cumberland District, L. Garrett presiding elder. Brother Young returned sixty-seven members.

At this Conference I was appointed by Bishop Asbury to the Wabash District, which was then composed of the following circuits, namely: Vincennes, in the State of Indiana; and Little Wabash and Fort Massack, in Illinois. These three circuits were north of the Ohio River; the balance of the district was in Kentucky, namely, Livingston, Christian, Henderson, Hartford, and Breckenridge Circuits. In traveling the district I had to cross the Ohio River sixteen times during the year.

I told Bishop Asbury that I deliberately believed that I ought not to be appointed presiding elder, for I was not qualified for the office; but he told me there was no appeal from his judgment. At the end of six months I wrote to him, begging a release from the post he had assigned me; but when he returned an answer, he said I must abide his judgment, and stand in my lot to the end of the time. I continued accordingly in the service, but the most of the year was gloomy to me, feeling that I had not the first qualification for the office of a presiding elder. Perhaps I never spent a more gloomy and sad year than this in all my itinerant life; and from that day to this I can safely say the presiding elder's office has had no special charms for me; and I will remark, that I have often wondered at the aspirations of many, very many Methodist preachers for the office of presiding elder; and have frequently said, if I were a bishop, that such aspirants should always go without office under my administration. I look upon this disposition as the out-cropping of fallen and unsanctified human nature, and whenever this spirit, in a large degree, gets into a preacher, he seldom ever does much good afterward.

We had through the summer and fall of this conference year some splendid camp-meetings, many conversions, and many accessions to the Church. In the fall we met at Conference, October 1st, 1813, at Rees's Chapel, Tennessee. The name of Wabash District was changed to Green River District, and Vincennes, Little Wabash, and Fort Massack Circuits, north of the Ohio River, were stricken off and attached to the Illinois District, and Dixon and Dover Circuits, south of the Cumberland River, that had belonged to Nashville District, were attached to Green River District. I was appointed by Bishop Asbury presiding elder of this district, some time in the course of the summer of this conference year, 1813. We had a camp-meeting in the Breckenridge Circuit, and a glorious good work of religion was manifest throughout the meeting. It was at this meeting that Benjamin Ogden, one of the early preachers sent to the West, who became disaffected, and left the Methodist Episcopal Church under the secession of J. O'Kelly, and backslid, professed to be reclaimed, and returned to his mother Church.

Slavery had long been agitated in the Methodist Episcopal Church, and our preachers, although they did not feel it to be their duty to meddle with it politically, yet, as Christians and Christian ministers, be it spoken to their eternal credit, they believed it to be their duty to bear their testimony against slavery as a moral evil, and this is the reason why the General Conference, from time to time, passed rules and regulations to govern preachers and members of the Church in regard to this great evil. The great object of the General Conference was to keep the ministry clear of it, and there can be no doubt that the course pursued by early Methodist preachers was the cause of the emancipation of thousands of this degraded race of human beings; and it is clear to my mind, if Methodist preachers had kept clear of slavery themselves, and gone on bearing honest testimony against it, that thousands upon thousands more would have been emancipated who are now groaning under an oppression almost too intolerable to be borne. Slavery is certainly a domestic, political, and moral evil. Go into a slave community, and you not only see the dreadful evils growing out of the system in the almost universal licentiousness which prevails among the slaves themselves, but their young masters are often tempted and seduced from the paths of virtue, from the associations in which they are placed; and there is an under-current of heart-embittering feeling of many ladies of high and noble virtue, growing out of the want of fidelity of their husbands, and the profligate course of their sons. Let any one travel through slave states, and see the thousands of mixed blood, and then say if I have misrepresented the dreadful causes of domestic disquietude that often falls with mountain weight on honorable wives and mothers. And although, in the infancy of this republic, it seemed almost impossible to form a strong and democratic confederacy, and maintain their independence without compromising constitutionally this political evil, and thereby fixing a stain on this "Land of the free and home of the brave," yet it was looked upon as a great national or political evil, and by none more so than General Washington, the father of the republic. I will not attempt to enumerate the moral evils that have been produced by slavery; their name is legion. And now, notwithstanding these are my honest views of slavery, I have never seen a rabid abolition or free-soil society that I could join, because they resort to unjustifiable agitation, and the means they employ are generally unchristian. They condemn and confound the innocent with the guilty; the means they employ are not truthful, at all times; and I am perfectly satisfied that if force is resorted to, this glorious Union will be dissolved, a civil war will follow, death and carnage will ensue, and the only free nation on the earth will be destroyed. Let moral suasion be used to the last degree for the sake of the salvation of the slaveholders, and the salvation of the slaves. Let us not take a course that will cut off the Gospel from them, and deliver them over to the uncovenanted mercies of God, or the anathemas of the devil. I have had glorious revivals of religion among the slaves, and have seen thousands of them soundly converted to God, and have stood by the bedside of the dying slave, and have heard the swelling shout of Christian victory from the dying negro as he entered the cold waters of the river of Jordan. . . .

Our Pottawattomie Mission was located on Fox River. Jesse Walker was missionary, and I was appointed superintendent; and it belonged to the Illinois District. During the two years that I superintended this mission [1827–1828] I received not one cent from the missionary funds. We had near one hundred miles of unbroken wilderness country to pass through to get to this mission. I had to pack provisions for myself and horse to and from the mission. There being no roads, I had to hire my pilot, and camp out.

Having made preparations for the journey, and an appointment to meet the chiefs of the nation at the mission, I started from the Peoria Quarterly Meeting with my pilot and several volunteers for the mission. We shaped our course from point to point of timber. Late in the evening we struck the timber of the Illinois Vermillion, and finding plenty of water, we camped, struck fire, cooked, and took supper and dinner all under one. We had prayer, fixed our blankets and overcoats, and laid us down, and slept soundly and sweetly till next morning. We rose early, took breakfast, fed our horses, and started on our way across the Illinois River, swimming our horses beside a canoe, and just at night reached the mission. We called the mission family together and preached to them. The next day the chiefs appeared; we smoked the pipe of friendship with them, and, through an interpreter, I made a speech to them, explaining our object in establishing a mission among them. All the chiefs now shook hands with us, as their custom is, and gave us a very sociable talk, and all bid us a cordial welcome save one, who was strongly opposed to our coming among them. He did not wish to change their religion and their customs, nor to educate their children. I replied to him, and met all his objections. I tried to show them the benefits of civilization and the Christian religion. There was present a Chippewa chief, with his two daughters, at the mission. This chief made a flaming speech in favor of the mission, and in favor of our "Great Father," the President, and the American people. He had fought under the American colors in the last war with England, and had his diploma from the President as a brave captain, and showed it with great exultation. His two daughters were dressed like the whites, and could read pretty well. When our "great talk" was over, I asked them the liberty to preach to them, which was granted. I tried to explain to them the original state of man, the fall of man, and the redemption through Christ; the condition of salvation, namely, faith in Christ, and obedience to all the precepts of the Gospel, as revealed in the Holy Scriptures; and urged them to repent, and forsake all their sins, and come to Christ.

It was an awkward and slow way to preach, through an interpreter, but I succeeded much better than I anticipated. One Indian woman, who had obtained religion, as we believed, desired baptism, and the ordinance was administered to her. Several couples, from the scattering white people that hung around the mission, applied to be married.

After directing matters, according to my instructions as superintendent, we started for home. After traveling near fifty miles, night came on at a point of timber called Crow Point, and there we camped. A dreadful storm of wind arose, which blew a severe gale, but Providence favored us in withholding the rain, and we considered this a great blessing. The next day we reached the settlement, in health and safety.

We expended several thousand dollars of missionary money in improving these mission premises, and succeeded in civilizing and Christianizing a few of these Indians, but the whites kept constantly encroaching on them till they became restless, and, finally, the government bought them out. The mission premises, with a section of land, was reserved for one of the half breed, so that the Missionary Society lost all that they had expended. It is true, the chiefs of the nation gave Brother Walker a thousand dollars of their annuities, as a compensation for the improvements he had made with the missionary money; and this money properly belonged to the Missionary Society, but they never realized it; and the Indians moved, finally, west of the Mississippi. There is still a lingering, wasting remnant of that nation; they have a missionary among them, and a good many of them are pious Christians. . . .

4.

Lyman Beecher

"The Faith Once Delivered to the Saints"

(1823)

Lyman Beecher was the outstanding revivalist produced by New England Calvinism during the Second Great Awakening. He was also a leading figure in the moral reform movements and missionary activities of the day in which the Congregationalists played such an important role. But his most important contribution to Evangelicalism was to transform the abstract theological modifications of Edwardsean Calvinism, which Nathaniel W. Taylor had worked out at the Yale Divinity School, into an effective revivalistic technique. This sermon, preached in Worcester, Massachusetts, on October 15, 1823, was a resounding defense of the Trinity and of Calvin's view of a stern, judging God against Unitarianism. It is a classic document of the Protestant Counter Reformation. But, at the same time, it undercut the hyper-Calvinist doctrine of the predestined elect by defining "the evangelical system" according to Taylor's theories of free will and the power of moral suasion. Evangelicalism is not only the religion of the common man, Beecher asserts here, but it is the religion of revivalism. Written ten years before the Congregational churches of Massachusetts were finally disestablished (but five years after this had occurred in his own state of Connecticut), this sermon indicates the willingness of some New School Calvinists to abandon the established church system devised by the Puritans for the voluntary system of affiliation espoused by Evangelicalism. Yet at the same time, Beecher tries hard to claim that he is merely defending the fundamental tenets of the Gospel and not advocating any heretical new notions. Until his death in 1863 Beecher always considered himself an orthodox Calvinist.

[This selection is taken from his *Sermons Delivered on Various Occasions*, published in Boston in 1828.]

SERMON VII. THE FAITH ONCE DELIVERED TO THE SAINTS

Beloved, when I gave all diligence to write unto you of the common salvation, it was needful for me to write unto you, and exhort you that ye should earnestly contend for the faith which was once delivered unto the saints.—Jude, 3.

By the faith once delivered to the saints, is to be understood the doctrines of the Gospel. These were delivered to the saints by holy men, who spake as they were moved by the Holy Ghost. The saints to whom they were delivered, were those who constituted the church under the old dispensation, and the new. The exhortation to contend for them earnestly, supposes that they would be powerfully assailed; and yet, that they might be known and defended.

It is proposed, in this discourse,

To give an epitome of what is supposed to be the faith delivered to the saints;—to state the reasons for believing it such;—and to point out the manner in which it becomes the churches of our Lord to contend for it.

The faith once delivered to the saints includes, it is believed, among other doctrines, the following:—

That men are free agents, in the possession of such faculties, and placed in such circumstances, as render it practicable for them to do whatever God requires, reasonable that he should require it, and fit that he should inflict, literally, the entire penalty of disobedience. Such ability is here intended, as lays a perfect foundation for government by law, and for rewards and punishments according to deeds.

That the divine law requires love to God with all the heart, and impartial love for men; together with certain overt duties to God and men, by which this love is to be expressed; and that this law is supported by the sanctions of eternal life and eternal death.

That the ancestors of our race violated this law;—that, in some way, as a consequence of their apostacy, all men, as soon as they become capable of accountable action, do, *of their own accord, most freely* and *most wickedly* withhold from God the *supreme love*, and from man the *impartial love*, which the law requires, besides violating many of its practical precepts: and that the obedience of the heart, which the law requires, has ceased entirely from the whole race of man.

That, according to the principles of moral government, obedience, either antecedent or subsequent to transgression, cannot avert the penalty of law; and that pardon, upon condition of repentance merely, would destroy the efficacy of moral government.

That an atonement has been made for sin by Jesus Christ, with reference to which, God can maintain the influence of his law and forgive sin, upon condition of repentance towards God, and faith in our Lord Jesus Christ:—that all men are invited sincerely, in this way to return to God, with an assurance of pardon and eternal life if they comply.

That a compliance with these conditions is practicable, in the regular exercise of the powers and faculties given to man as an accountable creature; and is prevented only by the exercise of a voluntary, criminal aversion to God, so inflexibly obstinate, that, by motives merely, men are never persuaded to repent and believe.

That God is able, by his Spirit, to make to the mind of man such an application of the truth, as shall unfailingly convince him of sin, render him willing to obey the Gospel, and actually and joyfully obedient.

That this special influence of the Holy Spirit is given according to the supreme discretion or good pleasure of God; and yet, ordinarily, is so inseparably associated with the use of means by the sinner, as to create ample encouragement to attend upon them, and to render all hopes of conversion, while neglecting or rejecting the truth, or while living in open sin, eminently presumptuous.

That believers are justified by the merits of Christ through faith; and are received into a covenant with God, which secures their continuance in holiness forever;—while those, who die in their sins, will continue to sin wilfully, and to be punished justly, forever.

That God exercises a providential government, which extends to all events in such a manner, as to lay a just foundation for resignation to his will in afflictions brought upon us by the wickedness of men, and for gratitude in the reception of good in all the various modes of human instrumentality;—that all events shall illustrate his glory, and be made subservient to the good of his kingdom;—and that this government is administered in accordance with a purpose or plan known and approved of by him from the beginning.

Finally, that the God of the universe has revealed himself to us as existing in three persons, the Father, the Son, and the Holy Ghost; possessing distinct and equal attributes, and, in some unrevealed manner, so united, as to constitute *one God.*

These are the doctrines, which, it is believed, were delivered to the saints, and which have been held, substantially, though with some variety of modification, by the true church of God in all ages. To prevent circumlocution, I shall, in this discourse, call them *the Evangelical System,* and for the same reason, I shall call the opposite doctrines *the Liberal System.*[1]

It has been common to support these doctrines by the quotation of proof texts. But to these a different exposition is given, more reasonable it is said, and carrying with it a higher probability of truth; which leads to critical exposition, opens a wide field for evasion, and creates perplexity and indecision. My design at present, is to avail myself of collateral evidence only, with the view of attempting to decide, in this way, which is the correct exposition of the proof texts, the evangelical, or the liberal exposition.

For the sake of argument, I shall suppose the evidence from exposition to be, on each side, exactly balanced; and proceed to lay into the scale of evangelical exposition, those arguments which seem to furnish evidence of its correctness. I observe, then;

1. That the doctrines of the evangelical system are in accordance with the most direct and obvious meaning of the sacred text. By *obvious meaning,* I intend that which is actually suggested, without note or comment, to the minds of honest and unlettered men. That the proof texts teach the doctrines of the evangelical system in this manner, is alleged by learned infidels as a reason for rejecting the inspiration of the Bible; by Unitarian commentators and writers,

[1] I choose to call these doctrines the evangelical system, not only because I believe them to be the Gospel; but because no man or denomination has held them so exclusively, as to render it proper to designate them by the name of an individual or a sect. It is a select system, which some of almost every denomination hold, and some reject; and which ought to be characterised by some general term indicative of the system as held in all ages, and among all denominations of Christians. I call the opposite doctrines the liberal system, not as admitting that these doctrines, or their advocates, possess any peculiar claims to liberality, in any just acceptation of the term; but simply, because it is the epithet by which its friends have chosen to distinguish their religious opinions.

as a reason for restraining, modifying, and turning aside, the text;
and by critics, who translate or expound without reference to theological opinions; and by the better part of the Unitarian German
critics, after having denied the inspiration of the Bible.[2] No trans-
lators have been able to maintain a reputation for classical literature,
and to sink, in a translation, the obvious meaning below, and bring
up the philosophical meaning upon, the surface.[3] The editors of
the "Improved Version" have manifested as much good will, with
as little conscience, in the attempt, as has ever appeared; and yet
have been compelled to allow the proof texts, in most instances, to
speak the offensive doctrines, and to content themselves with a
simple contradiction of them in notes and comments. Interpretation
according to the obvious import, has always resulted in the evangelical system; while expositors according to the supposed rational
and philosophical mode of exposition, have differed indefinitely. It
is not the evangelical, but the liberal rule of interpretation, which
has filled the world with divers doctrines, perplexity and doubt.
All versions, and all expositions according to the obvious meaning,
of whatever country or age, do substantially agree in the evangelical
system; and agree with the understanding of mankind at large who
read the Bible. The Bible also, for the most part, was written by
men who understood language only according to its obvious import;
—and for the use of men, to whom it must have been a sealed book
upon any other principle of interpretation. Add to this, the testimony
of the Bible to its own plainness; that it can be read by him that
runs, and understood by the wayfaring man though a fool;—that it
is a lamp to the path;—that it furnishes the man of God thoroughly;—that it is profitable for doctrine;—that it is able to make
wise to salvation;—that it creates obligation to know the truth, and
renders error inexcusable. Now if the obvious meaning of the proof
texts be not the true one, and if the true meaning be one which
can be seen only by men of classical and philosophical vision, then
the common people have *no Bible*. For the book itself teaches *them*

[2]See Stuart's Letters, p. 155.

[3]This fact shows that these remarks are as applicable to the original text, as
to the translation; for surely, if the evangelical were not the obvious import
in the original, nothing would be easier than to give a literal translation which
should leave them out of sight entirely.

nothing; and the critical expositions of uninspired men are not a revelation. The character of God is also implicated, as having practised on his subjects a most deplorable deception; as having taught them falsehood in their own tongue, and the truth in an unknown tongue; for, to the common people, the obvious, is the only meaning of terms. If, therefore, the truth is not contained in the obvious meaning, it is not revealed to them in any form. Indeed, if the obvious be not the true import, the Bible teaches them falsehood. And yet, with a book, whose only intelligible meaning on the subject of doctrines is false, and whose real import is necessarily unknown, the common people are required, upon pain of his eternal displeasure, to abhor error, and to love and obey the truth. Was the glorious God ever more scandalized than by such an imputation? We have heard of his having made a great part of mankind on purpose to damn them, and of his sending to hell infants and help-less victims, for the non-performance of impossibilities: and, if such were indeed his character and conduct, I know not what other Bible we could expect, than one impossible to be understood, and framed to deceive. But, on this subject, we adopt the language of a distinguished advocate of the liberal system. "It is impossible that a teacher of infinite wisdom should expose those, whom he would teach, to infinite error. He will rather surpass all other in-structors in bringing down truth to our apprehension. A revelation is a gift of light; it cannot thicken and multiply our perplexities."[4]

2. It is the uniform testimony of the Bible, that the righteous love the truth, and that the wicked are opposed to it.

If then, we can decide who are the wicked in the scriptural sense, which system they approve, and which they oppose; we have an inspired decision which is the faith delivered to the saints. But the scriptures have decided that the irreligious and profane, and all persons of confirmed vicious habits, are wicked men. They have placed in the same class the ambitious, who love the praise of men more than the praise of God; and the voluptuous, who love pleasure more than God. Now that some of this description of sinners are found among the professed believers of both systems, is admitted; but which system do they, as a body, prefer, and against which do

---

[4]Channing's Sermon, second Baltimore ed. pp. 12, 13.

they manifest unequivocal hostility? It requires no proof but universal observation, to support the position, that the irreligious, immoral and voluptuous part of the community prefer the liberal
system, and are vehement in their opposition to the evangelical
system.[5] If this assertion needs confirmation, assemble the pleasure-
loving and licentious community of the world;—the patrons of
balls, and theatres, and masquerades, and let the doctrines of the
evangelical system be preached plainly to them. Would they be
pleased with them? Would they endure them? Do this class of the
community, anywhere in the wide world, where their numbers or
influence preponderate, settle and support an evangelical minister;
and if they support the preaching of any system of doctrines, is it
not substantially the liberal system? Go to the voluntary evening
association for conference and prayer, and which system will you
hear breathed out in supplication? Then go to the voluntary evening association for gambling or inebriation, and which system, with
its patrons, will you hear loaded with execration and ridicule? When
a division is made in a town or parish, by the settlement of a
minister of liberal or evangelical opinions, which side do a majority
of the pious take, if there be on earth any such thing as piety manifested by credible evidence; and which side do the wicked take, if
there be on earth any such class of persons as wicked men—proved
to be such by their deeds? If a majority is obtained against evangelical opinions, was it ever known to be done by the most pious
and moral part of the community, in opposition to the suffrages of
the most irreligious and flagitious?[6] There is, then, some powerful

[5]The reader will observe, that we do not say, nor do we believe it to be true,
that all, or even the majority, who professedly embrace the liberal system are
wicked in the sense explained. We know, and we gladly embrace the opportunity to acknowledge, that there are among them many, whose talents and
learning, whose amiable and generous dispositions, and whose devotedness to
the public good, on many accounts, deserve our respect and commendation.
There are, in the class of the community, many whom we not only respect and
esteem, but whom, as connexions and friends we tenderly love. Our assertion
is, that those who are wicked in the Scripture sense of that term, do, as a body,
whatever preaching they attend, and with whatever denomination they are
classed, dislike the doctrines of the evangelical faith and prefer those of the
liberal system.

[6]It may not be known to all who read this discourse, that, according to a
late construction given to the laws of Massachusetts, the town or society may
dispose of the funds which were given to the church; and dismiss or settle a

cause of universal operation, which arrays the irreligious part of the community against the evangelical system. But, according to the Bible, of two opposing systems, one of which must be true, that which the wicked approve is false, and that which they oppose and hate is true;—"for he that doeth evil hateth the light, neither cometh to the light, lest his deeds should be reproved."

3. The evangelical system produces the same effects, universally, as were produced by the faith delivered to the saints.

The maxim, that *the same cause in the same circumstances, will produce the same effect*, is as true in the moral, as in the natural world; the laws of mind, and the operation of moral causes, being just as uniform as the laws of matter. The Gospel, the greatest moral cause which ever operated in the world, is the same now as in the apostolic age; and the heart of man, civilized or uncivilized, is also the same. So that this great cause is operating now, in sub-

---

minister without the concurrence, and in opposition to the suffrage of the church. And that, in consequence of this decision, Unitarian ministers have often been settled by towns and societies in opposition to the efforts of evangelical churches: by which means, the latter have been stripped of their funds, and exiled from their place of worship, and subjected to the necessity of forming a new society, and erecting another house of worship, unless they would consent to set under Unitarian ministrations, and forego that instruction which they considered an important means of salvation. Now, in every one of these instances, it is believed, that the immoral and irreligious part of the town or society, have united with Unitarians; and sometimes, if not always, have contributed to the formation of a majority which could not have been obtained without them.

If it should be said, that these men united with Unitarians from a restless spirit of opposition to religious institutions generally, and not with any reference to doctrinal opinions: the answer is that, when Unitarians obtain the ascendancy, the external religious order of the society remains as it was, and is supported by these wicked men with more ardor than before. But when the evangelical part of the society with the church prevails, and the liberal part secedes; these same wicked men secede with them; so that, whether Unitarians prevail or act as a minority, the irreligious and profligate uniformly act with them; and never, in any case, act with the evangelical party. The wicked then will *support* religious order under Unitarian auspices, and, with Unitarians, will *abandon* it under evangelical auspices. Does this look like a mere restless opposition to religious order, without reference to doctrinal opinions? Are Unitarians so notoriously and always opposed to religious order, as to attach the enemies of religious institutions uniformly to their party; or is the evangelical system hated by wicked men because it is the truth, and the liberal system patronised by them, because they, whose deeds are evil, "love darkness rather than light"?

stantially the same circumstances as it did in the primitive age;—
for the heart of man is the moral world, and is the same now, as
in the time of the apostles. If there be a system of doctrines, then,
at the present time, whose effects are universally the same with
those produced by the faith once delivered to the saints; that system,
demonstrably, *is the faith* which was once delivered to the saints.
Identity of moral effect proves identity of moral cause. . . .

I observe then, that the evangelical system occasions the same
objections now, which were occasioned by the faith once delivered
to the saints.

Such an exhibition was given of old of the particular providence
of God, as occasioned, on the part of thieves, and liars, and adul-
terers, and idolaters, the extenuating plea, "We are delivered to do
all these abominations."[7] God governs the moral world by such
irresistible influence, that crimes are as much a matter of physical
necessity, as rain and sunshine. Do I need to say to this audience,
that the charge constantly urged against the decrees of God, as an
article of the evangelical system, is, that it destroys accountable
agency, and makes men machines, and all actions necessary by an
irresistible fatality? The faith delivered to the saints then, and the
evangelical faith, are perverted in this article, exactly alike.

The ancient faith included an article, which led the wicked among
the Jews, to extenuate their crimes by the allegation, "The fathers
have eaten sour grapes, and the children's teeth are set on edge";[8]
i. e. 'Sin in man, is a physical property transmitted from father to
son, as bones and sinews are, and alike inconsistent with choice or
blame.' And is not the objection urged against the doctrine of
original sin as contained in the evangelical system, the same? The
inspired answer to the objection of old was, That children are
accountable only for their own voluntary exercises and deeds; and
this is the reply returned now by the patrons of the evangelical
system.

The doctrine of human depravity as taught in the Bible, led the
people in a time of great wickedness, to say, "If our transgressions
and our sins be upon us, and we pine away in them, how should we

[7] Jer. vii. 10.
[8] Ezek. xviii. 2.

then live?"[9] i.e. 'If we be dead in sin, to the exclusion of all spiritual life, how can we be free agents, and how can we help ourselves, or be justly blamed?' And, as if they had been told by the prophet, that their death in sin was voluntary and criminal, though entire, and certain in its efficacy, they seem to say; 'Well, if we are so wicked that we certainly shall pine away in our sins, how can we be to blame? If we shall not turn of ourselves, how can we turn; and of what use is ability, that will never be exerted?' Now, are not these precisely the objections which are at this day constantly alleged against the doctrines of man's entire depravity, and moral inability, as articles of the evangelical system?

Our Saviour asserts the necessity of some great change to qualify a man for the kingdom of heaven, which, to a ruler in Israel, appeared mysterious, and even impossible. And in the evangelical system, is there not a great change insisted on, as indispensable to salvation; to which masters in Israel now, confess that they are strangers; and which they regard as impossible, without the destruction of free agency and accountability?

The manner of a sinner's justification was delivered to the saints in such terms as occasioned the objection, that it made void the law; superseding the obligations and motives to a moral life, and leading to licentiousness. "Do we then make void the law through faith?" "Shall we continue in sin that grace may abound?" And is not this precisely the objection which has been urged against the doctrine of justification by faith, as contained in the evangelical system, from the time of the reformation to this day?

The saints were taught something concerning the sovereignty of God, as having mercy on whom he would, and punishing whom he would;—which produced the objection, "Why then doth he yet find fault; for who hath resisted his will?" 'If wicked men receive their destination as God appoints, why does he blame them? If it be his will that they perish, and they do perish; are they not obedient; and why does he find fault?' And is not this the objection which is urged, unceasingly, against the doctrine of election as taught in the evangelical system? To our reply, that the will of God, as a moral rule to man, and the will of God, as a rule of administration to himself in disposing of rebels, are distinct; the

[9]Ezek. xxxiii. 10.

answer is, 'Metaphysics! metaphysics! The will of God is the will of God; and if sinners act, in any sense, in accordance with any will of God, they are obedient; and he has no cause to find fault.' Now, did the liberal exposition of the ninth of Romans ever produce, in the whole history of man, the objection which this chapter produced as written by the apostle; or do liberal preachers ever have occasion to adopt the reply of Paul to objections produced by their exposition? But the evangelical exposition produces, invariably, the same objection which the apostle encountered, and this objection receives, invariably, the same reply. "Nay, but, O man, who art thou that repliest against God?" 'Shall a being of yesterday arraign the conduct of his Maker? Shall a rebel sit in judgment upon his God? Are not men rebels, justly doomed to die; and, in reference to their character and condition as condemned criminals, all clay of the same lump? And is not the discretion of God to pardon or reprieve, as absolute, as that of the potter over his clay, to make one vessel to honor and another to dishonor?' Do you object, that the punishment threatened is unjust? But how could God make a vessel of *mercy* of one whose punishment would be unjust; or a vessel of *wrath* of one whose punishment would be undeserved? Do you call men impotent, because they are compared to clay; or assert, that the sovereignty of God, in saving some, *causes*, and renders unavoidable, the destruction of others? We reply, those who perish, perish *for their sins*, for which they might have been justly punished, without an offer of pardon. They might, if they would, comply with the terms of pardon, and are punished for rejecting them. Nor are they cut down in haste. With much longsuffering they are endured, while, by despising the riches of the goodness of God they *fit themselves* for destruction. Such is the evangelical reply; and such, as we understand his language and argument, is the reply of Paul.

It was objected to the Gospel, and in the early age, conceded, that few embraced it but the poor, and the common people. "To the poor the Gospel is preached." "Have any of the Scribes and Pharisees believed on him?" "The common people heard him gladly." "Not many wise men after the flesh, not many mighty, not many noble, are called." Celsus, in the second century, exulted in the fact, that so few in the higher classes of society had professed christianity; and poured contempt upon the cause, as patronized only by mechanics and vulgar people.[10] Now, is it not notorious, that the liberal system of doctrines, unpatronized by the civil power, has never been the religion of the common people in any country; but rather the religion of men of philosophical minds and literary habits? i. e. the evangelical system has been chiefly patronized by that class of society which patronized the faith delivered to the saints; while the opposite system has more commonly relied for patronage on the arm of government, and on that class of men in society who, as a body, rejected the Gospel. A late writer in this country, of high reputation on the liberal side, says, "It is not to be doubted, that, throughout our country, a very large proportion of those men, who, for their talents and learning and virtues, have the most influence in the community, and have it in their power to do the most towards giving a right direction to the public feeling and the public sentiment, are dissatisfied with the Calvinistic and Trinitarian form in which they have had religion presented to them; but are prevented from making a public avowal of their opinions, by an unwillingness to encounter opposition and obloquy, and loss of confidence, and the power of being useful."[11] The evangelical system in this country, then, is extensively embraced by the same classes which embraced the Gospel; and is extensively disapproved by that class of men who rejected the Gospel.[12] . . .

[10]Are there no attempts making to create an impression now, that the liberal system is patronized peculiarly by persons in high life, by men of taste and talents, of wealth and refinement; and that the opposite system is fast going down, to be the religion of the common people only, and of the poor?

[11]Dr. Ware's Letters to Trinitarians and Calvinists, pp. 146, 147.

[12]If, to any, it should seem improbable that the unlearned and obscure should be more likely to have the truth than men of talents and learning; we are ready to admit, that the apprehension would be just, if the perception of the truth depended, exclusively, upon capacity and knowledge. But if, as the Bible declares, the truth is so plain that the feeble and unlearned are able to perceive it, and its rejection is caused chiefly by the state of the heart; and if talents, and learning, and wealth, and power, occasion self-sufficiency, and ambition, and love of pleasure; with the cares of this world, diverting the attention from the truth, and increasing the prejudice of the heart against it; then men in the highest orders of society, are not as likely to have the truth as the common people: for the heart governs the understanding; and the peculiar aversion of learned and worldly men to the truth, throws more darkness upon it, than their superior intelligence serves to dispel; and creates a greater impediment to the perception of the truth, than is occasioned by any relative deficiency of capacity and knowledge among the common people. The argument, however, does not demand this explanation; for we do not infer the truth of the evangelical

The faith delivered to the saints produced revivals of religion. The preaching of it was attended with sudden anxieties, and deep convictions of sin, and sudden joy in believing, followed by reformation and a holy life. Nor was this the effect of miracles, or itself a miraculous event, in the common acceptation of the term. Miracles merely, produced no such effects. It was under the preaching of the word, that men were pricked in their hearts, and cried out, "Men and brethren, what shall we do to be saved?" And it was by the moral transformation which attended the apostolic answer to this question, and not by the power of miracles, that the Gospel defied opposition, and spread during the first three hundred years. There was no resisting it. Conviction attended the word, and a joyful obedience to the faith followed. The very chiefs of opposition exchanged their weapons of annoyance for the shield of faith, and the sword of the Spirit. And do not the same convictions of sin attend the preaching of the evangelical system; and does it not extend its victories in the same manner? By argument, merely, we convince few, and reclaim none. But there is an efficacy in evangelical preaching on the conscience and on the heart, against which neither learning, nor talents, nor prejudice, nor wrath itself, afford effectual protection. Multitudes who virulently hated, and verily thought that they ought to oppose evangelical doctrines and revivals of religion, have been convinced of their mistake and their sin; and have embraced, joyfully, the doctrines which they reviled. Many who preach the liberal system can bear witness, that they have lost, in this way, again and again, the very pillars of their societies. Defections of the same kind are frequent still, and clothe evangelical doctrines and revivals of religion with a terrifying power.

The faith delivered to the saints was efficacious in the sudden reformation of those who had been long under the dominion of vicious habits. The apostle enumerates the habits of crime which prevailed among Pagans; and then, writing to the church of Corinth, says, "And such were some of you." But, while the liberal system

---

system from the fact, that, either class is more likely to have the truth; but, from the fact, that the same sort of men reject the evangelical system now, who rejected the Gospel; and the same sort embrace it now, who embraced the Gospel: furnishing a strong presumptive argument, that the evangelical system and the Gospel are the same, because they produce the same effects.

despairs, professedly, of any sudden reformation from vicious habits, as against the established laws of the moral world; and is unable to produce an instance in which a vicious person has been reformed by *abandoning the evangelical, and adopting the liberal system*; and while reformation from vicious habits is a rare event, if it exists at all, under liberal preaching; it is a frequent event for profligates, on *abandoning their confidence in the liberal system and adopting the evangelical, to manifest a most salutary and abiding change of character and conduct.* In almost all the revivals of religion which are now prevailing in our land, there are some to whom it may be said, "And such were some of you, but ye are washed," &c. Dr. Chalmers, who preached the liberal system twelve years, and after this the evangelical, says, "And here I cannot but record the effect of an actual, though undesigned, experiment, which I prosecuted for upwards of twelve years, among you. For the greater part of that time, I could expatiate on the meanness of dishonesty, on the villany of falsehood, on the despicable arts of calumny; in a word, upon all those deformities of character, which awaken the natural indignation of the human heart against the pests and the disturbers of human society. Even at this time, I certainly did press the reformations of honor, and truth, and integrity, among my people; but I never once heard of any such reformations having been effected amongst them. If there was any thing at all brought about in this way, it was more than ever I got any account of. I am not sensible that all the vehemence with which I urged the virtues and the proprieties of social life, had the weight of a feather on the moral habits of my parishioners. And it was not till I got impressed by the utter alienation of the heart, in all its desires and affections, from God; it was not till reconciliation to him became the distinct and the prominent object of my ministerial exertions; it was not till I took the scriptural way of laying the method of reconciliation before them; it was not till the free offer of forgiveness through the blood of Christ was urged upon their acceptance; and the Holy Spirit, given through the channel of Christ's mediatorship to all who ask him, was set before them as the unceasing object of their dependence and their prayers; it was not, in one word, till the contemplations of my people were turned to these great and essential elements in the business of a soul providing for its interest with

God, and the concerns of its eternity; that I ever heard of any of those subordinate reformations which I aforetime made the earnest and the zealous, but I am afraid, at the same time, the ultimate object of my earlier ministrations."[13]

The faith delivered to the saints produced a spirit of missions. On the day of Pentecost the number of disciples was one hundred and twenty. And on that day the scales of Jewish prejudice fell from their eyes; and the spirit of missions descended upon their hearts; and, in three hundred years, without colleges, or theological seminaries, or the press, or governmental aid, but in opposition to its dire hostility, they evangelized the world. And are not the great movements now making to evangelize the world, conducted chiefly under the auspices, and by the charities of those, who adopt substantially the evangelical system? Are not all the denominations in the world, who believe in the Divinity of Christ and his atonement, in the depravity of man and his need of a moral renovation by the Spirit, and in the doctrine of justification by faith, and future eternal punishment, more or less engaged in the work of missions? And is there, in the wide world, a denomination which rejects these doctrines, that is thus engaged? And is this system, which does nothing to evangelize the world, the Gospel; and that, which does all that is done in accordance with the efforts of the primitive church, not the Gospel?

The faith delivered to the saints produced a piety of great solemnity, and ardor, and decision. It was a piety which took delight in the public worship of God, and in frequent private association for religious conference and prayer; a piety, which included a deep solicitude, and made vigorous exertions for the conversion of sinners, and experienced peculiar joy in the event; a piety, which espoused openly the cause of Christ, encountered obloquy and the loss of all things, and stood undaunted in the face of danger, and produced joy unspeakable in the hour of death. And is not this, precisely, the same cast of piety which the evangelical system does, and which the liberal system does not, produce? Is not the deeply serious cast of the one regarded as constituting the evangelical a gloomy religion; and the lighter cast of the other, as giving to it vastly the

[13]Chalmers' Farewell Discourse addressed to his parishioners of Kilmany, in his series of Discourses, pp. 110, 111, 112.

preference on the score of cheerfulness? Is not the ardor of the one stigmatized as enthusiasm; and the cool, deliberate, intellectual cast of the other regarded as giving to it the enviable pre-eminence of a rational religion? Does not the one delight in, and the other deprecate, frequent voluntary associations for religious conference and prayer? Does not the one ridicule the supposed work of sudden conversion by the Spirit of God, and the other hold it in the highest estimation? . . .

The doctrine of the incarnation of Christ was the received opinion of the church, when denied by the Gnostics, towards the close of the first century. The divinity of Christ was the received opinion of the church when denied by Arius, A. D. 315; who, soon after, was condemned as a heretic in a council of 380 Fathers. And the doctrines of original sin, entire depravity, regeneration by special grace, and justification by faith, continued to be the received doctrines of the church until the time of Pelagius, about A. D. 400.

The doctrines of the evangelical system, then, commenced their journey down to us from the apostolic age: and as each doctrine of the liberal system encountered any one of them, *that* was declared by the church to be a novelty, and the other the antecedently received opinion of the church. . . .

The faith, then, which the martyrs held under Pagan and Papal Rome, and for which they suffered, was the same; and was the WORD OF GOD AND THE FAITH OF JESUS. But we know, by evidence unequivocal and undeniable, that the doctrinal opinions of the martyrs under Papal Rome, were the doctrines of the evangelical system, and not those of the liberal system. They exist now upon historical records, and in public creeds; and are denominated the doctrines of the Reformation. The doctrines of the Reformation then, which we denominate the evangelical system, have the seal of heaven impressed upon them, as being the WORD OF GOD AND THE FAITH OF JESUS;—THE FAITH WHICH WAS ONCE DELIVERED TO THE SAINTS.

5.

Charles Grandison Finney

"What A Revival of Religion Is"
(1834)

Rather than quarrel among themselves over the formation of new churches in western New York, the Presbyterians and Congregationalists formed a union in 1801 to allow home missionaries in this area to work cooperatively. Charles Grandison Finney was ordained as a "Presbygational" home missionary in Oneida, New York, in 1824 and ostensibly adhered to the Calvinism of the Westminster Confession of Faith. But by 1835, when he published his famous *Lectures on Revivals of Religion,* Finney had repudiated both the Confession and the Calvinism based upon it. The outstanding revivalist in America for almost half a century, Finney's theology and "new measures" were halfway between those of Peter Cartwright and Lyman Beecher. Beecher at first opposed him as too radical, then cooperated with him during a revival campaign in Boston in 1831, and then denounced his "Perfectionist" heresies after 1835.

Finney delivered this lecture to his New York Presbyterian Church in December, 1834, in order to take people's minds off antislavery and keep them on the main theme of soul saving. But this lecture series achieved fame primarily because it defined so clearly the new "philosophic" or scientific principles upon which all modern revival techniques have built since his day. Old School Presbyterians at Princeton Seminary denounced the lectures as Arminian, if not Pelagian, and were glad when Finney left their denomination to become a Congregationalist in 1836. But for most Evangelicals Finney had, at last, made the principles of conversion and of revivalism systematic and pragmatic. As Finney told his Old School opponents, "the results justify my methods." Even Baptist evangelists like Jacob Knapp and Jabez Swan abandoned their Calvinism after 1835 to adopt Finney's methods. The

lectures became the "how-to-do-it" handbook for professional revivalists in all denominations.
[This lecture is taken from the original edition published in New York in 1835.]

I. WHAT A REVIVAL OF RELIGION IS

Text.—O Lord, revive thy work in the midst of the years, in the midst of the years make known; in wrath remember mercy.—Hab. iii. 2.

It is supposed that the prophet Habakkuk was contemporary with Jeremiah, and that this prophecy was uttered in anticipation of the Babylonish captivity. Looking at the judgments which were speedily to come upon his nation, the soul of the prophet was wrought up to an agony, and he cries out in his distress, "O Lord, revive thy work." As if he had said, "O Lord, grant that thy judgments may not make Israel desolate. In the midst of these awful years, let the judgments of God be made the means of reviving religion among us. In wrath remember mercy."

Religion is the work of man. It is something for man to do. It consists in obeying God. It is man's duty. It is true, God induces him to do it. He influences him by his Spirit, because of his great wickedness and reluctance to obey. If it were not necessary for God to influence men—if men were disposed to obey God, there would be no occasion to pray, "O Lord, revive thy work." The ground of necessity for such a prayer is, that men are wholly indisposed to obey; and unless God interpose the influence of his Spirit, not a man on earth will ever obey the commands of God.

A "Revival of Religion" presupposes a declension. Almost all the religion in the world has been produced by revivals. God has found it necessary to take advantage of the excitability there is in mankind, to produce powerful excitements among them, before he can lead them to obey. Men are so sluggish, there are so many things to lead their minds off from religion, and to oppose the influence of the gospel, that it is necessary to raise an excitement among them, till the tide rises so high as to sweep away the opposing obstacles. They must be so excited that they will break over these counteracting influences, before they will obey God.

Look back at the history of the Jews, and you will see that God

used to maintain religion among *them* by special occasions, when
there would be a great excitement, and people would turn to the
Lord. And after they had been thus revived, it would be but a short
time before there would be so many counteracting influences brought
to bear upon them, that religion would decline, and keep on declining, till God could have time—so to speak—to shape the course
of events so as to produce another excitement, and then pour out
his Spirit again to convert sinners. Then the counteracting causes
would again operate, and religion would decline, and the nation
would be swept away in the vortex of luxury, idolatry, and pride.

There is so little *principle* in the church, so little firmness and
stability of purpose, that unless they are greatly excited, they will
not obey God. They have so little knowledge, and their principles
are so weak, that unless they are excited, they will go back from
the path of duty, and do nothing to promote the glory of God.
The state of the world is still such, and probably will be till the
millennium is fully come, that religion must be mainly promoted
by these excitements. How long and how often has the experiment
been tried, to bring the church to act steadily for God, without
these periodical excitements! Many good men have supposed, and
still suppose, that the best way to promote religion, is to go along
uniformly, and gather in the ungodly gradually, and without excitement. But however such reasoning may appear in the abstract,
facts demonstrate its futility. If the church were far enough advanced in knowledge, and had stability of principle enough to *keep
awake*, such a course would do; but the church is so little enlightened, and there are so many counteracting causes, that the church
will not go steadily to work without a special excitement. As the
millennium advances, it is probable that these periodical excitements
will be unknown. Then the church will be enlightened, and the
counteracting causes removed, and the entire church will be in a
state of habitual and steady obedience to God. The entire church
will stand and take the infant mind, and cultivate it for God. Children will be trained up in the way they should go, and there will be
no such torrents of worldliness, and fashion, and covetousness, to
bear away the piety of the church, as soon as the excitement of a
revival is withdrawn.

It is very desirable it should be so. It is very desirable that the church should go on steadily in a course of obedience without these excitements. Such excitements are liable to injure the health. Our nervous system is so strung that any powerful excitement, if long continued, injures our health and unfits us for duty. If religion is ever to have a pervading influence in the world, it can't be so; this spasmodic religion must be done away. Then it will be uncalled for. Christians will not sleep the greater part of the time, and once in a while wake up, and rub their eyes, and bluster about, and vociferate, a little while, and then go to sleep again. Then there will be no need that ministers should wear themselves out, and kill themselves, by their efforts to roll back the flood of worldly influence that sets in upon the church. But as yet the state of the Christian world is such, that to expect to promote religion without excitements is unphilosophical and absurd.[1] The great political, and other worldly excitements that agitate Christendom, are all unfriendly to religion, and divert the mind from the interests of the soul. Now these excitements can only be counteracted by *religious* excitements. And until there is religious principle in the world to put down irreligious excitements, it is in vain to try to promote religion, except by counteracting excitements. This is true in philosophy, and it is a historical fact.

It is altogether improbable that religion will ever make progress among *heathen* nations except through the influence of revivals. The attempt is now making to do it by education, and other cautious and gradual improvements. But so long as the laws of mind remain what they are, it cannot be done in this way. There must be excitement sufficient to wake up the dormant moral powers, and roll back the tide of degradation and sin. And precisely so far as our own land approximates to heathenism, it is impossible for God or man to promote religion in such a state of things but by powerful excite-

[1]Finney lived in the era when there was no academic distinction between the humanities and the sciences. Consequently he uses the adjective "philosophical" throughout these lectures in the old sense of "logical," "rational," or "scientific." And he includes in the word "philosophy" what would now be designated as the science of psychology. Finney would accept Webster's first definition of philosophy as "the science which investigates the facts and principles of reality and of human nature and conduct." The crux of Finney's attack on Calvinism in these lectures is that its doctrines are contrary to the laws of philosophy and to "the laws of mind" and hence, in modern terms, Calvinism is "unscientific."

ments.—This is evident from the fact that this has always been the way in which God has done it. God does not create these excitements, and choose this method to promote religion for nothing, or without reason. Where mankind are so reluctant to obey God, they will not act until they are excited. For instance, how many there are who know that they ought to be religious, but they are afraid if they become pious they shall be laughed at by their companions. Many are wedded to idols, others are procrastinating repentance, until they are settled in life, or until they have secured some favorite worldly interest. Such persons never will give up their false shame, or relinquish their ambitious schemes, till they are so excited that they cannot contain themselves any longer.

These remarks are designed only as an introduction to the discourse. I shall now proceed with the main design, to show,

I. What a revival of religion is not;

II. What it is; and

III. The agencies employed in promoting it.

I. A Revival of Religion is Not a Miracle

1. A miracle has been generally defined to be, a Divine interference, setting aside or suspending the laws of nature. It is not a miracle, in this sense. All the laws of matter and mind remain in force. They are neither suspended nor set aside in a revival.

2. It is not a miracle according to another definition of the term miracle—*something above the powers of nature*. There is nothing in religion beyond the ordinary powers of nature. It consists entirely in the *right exercise* of the powers of nature. It is just that, and nothing else. When mankind becomes religious, they are not *enabled* to put forth exertions which they were unable before to put forth. They only exert the powers they had before in a different way, and use them for the glory of God.

3. It is not a miracle, or dependent on a miracle, in any sense. It is a purely philosophical result of the right use of the constituted means—as much so as any other effect produced by the application of means. There may be a miracle among its antecedent causes, or there may not. The apostles employed miracles, simply as a means by which they arrested attention to their message, and established

its Divine authority. But the miracle was not the revival. The miracle was one thing; the revival that followed it was quite another thing. The revivals in the apostles' days were connected with miracles, but they were not miracles.

I said that a revival is the result of the *right* use of the appropriate means. The means which God has enjoyed for the production of a revival, doubtless have a natural tendency to produce a revival. Otherwise God would not have enjoined them. But means will not produce a revival, we all know, without the blessing of God. No more will grain, when it is sowed, produce a crop without the blessing of God. It is impossible for us to say that there is not as direct an influence or agency from God, to produce a crop of grain, as there is to produce a revival. What are the laws of nature, according to which, it is supposed, that grain yields a crop? They are nothing but the constituted manner of the operations of God. In the Bible, the word of God is compared to grain, and preaching is compared to sowing seed, and the results to the springing up and growth of the crop. And the result is just as philosophical in the one case, as in the other, and is as naturally connected with the cause.

I wish this idea to be impressed on all your minds, for there has long been an idea prevalent that promoting religion has something very peculiar in it, not to be judged of by the ordinary rules of cause and effect; in short, that there is no connection of the means with the result, and no tendency in the means to produce the effect. No doctrine is more dangerous than this to the prosperity of the church, and nothing more absurd.

Suppose a man were to go and preach this doctrine among farmers, about their sowing grain. Let him tell them that God is a sovereign, and will give them a crop only when it pleases him, and that for them to plow and plant and labor as if they expected to raise a crop is very wrong, and taking the work out of the hands of God, that it interferes with his sovereignty, and is going on in their own strength; and that there is no connection between the means and the result on which they can depend. And now, suppose the farmers should believe such doctrine. Why, they would starve the world to death.

Just such results will follow from the church's being persuaded that promoting religion is somehow so mysteriously a subject of Divine sovereignty, that there is no natural connection between the means and the end. What *are* the results? Why, generation after generation have gone down to hell. No doubt more than five thousand millions have gone down to hell, while the church has been dreaming, and waiting for God to save them without the use of means. It has been the devil's most successful means of destroying souls. The connection is as clear in religion as it is when the farmer sows his grain.

There is one fact under the government of God, worthy of universal notice, and of everlasting remembrance; which is, that the most useful and important things are most easily and certainly obtained by the use of the appropriate means. This is evidently a principle in the Divine administration. Hence, all the *necessaries* of life are obtained with great *certainty* by the use of the simplest means. The luxuries are more difficult to obtain; the means to procure them are more intricate and less certain in their results; while things absolutely hurtful and poisonous, such as alcohol and the like, are often obtained only by torturing nature, and making use of a kind of infernal sorcery to procure the death-dealing abomination. This principle holds true in moral government, and as spiritual blessings are of surpassing importance, we should expect their attainment to be connected with *great certainty* with the use of the appropriate means; and such we find to be the fact; and I fully believe that could facts be known, it would be found that when the appointed means have been *rightly* used, spiritual blessings have been obtained with greater uniformity than temporal ones.

II. I Am to Show What a Revival Is

It presupposes that the church is sunk down in a backslidden state, and a revival consists in the return of the church from her backslidings, and in the conversion of sinners.

1. A revival always includes conviction of sin on the part of the church. Backslidden professors cannot wake up and begin right away in the service of God, without deep searchings of heart. The fountains of sin need to be broken up. In a true revival, Christians are always brought under such convictions; they see their sins in

such a light, that often they find it impossible to maintain a hope of their acceptance with God. It does not always go to that extent; but there are always, in a genuine revival, deep convictions of sin, and often cases of abandoning all hope.

2. Backslidden Christians will be brought to repentance. A revival is nothing else than a new beginning of obedience to God. Just as in the case of a converted sinner, the first step is a deep repentance, a breaking down of heart, a getting down into the dust before God, with deep humility, and forsaking of sin.

3. Christians will have their faith renewed. While they are in their backslidden state they are blind to the state of sinners. Their hearts are as hard as marble. The truths of the Bible only appear like a dream. They admit it to be all true; their conscience and their judgment assent to it; but their faith does not see it standing out in bold relief, in all the burning realities of eternity. But when they enter into a revival, they no longer see men as trees walking, but they see things in that strong light which will renew the love of God in their hearts. This will lead them to labor zealously to bring others to him. They will feel grieved that others do not love God, when they love him so much. And they will set themselves feelingly to persuade their neighbors to give him their hearts. So their love to men will be renewed. They will be filled with a tender and burning love for souls. They will have a longing desire for the salvation of the whole world. They will be in agony for individuals whom they want to have saved; their friends, relations, enemies. They will not only be urging them to give their hearts to God, but they will carry them to God in the arms of faith, and with strong crying and tears beseech God to have mercy on them, and save their souls from endless burnings.

4. A revival breaks the power of the world and of sin over Christians. It brings them to such vantage ground that they get a fresh impulse towards heaven. They have a new foretaste of heaven, and new desires after union to God; and the charm of the world is broken, and the power of sin overcome.

5. When the churches are thus awakened and reformed, the reformation and salvation of sinners will follow, going through the same stages of conviction, repentance, and reformation. Their hearts will be broken down and changed. Very often the most

abandoned profligates are among the subjects. Harlots, and drunkards, and infidels, and all sorts of abandoned characters, are awakened and converted. The worst part of human society are softened, and reclaimed, and made to appear as lovely specimens of the beauty of holiness.

III. I Am to Consider the Agencies Employed in Carrying Forward a Revival of Religion

Ordinarily, there are three agents employed in the work of conversion, and one instrument. The agents are God,—some person who brings the truth to bear on the mind,—and the sinner himself. The instrument is the truth. There are *always two* agents, God and the sinner, employed and active in every case of genuine conversion.

1. The agency of God is two-fold; by his Providence and by his Spirit.

(1.) By his providential government, he so arranges events as to bring the sinner's mind and the truth in contact. He brings the sinner where the truth reaches his ears or his eyes. It is often interesting to trace the manner in which God arranges events so as to bring this about, and how he sometimes makes every thing seem to favor a revival. The state of the weather, and of the public health, and other circumstances concur to make every thing just right to favor the application of truth with the greatest possible efficacy. How he sometimes sends a minister along, just at the time he is wanted! How he brings out a particular truth, just at the particular time when the individual it is fitted to reach is in the way to hear!

(2.) God's special agency by his Holy Spirit. Having direct access to the mind, and knowing infinitely well the whole history and state of each individual sinner, he employs that truth which is best adapted to his particular case, and then sets it home with Divine power. He gives it such vividness, strength, and power, that the sinner quails, and throws down his weapons of rebellion, and turns to the Lord. Under his influence, the truth burns and cuts its way like fire. He makes the truth stand out in such aspects, that it crushes the proudest man down with the weight of a mountain. If men were *disposed* to obey God, the truth is given with sufficient clearness in the Bible; and from preaching they could learn all that is necessary for them to know. But because they are wholly *disinclined* to obey it, God clears it up before their minds, and pours in a blaze of convincing light upon their souls, which they cannot withstand, and they yield to it, and obey God, and are saved.

2. The agency of men is commonly employed. Men are not mere *instruments* in the hands of God. Truth is the instrument. The preacher is a moral agent in the work; he acts; he is not a mere passive instrument; he is voluntary in promoting the conversion of sinners.

3. The agency of the sinner himself. The conversion of a sinner consists in his obeying the truth. It is therefore impossible it should take place without his agency, for it consists in *his* acting right. He is influenced to this by the agency of God, and by the agency of men. Men act on their fellow-men, not only by language, but by their looks, their tears, their daily deportment. See that impenitent man there, who has a pious wife. Her very looks, her tenderness, her solemn, compassionate dignity, softened and moulded into the image of Christ, are a sermon to him all the time. He has to turn his mind away, because it is such a reproach to him. He feels a sermon ringing in his ears all day long.

Mankind are accustomed to read the countenances of their neighbors. Sinners often read the state of a Christian's mind in his eyes. If his eyes are full of levity, or worldly anxiety and contrivance, sinners read it. If they are full of the Spirit of God, sinners read it; and they are often led to conviction by barely seeing the countenance of Christians.

An individual once went into a manufactory to see the machinery. His mind was solemn, as he had been where there was a revival. The people who labored there all knew him by sight, and knew who he was. A young lady who was at work saw him, and whispered some foolish remark to her companion, and laughed. The person stopped and looked at her with a feeling of grief. She stopped, her thread broke, and she was so much agitated she could not join it. She looked out at the window to compose herself, and then tried again; again and again she strove to recover her self-command. At length she sat down, overcome with her feelings. The person then approached and spoke with her; she soon manifested a deep sense of sin. The feeling spread through the establishment like fire, and in a few hours almost every person employed there was under conviction, so much so, that the owners, though worldly men, were astounded, and requested to have the works stop and have a prayer meeting; for they said it was a great deal more important to have these people converted than to have the works go on. And in a few days, the owners and nearly every person employed in the establishment were hopefully converted. The eye of this individual, his solemn countenance, his compassionate feeling, rebuked the levity of the young woman, and brought her under conviction of sin; and this whole revival followed, probably in a great measure, from so small an incident.[2]

If Christians have deep feeling on the subject of religion themselves, they will produce deep feeling wherever they go. And if they are cold, or light and trifling, they inevitably destroy all deep feeling, even in awakened sinners.

I knew a case, once, of an individual who was very anxious, but one day I was grieved to find that her convictions seemed to be all gone. I asked her what she had been doing. She told me she had been spending the afternoon at such a place, among some professors of religion, not thinking that it would dissipate her convictions to spend an afternoon with professors of religion. But they were trifling and vain, and thus her convictions were lost. And no doubt those professors of religion, by their folly, destroyed a soul, for her convictions did not return.

The church is required to use the means for the conversion of sinners. Sinners cannot properly be said to use the means for their own conversion. The church uses the means. What sinners do is to submit to the truth, or to resist it. It is a mistake of sinners, to think they are using means for their own conversion. The whole drift of a revival, and every thing about it, is designed to present the truth *to* your mind, for your obedience or resistance.

[2]The "individual" in this story was Finney himself; the manufactory was the Oriskany Woolen Mill in Oriskany, New York; the year was 1826. Finney tells the story in his *Memoirs*, pp. 183–184.

Remarks

1. Revivals were formerly regarded as miracles. And it has been so by some even in our day. And others have ideas on the subject so loose and unsatisfactory, that if they would only *think*, they would see their absurdity. For a long time, it was supposed by the church, that a revival was a miracle, an interposition of Divine power which they had nothing to do with, and which they had no more agency in producing, than they had in producing thunder, or a storm of hail, or an earthquake. It is only within a few years that ministers generally have supposed revivals were to be *promoted*, by the use of means designed and adapted specially to that object. Even in New England, it has been supposed that revivals came just as showers do, sometimes in one town, and sometimes in another, and that ministers and churches could do nothing more to produce them, than they could to make showers of rain come on their own town, when they are falling on a neighboring town.

It used to be supposed that a revival would come about once in fifteen years, and all would be converted that God intended to save, and then they must wait until another crop came forward on the stage of life. Finally, the time got shortened down to five years, and they supposed there might be a revival about as often as that.

I have heard a fact in relation to one of these pastors, who supposed revivals might come about once in five years. There had been a revival in his congregation. The next year, there was a revival in a neighboring town, and he went there to preach, and staid several days, till he got his soul all engaged in the work. He returned home on Saturday, and went into his study to prepare for the Sabbath. And his soul was in an agony. He thought how many adult persons there were in his congregation at enmity with God —so many still unconverted—so many persons *die* yearly—such a portion of them unconverted—if a revival does not come under five years, so many adult heads of families will be in hell. He put down his calculations on paper, and embodied them in his sermon for the next day, with his heart bleeding at the dreadful picture. As I understood it, he did not do this with any expectation of a revival, but he felt deeply, and poured out his heart to his people. And that sermon awakened *forty heads of families*, and a powerful revival followed; and so his theory about a revival once in five years was all exploded.

Thus God has overthrown, generally, the theory that revivals are miracles.

2. Mistaken notions concerning the sovereignty of God, have greatly hindered revivals.

Many people have supposed God's sovereignty to be something very different from what it is. They have supposed it to be such an arbitrary disposal of events, and particularly of the gift of his Spirit, as precluded a rational employment of means for promoting a revival of religion. But there is no evidence from the Bible, that God exercises any such sovereignty as that. There are no facts to prove it. But every thing goes to show, that God has connected means with the end through all the departments of his government —in nature and in grace. There is no *natural* event in which his own agency is not concerned. He has not built the creation like a vast machine, that will go on alone without his further care. He has not retired from the universe, to let it work for itself. This is mere atheism. He exercises a universal superintendence and control. And yet every event in nature has been brought about by means. He neither administers providence nor grace with that sort of sovereignty, that dispenses with the use of means. There is no more sovereignty in one than in the other.

And yet some people are terribly alarmed at all direct efforts to promote a revival, and they cry out, "You are trying to get up a revival in your own strength. Take care, you are interfering with the sovereignty of God. Better keep along in the usual course, and let God give a revival when he thinks it is best. God is a sovereign, and it is very wrong for you to attempt to get up a revival, just because *you think* a revival is needed." This is just such preaching as the devil wants. And men cannot do the devil's work more effectually, than by preaching up the sovereignty of God, as a reason why we should not put forth efforts to produce a revival.

3. You see the error of those who are beginning to think that religion can be better promoted in the world without revivals, and who are disposed to give up all efforts to produce religious excitements. Because there are evils arising in some instances out of great excitements on the subject of religion, they are of opinion

that it is best to dispense with them altogether. This cannot, and must not be. True, there is danger of abuses. In cases of great *religious* as well as all other excitements, more or less incidental evils may be expected of course. But this is no reason why they should be given up. The best things are always liable to abuses. Great and manifold evils have originated in the providential and moral governments of God. But these *foreseen* perversions and evils were not considered a sufficient reason for giving them up. For the establishment of these governments was on the whole the best that could be done for the production of the greatest amount of happiness. So in revivals of religion, it is found by experience, that in the present state of the world, religion cannot be promoted to any considerable extent without them. The evils which are sometimes complained of, when they are real, are incidental, and of small importance when compared with the amount of good produced by revivals. The sentiment should not be admitted by the church for a moment, that revivals may be given up. It is fraught with all that is dangerous to the interests of Zion, is death to the cause of missions, and brings in its train the damnation of the world.

FINALLY—I have a proposal to make to you who are here present. I have not commenced this course of Lectures on Revivals to get up a curious theory of my own on the subject. I would not spend my time and strength merely to give you instructions, to gratify your curiosity, and furnish you something to talk about. I have no idea of preaching *about* revivals. It is not my design to preach so as to have you able to say at the close, "We *understand* all about revivals now," while you do *nothing*. But I wish to ask you a question. What do you hear lectures on revivals for? Do you mean that whenever you are convinced what your duty is in promoting a revival, you will go to work and practise it?

Will you follow the instructions I shall give you from the word of God, and put them in practice in your own hearts? Will you bring them to bear upon your families, your acquaintances, neighbors, and through the city? Or will you spend the winter in learning *about* revivals, and do nothing *for* them? I want you, as fast as you learn any thing on the subject of revivals, to put it in practice, and go to work and see if you cannot promote a revival among sinners here. If you will not do this, I wish you to let me know at the beginning, so that I need not waste my strength. You ought to decide *now* whether you will do this or not. You know that we call sinners to decide on the spot whether *they* will obey the gospel. And we have no more authority to let you take time to deliberate whether *you* will obey God, than we have to let sinners do so. We call on you to unite now in a solemn pledge to God, that you will do your duty as fast as you learn what it is, and to pray that He will pour out his Spirit upon this church and upon all the city this winter.

6.

Francis Wayland

The Elements of Moral Science (1835)
and
The Elements of Political Economy (1840)

Francis Wayland, the Baptist minister who was president of Brown
University from 1827 to 1855, is remembered now chiefly for his
efforts to reform higher education. But in his day he was famous primarily as a Christian economist and author of the two most widely
used textbooks of moral science and political economy. Growing out
of his own teaching as Professor of Moral and Intellectual Philosophy
at Brown, these works captured so perfectly the philosophic bases
of the Scottish Realism which underlay Evangelical thought of Wayland's day that they became the prescribed textbooks for two generations of American college students. While ostensibly nontheological,
both volumes are in essence efforts to deduce the truth of Evangelical
Christianity from Natural Law and Common Sense. Or, as one review
of his work on political economy put it, "It is metaphysics reduced
to practical common sense and made subservient to Christianity."
Wayland considered himself an Evangelical Calvinist and it was in
defense of that position that he preached and wrote. Just as Charles
Finney's *Lectures on Revivals* had provided the "philosophic" under-
pinning for the promotion of revivals, so Wayland's *Elements of
Moral Science* provided the psychological and ethical theory underlying Evangelical preaching on the moral behavior of the individual
while his *Elements of Political Economy* provided the basis for Evangelical judgment of the secular life of their society. Chancellor James
Kent, the pre-eminent jurist of Wayland's day, said of his book on
moral science, "I do not know of any ethical treatise in which our
duties to God and to our fellow-men are laid down with more preci-
sion, simplicity, clearness, energy, and truth." His work on political
economy applies this ethical theory to such topics as the failure of

the French Revolution, the economic ineptitude of the Indians, "the tyranny of trades-unions," the evils of helping the undeserving poor, the necessity of universal education, and the virtues of the economic whip of work-or-starve in a laissez-faire system of free enterprise capitalism. To have read these works of Wayland is to understand the fundamental assumptions of the Evangelical mind in America in their purest form.

[These selections are from the first edition of *Moral Science* in 1835 and the second edition of *Political Economy* in 1852.]

(a) THE ELEMENTS OF MORAL SCIENCE

Chapter I. of the Origin of Our Notion of the Moral Quality of Actions
Section I. of Moral Law.

Ethics, or Moral Philosophy, is the Science of Moral Law.

The first question which presents itself is, what is moral law? Let us inquire, first, what is *law*, and secondly, what is *moral* law.

By the term *Law*, I think we generally mean, a form of expression, denoting either a mode of existence, or an order of sequence.

Thus, the first of Sir Isaac Newton's laws, namely, that every body will continue in a state of rest, or of uniform motion in a right line, unless compelled by some force to change its state, denotes a *mode of existence*.

The third law of motion, that, to every action of one body upon another, there is an equal and contrary re-action, denotes *an order of sequence*; that is, it declares the general fact, that, if one event occurs, the constitution of things under which we exist, is such, that the other event will also occur.

The axioms in mathematics are laws of the same kind. Thus, the axiom, if equals be added to equals, the wholes will be equal, denotes an order of sequence, in respect to quantity.

Of the same nature are the laws of chemistry. Such, for instance, is the law that, if soda be saturated with muriatic acid, the result will be common salt.

Thus in intellectual philosophy. If a picture of a visible object be formed upon the retina, and the impression communicated, by the nerves, to the brain, the result will be an act of perception.

The meaning of law, when referring to civil society, is substantially the same. It expresses an established order of sequence between a specified action, and a particular mode of reward or of punishment. Such, in general, is the meaning of *law*.

Moral philosophy takes it for granted that there is in a human action a moral quality; that is, that a human action may be right or wrong. Every one knows that we may contemplate the same action as wise or unwise; as courteous or impolite; as graceful or awkward; and, also, as right or wrong. It can have escaped the observation of no one, that there are consequences distinct from each other, which follow an action, and which are connected, respectively, with each of its attributes. To take, for instance, a moral quality. Two men may both utter what is false; the one intending to speak the truth, the other intending to deceive. Now, some of the consequences of this act are common to both cases, namely, that the hearers may, in both cases, be deceived. But it is equally manifest, that there are also consequences peculiar to the case in which the speaker intended to deceive; as, for example, the effects upon his own moral character, and the estimation in which he is held by the community. And thus, in general, moral philosophy proceeds upon the supposition that there may exist in the actions of men a moral quality, and that there are certain sequences connected by our Creator with the exhibition of that quality.

A moral law is therefore a form of expression denoting an order of sequence established, between the moral quality of actions, and their results.

Moral philosophy, or Ethics, is the science which classifies and illustrates moral law.

Here it may be worth while to remark, that an order of sequence established, of necessity supposes an Establisher. Hence moral philosophy, as well as every other science, proceeds upon the supposition of the existence of an universal cause, the Creator of all things, who has made every thing as it is, and who has subjected all things to the relations which they sustain. And hence, as all relations, whether moral or physical, are the result of His enactment, an order of sequence, once discovered in morals, is just as invariable as an order of sequences in physics.

Such being the fact, it is evident, that the moral laws of God, can never be varied by the institutions of man, any more than the physical laws. The results which God has connected with actions, will inevitably occur; all the created power in the universe to the contrary notwithstanding. Nor can these consequences be eluded or averted any more than the sequences which follow by the laws of gravitation. What should we think of a man who expected to leap off from a precipice, and, by some act of sagacity, elude the effect of the accelerating power of gravity; or, of another, who, by the exercise of his own will, determined to render himself imponderable. Every one who believes God to have established an order of sequences in morals, must see that it is equally absurd, to expect to violate, with impunity any moral law of the Creator.

Yet men have always flattered themselves with the hope that they could violate *moral* law and escape the consequences which God has established. The reason is obvious. In *physics*, the consequent follows the antecedent, frequently, immediately, and, most commonly, after a stated interval. In *morals*, the result is frequently long delayed; and the *time* of its occurrence is always uncertain. Hence, because sentence against an evil work is not executed *speedily*, therefore the hearts of the sons of men are fully set in them to do evil. But time, whether long or short, has neither *power* nor *tendency* to change the order of an established sequence. The time required for vegetation in different orders of plants, may vary, but yet wheat will always produce wheat, and an acorn will always produce an oak. That such is the case in morals, a heathen poet has taught us.

> Raro, antecedentem scelestum
> Deseruit, pede poena clauda.

A higher authority has admonished us, Be not deceived, God is not mocked; *whatsoever* a man *soweth, that, shall he* also *reap*. It is also to be remembered, that, in morals as well as in physics, the harvest is always more abundant than the seed from which it springs. . . .

Chapter II. Conscience or the Moral Sense

Section I. Is There a Conscience?

By conscience, or the moral sense, is meant, that faculty, by which we discern the moral quality of actions, and by which, we are capable of certain affections in respect to this quality.

By *faculty*, is meant any particular part of our constitution, by which we become affected, by the various qualities and relations of beings around us. Thus, by taste, we are conscious of the existence of beauty and deformity; by perception, we acquire a knowledge of the existence and qualities of the material world. And, in general, if we discern any quality in the universe, or produce, or suffer any change, it seems almost a truism, to say that we have a faculty, or power, for so doing. A man who sees, must have eyes, or the faculty for seeing, and, *if he have not eyes*, this is considered a sufficient reason why *he should not see*. And thus, it it universally admitted, that there may be a thousand qualities in nature, of which we have no knowledge, for the simplest reason, that we have not been created with the faculties for discerning them. There is a world without us, and a world within us, which exactly correspond to each other. Unless *both exist*, we can never be conscious of the existence of either.

Now, that we do actually observe a moral quality in the actions of men, must, I think, be admitted. Every human being is conscious, that, from childhood, he has observed it. We do not say, that all men discern this quality with equal accuracy, any more than that they all see with equal distinctness; but we say, that all men perceive it in some actions; and that there is a multitude of cases in which their perception of it, will be found universally to agree. And, moreover, this quality, and the feeling which accompanies the perception of it, are unlike those derived from every other faculty.

The question would then seem reduced to this, do we perceive this quality of actions by a single faculty, or by a combination of faculties. I think it must be evident, from what has been already stated, that this notion is, in its nature, simple and ultimate, and *distinct from every other notion*. Now, if this be the case, it seems self-evident, that we must have a *distinct and separate faculty*, to make us acquainted with the existence of this *distinct and separate quality*. This is the case in respect to all other distinct qualities: it is, surely, reasonable to suppose, that it would be the case with this, unless some reason can be shown to the contrary. . . .

Chapter IV. Human Happiness

We have already, on several occasions, alluded to the fact that God has created every thing double; a world without us, and a corresponding world within us. He has made light without, and the eye within; beauty without, and taste within; moral qualities in actions, and conscience to judge of them; and so of every other case. By means of this correspondence, our communication with the external world exists.

These internal powers are called into exercise, by the presence of their corresponding external objects. Thus, the organ of vision is excited by the presence of light, the sense of smell by odors, the faculty of taste by beauty or deformity, and so of the rest.

The first effect of this exercise of these faculties is, that we are conscious of the existence and qualities of surrounding objects. Thus, by sight, we become conscious of the existence and colors of visible objects, by hearing of the existence and sound of audible objects, &c.

But, it is manifest, that this knowledge of the existence and qualities of external objects, is far from being all the intercourse which we are capable of holding with them. This knowledge of their existence and qualities, is, most frequently, attended with pleasure or pain, desire or aversion. Sometimes the mere perception itself is immediately pleasing; in other cases, it is merely the sign of some other quality which has the power of pleasing us. In the first case, the perception produces gratification, in the other, it awakens desire.

That is, we stand in such relations to the external world, that certain objects, besides being capable of being perceived, are also capable of giving us pleasure, and certain other objects besides being perceived are capable of giving us pain. Or, to state the same truth, in the other form, we are so made, as to be capable, not only of perceiving, but, also, of being pleased with, or pained by, the various objects by which we are surrounded.

This general power of being pleased or pained, may be, and I think frequently is, termed sensitiveness.

This sensitiveness, or the power of being made happy, by surrounding objects, is intimately connected with the *exercise* of our various faculties. Thus, the pleasure of vision cannot be enjoyed in any other manner, than by the *exercise* of the faculty of sight. The pleasure of knowledge can be enjoyed in no other way, than by the exercise of the intellectual powers. The pleasure of beauty can be enjoyed in no other manner, than by the exercise of the faculty of taste, and of the other subordinate faculties, on which this faculty depends. And, thus, in general, our sensitiveness derives pleasure from the *exercise of those powers which are made necessary* for our existence and well-being in our present state.

Now, I think that we can have no other idea of happiness, than the exercise of this sensitiveness upon its corresponding objects and qualities. It is the gratification of desire; the enjoyment of what we love; or, as Dr. Johnson remarks: "Happiness consists in the multiplication of agreeable consciousness."

It seems, moreover, evident, that this very constitution is, to us, an indication of the will of our Creator; that is, inasmuch as he has created us, with these capacities for happiness, and has also created objects around us precisely adapted to these capacities, he meant that the one should be exercised upon the other; that is, that we should be made happy in this manner.

And, this is more evident, from considering that this happiness is intimately connected with the exercise of those faculties, the employment of which is necessary to our existence, and our well-being. It thus becomes the incitement to, or the reward of, certain courses of conduct, which, it is necessary to our own welfare, or to that of society, that we should pursue.

And, thus, we arrive at the general principle that our desire for a particular object, and the existence of the object adapted to this desire, is, in itself, a reason why we should enjoy that object, in the same manner as our aversion to another object is a reason why we should avoid it. There may be, it is true, other reasons to the contrary, which may be more authoritative than that emanating from this desire or aversion, and these may and ought to control it; but this does not show that the desire is not *a reason*, and a sufficient one, if no better reason can be shown to the contrary.

But, if we consider the subject a little more minutely, we shall find that the simple gratification of desire, in the manner above stated, is not the only condition on which our happiness depends.

We find, by experience, that a desire or appetite may be so gratified as forever afterwards to destroy its power of producing happiness. Thus, a certain kind of food is pleasant to me, this is a reason why I should partake of it. But, I may eat of it to excess, so as to loathe it forever afterwards, and thus annihilate, in my constitution, this mode of gratification. Now, the same reasoning which proves that God intended me to *partake* of this food, namely, because it will promote my happiness, also proves that he did not intend me to partake of it after this manner, for, by so doing, I have diminished, by this whole amount, my capacity for happiness, and thus defeated, in so far, the very end of my constitution. Or, again, though I may not destroy my desire for a particular kind of food, by a particular manner of gratification, yet, I may so derange my system that the eating of it shall produce pain and distress, so that it ceases to be to me a source of happiness *upon the whole*. In this case, I equally defeat the design of my constitution. The result equally shows, that, although he means that I should eat it he does not mean that I should eat it in this manner.

Again, every man is created with various and dissimilar forms of desire, corresponding with the different external objects designed to promote his happiness. Now, it is found that one form of desire may be gratified in such a manner, as to destroy the power of receiving happiness from another; or, on the contrary, the first may be so gratified as to leave the other powers of receiving happiness unimpaired. Since then, it is granted, that these were all given us for the same end, namely, to promote our happiness, if, by one manner of gratification, we destroy another power of gratification, while, by another manner of gratification, we leave this first power of gratification uninjured, it is, evidently, the design of our Creator that we should limit ourselves to this latter mode of gratification. . . .

Hence, while it is *the truth*, that human happiness consists in the gratification of our desires, it is not *the whole truth*. It consists in the *gratification of our desires within the limits assigned to them by our Creator*. And, the happiness of that man will be the most perfect, who regulates his desires most perfectly in accordance with the laws under which he has been created. And, hence, the greatest happiness of which man is in his present state capable, is to be attained by conforming our whole conduct to the laws of virtue, that is, to the will of God.

Chapter V. Of Self Love

By the term sensitiveness, I have designated the capacity of our nature, to derive happiness from the various objects and qualities of the world around us. Though intimately associated with those powers, by which we obtain a knowledge of external objects, it differs from them. When a desire for gratification is excited by its appropriate objects, it is termed appetite, passion, &c.

As our means of gratification are various, and are also attended by different effects, there is evidently an opportunity for choice between them. By declining a gratification at present, we may secure one of greater value, at some future time. That which is, at present, agreeable, may be of necessity followed by pain; and that which is, at present, painful, may be rewarded by pleasure which shall far overbalance it.

Now, it must be evident, to every one who will reflect, that my happiness, at any one period of my existence, is just as valuable as my happiness at the present period. No one can conceive of any reason, why the present moment should take the precedence, in any respect, over any other moment of my being. Every moment of my past life was once present, and seemed of special value; but in the retrospect, all seem so far as the happiness of each is concerned of equal value. Each of those to come may, in its turn, claim some pre-eminence; though, now, we plainly discover in anticipation, that no one is more than another entitled to it. Nay, if there be any difference, it is manifestly in favor of the most distant future, in comparison with the present. The longer we exist, the greater is our capacity for virtue and happiness, and the wider is our sphere of existence. To postpone the present for the future, seems, therefore, to be the dictate of wisdom, if we calmly consider the condition of our being.

But, it is of the nature of passion, to seize upon the present gratification, utterly irrespective of consequences, and, utterly regardless of other or more excellent gratifications, which may be obtained by self-denial. He, whose passions are inflamed, looks at nothing beyond the present gratification. Hence, he is liable to seize upon a present enjoyment, to the exclusion of a much more valuable one in future; and even in such a manner as to entail upon himself poignant and remediless misery. And, hence, in order to be enabled to enjoy all the happiness of which his present state is capable, the sensitive part of man needs to be combined with another, which upon a comparison of the present with the future, shall impel him towards that mode either of gratification or of self-denial, which shall most promote his happiness upon the whole.

Such is self-love. We give this name to that part of our constitution, by which we are incited to do, or to forbear, to gratify, or to deny our desires, simply on the ground of obtaining the greatest amount of happiness for ourselves, taking into view a limited future, or else our entire future existence. When we act from simple respect to present gratification, we act from passion. When we act from a respect to our whole individual happiness, without regard to the present, only as it is a part of the whole, and without any regard to the happiness of others, only as it will contribute to our own, we are then said to act from self-love.

The difference between these two modes of impulsion, may be easily illustrated.

Suppose a man destitute of self-love, and actuated only by passion. He would seize, without reflection, and enjoy without limit, every object of gratification which the present moment might offer, without regard to its value in comparison with others, which might be secured by self-denial; and without any regard to the consequences which might follow present pleasure, be they ever so disastrous.

On the contrary, we may imagine a being destitute of passions, and impelled only by self-love; that is, by a desire for his own happiness, on the whole. In this case, so far as I see, he would never act at all. Having no desires to gratify, there could be no gratification; and hence, there could be no happiness. Happiness is the result of the exercise of our sensitiveness upon its corresponding objects. But we have no sensitiveness which corresponds with any object in ourselves; nor do ourselves present any object to correspond with such sensitiveness. Hence, the condition of a being, destitute of passions, and actuated only by self-love, would be an indefinite and most painful longing after happiness, without the consciousness of any relation to external objects which could gratify it. Nor is this an entirely imaginary condition. In cases of deep melancholy, and of fixed hypochondria, tending to derangement, I think every one must have observed in others, and he is happy, if he have not experienced in himself, the tendencies to precisely such a state. The very power of affection, or sensitiveness, seems paralyzed. This state of mind, has, I think, been ascribed to Hamlet by Shakespeare, in the following passage.

"I have, of late, (but wherefore I know not,) lost all my mirth, foregone all custom of exercises; and, indeed, it goes so heavily with my dispositions, that this goodly frame, the earth, seems to me a sterile promontory; this most excellent canopy, the air—look you —this brave overhanging firmament; this majestical roof, fretted with golden fire; why, it appears no other thing to me, than a foul and pestilent congregation of vapours. Man delights me not, nor woman neither, though by your smiling you seem to say so." *Hamlet*, Act ii, Sc. 2.

It would seem, therefore, that self-love was not, in itself a faculty, or part of our constitution, in itself, productive of happiness; but rather, an impulse which, out of several forms of gratification that may be presented, inclines us to select that which will be the most for our happiness, considered as a whole. This seems the more evident, from the obvious fact, that a man, actuated by the most zealous self-love, derives no more happiness from a given gratification, than any other man. His pleasure, in any one act of enjoyment, is not in the ratio of his self-love, but of his sensitiveness. . . .

Chapter VI. Imperfection of Conscience; Necessity of Some Additional Moral Light

It has been already remarked, that a distinction may be very clearly observed between right and wrong, and guilt and innocence. Right and wrong depend upon the obligations under which we are created; and are, in their nature immutable. Guilt and innocence have respect to the individual, and are modified moreover, by the amount of his knowledge, of his duty; and are not decided solely by the fact, that the action was, or was not, performed.

It is, moreover, to be observed, that the results of these two attributes of actions, may be seen to differ. Thus, every right action, is followed, in some way, with pleasure or benefit to the individual; and every wrong one, by pain or discomfort, irrespective of the guilt or innocence of the author of the act. Thus, in the present constitution of things, it is evident, that a nation, which had no knowledge of the wickedness of murder, revenge, uncleanness, or theft, would, if it violated the moral law, in these respects, suffer the consequences which are attached to these actions by our Creator. And, on the contrary, a nation which practised forgiveness, mercy, honesty, and purity, without knowing them to be right, would enjoy the benefits which are connected with such actions.

Now, whatever be the object of this constitution, by which rewards or punishments are affixed to actions as right and wrong, whether it be as a monition, or to inform us of the will of God concerning us; one thing seems evident, it is not to punish actions as *innocent or guilty*, for the rewards and punishments, of which we speak, affect men simply in consequence of the *action*, and without any regard to the innocence or guilt of the actor.

Let us now, add another element. Suppose a man to know the obligations which bind him to his Creator; and also, what is his Creator's will respecting a certain action; and that he then deliberately violates this obligation. Now, every man feels that this violation of obligation deserves punishment; and, also, punishment in proportion to the greatness of the obligation violated. Hence, the consequences of any action, are to be considered in a two fold light; first, the consequences depending upon the present constitution of things; and, secondly, those which follow the action, as innocent or guilty; that is, as violating, or not, our obligations to our Creator. . . .

If such be our state, it is manifest, that, under such a moral constitution as we have above described, our condition must be sufficiently hopeless. Unless something be done, it would seem that we must all fail of a large portion of the happiness, to which we might otherwise in the present life attain, and still more, must be exposed to a condemnation greater than we are capable of conceiving.

Under such circumstances, it surely is not improbable, that a benevolent Deity should make use of some additional means, to inform us of our duty, and thus warn us of the evils which we were bringing upon ourselves. Still less is it improbable, that a God, delighting in right, should take some means to deliver us from the guilty habits which we have formed, and restore us to that love and practice of virtue, which can alone render us pleasing to him. That God was under any obligation to do this, is not asserted; but that a being of infinite compassion and benevolence should do it, though not under obligation, is surely not improbable. . . .

Chapter IX. *The Holy Scriptures*

This would be the place in which to present the proof of the authenticity of the Holy Scriptures, as a revelation from God. This, however, is only a particular exemplification of the general laws of evidence, and belongs to the course of instruction in intellectual philosophy. It must, therefore, be here omitted. We shall, in the remainder of these remarks, take it for granted, that the Scriptures of the Old and New Testament contain a revelation from God to man, and that these books contain all that God has been pleased to reveal unto us by language; and, therefore, all which is recorded in language that is ultimate in morals, and that is, by its own authority, binding upon the conscience. . . .

The whole of this volume taken together, teaches us the precepts, the sanctions and the rewards of the law of God with as great distinctness as we could desire, and also, a way of salvation, on different grounds from that revealed both by natural religion, and by the Old Testament; a way depending for *merit*, upon the doings and sufferings of another, but yet *available* to us, on no other conditions, than those of supreme, strenuous and universal moral effort after perfect purity of thought, and word, and action.

This being a remedial dispensation, is, in its nature, fixed. We have no reason to expect any other; nay, the idea of another, would be at variance with the belief of the truth of this. And hence, the Scriptures of the Old and New Testaments, contain all that God has revealed to us by language respecting his will. What is contained here alone, is binding upon the conscience. Or, in the words of Chillingworth, "THE BIBLE, THE BIBLE, THE RELIGION OF PROTESTANTS."

(b) THE ELEMENTS OF POLITICAL ECONOMY

Chapter Third. Of the Laws Which Govern the Application of Labor to Capital

. . . 1. God has created man with physical and intellectual faculties, adapted to labor. He has given us a mind, adapted to investigate the laws of the universe, and a body adapted to perform all those operations by which, in obedience to those laws, the objects of desire may be produced.

2. Labor has been made necessary to the attainment of the means of happiness. No valuable object of desire can be procured without it. Intellectual power cannot be attained without intellectual discipline; nor a knowledge of the laws of nature, without study. Neither physical comforts, nor even physical necessaries, can be obtained, unless labor be first expended to procure them. The universal law of our existence is, "In the sweat of thy face shalt thou eat thy bread."

3. Labor is necessary to the healthful condition of our powers, both physical and intellectual. Without intellectual labor, the mind becomes enfeebled; and, were this labor wholly intermitted, it would sink into idiocy or madness. Without physical labor, the body, feeble and enervated, becomes a prey to pain and disease.

4. That labor, *per se*, is pleasant, it is not necessary to assert. It is sufficient to our purpose, that it is less painful than idleness and the results of idleness. The laborer complains of his toil, but deprive him of his opportunity for toil, and he becomes miserable. . . .

5. On the contrary, the Creator has affixed several penalties, which those who disobey this law of their being, can never expect to escape. He who refuses to labor with his mind, suffers the penalty of ignorance. The amount of this penalty may be estimated, by considering the blessings, both physical and intellectual, of which ignorance deprives us; and by contrasting the comforts of savage with those of civilized nations, where the physical effort, made by both, is the same. He who refuses to labor with his hands, suffers, besides the pains of disease, all the evils of poverty, cold, hunger, and nakedness. The results which our Creator has attached to idleness, are all to be considered as punishments, which he inflicts for the neglect of this established law of our being.

6. And, on the other hand, God has assigned to industry, rich and abundant rewards. "The hand of the diligent maketh rich." "Seest thou a man diligent in his business, he shall stand before kings; he shall not stand before mean men." The pleasure, the independence, and the power arising from knowledge, are the rewards of intellectual industry. "*A wise man is strong, yea, a man of understanding*

increaseth strength." And it is only by physical labor, that the riches of the earth are appropriated, and the laws of nature made available to the happiness of man. At the first there existed nothing in our world but the earth, with its spontaneous productions, and capabilities, and helpless and defenceless man. All that now exists of capital, of convenience, of comfort, and of intelligence, is the work of industry, and is the reward which God has bestowed upon us for obedience to the law of our being.

7. If such be the facts; if God have given to all men faculties for labor; if he have made labor necessary to our happiness; if he have attached the severest penalties to idleness, and have proffered the richest rewards to industry; it would seem reasonable to conclude, that all that was required of us, was, so to construct the arrangements of society, as to give free scope to the laws of Divine Providence. If he have excited us to labor by sufficient rewards, and deterred us from indolence by sufficient penalties, it would seem that our business must be, to give to these rewards and penalties their free and their intended operation. . . .

Section II. Industry Will Be Applied to Capital, As Every Man Enjoys the Advantages of His Labor and His Capital

Although God has designed men to labor, yet he has not designed them to labor without reward. Hence, when men devise some form of labor, even for exercise, they always connect with it some result, as the game of the huntsman, or the watering place of the traveller or tourist. Thus, also, as it is unnatural to labor without receiving benefit from labor, men will not labor continuously nor productively, unless they receive such benefit. And, hence, the greater this benefit, the more active and spontaneous will be their exertion.

In order that every man may enjoy, in the greatest degree, the advantages of his labor. . . .

I. *It is necessary that every man be allowed to gain all that he can*; that is, that the arrangements of society be so constructed, that every man be able to render his labor, in the highest degree, available to himself. This will require,

1. *That property be divided.* When property is held in common, every individual of the society to which it belongs, has an equal, but an undivided and indetermined right to his portion of the revenue.

Hence, every one is at liberty to take what he will, and as much as he will, and to labor as much or as little as he pleases. There is, therefore, under such an arrangement, no *connexion* between *labor* and the *rewards* of labor. There is rather a premium for indolence than for industry. . . .

On the contrary, as soon as land with all other property is divided, a motive exists for regular and voluntary labor, inasmuch as the individual knows that he, and not his indolent neighbor, will reap the fruit of his toil. Henceforth he begins to create a regular supply of annual product. With increased skill, this annual product increases, and he begins to convert it into fixed capital, a form of wealth which could scarcely exist without division of property. Every accession to his fixed capital renders his labor more productive, and hence it creates a stronger stimulus to increased exertion. With increased exertion, his annual capital is increased, and a greater surplus remains to be changed into fixed capital. Thus, increased production stimulates industry, and increased industry results in more abundant production. Thus, division of property, or the appropriation, to each, of his particular portion of that which God has given to all, lays at the foundation of all accumulation of wealth, and of all progress in civilization. . . .

2. But the division of property would be of no avail unless the right of property *were enforced*. . . .

Hence, we see the economical importance of all means which shall prevent the *individual violation* of the right of property. These means are two.

The first is, the inculcation of those moral and religious principles, which teach men to respect the rights of others as their own, that is, to obey the law of reciprocity; and which present the strongest conceivable reasons for so doing. This is the *most certain* method of preventing the violation of the right of property, inasmuch as it aims to eradicate those dispositions of mind, from which all violation proceeds. It is also the *cheapest*, as it aims at *prevention*, which is always more economical than *cure*. It is also *necessary*, inasmuch as good laws will never be enacted, or if enacted, will never be obeyed, only in so far as there exists a moral character in the community sufficiently pure to sustain them. In proportion as these are efficacious, all other means are needless. Hence, we see the reason why moral and religious nations grow wealthy so much more rapidly than vicious and irreligious nations. The feeling of perfect tranquillity and security, which a high social morality diffuses over a whole community, is one of the most beneficial, as well as one of the strongest stimulants to universal industry. This is one of the temporal rewards which God bestows upon social virtue. And, inasmuch as no one can enjoy this reward, simply by being virtuous himself, but only as his fellow citizens also are virtuous, we see the indication in our constitution, that it is the duty, as well as the interest, of every man, to labor to render other men more virtuous.

3. But inasmuch as all men are not influenced in their conduct by moral and religious principles, it is necessary that aggression be somehow prevented, and violations of property, in so far as possible, redressed. Hence, the importance of wholesome and equitable laws, of an independent and firm judiciary, and an executive, which shall carry the decisions of law faithfully into effect. Hence the expense, necessary for the most perfect administration of justice, is among the most productive of all the expenditures of society. Good law, and the faithful administration of it, are always the cheapest law, and the cheapest administration of it. The interests of man require that law should be invariably executed, and that its sovereignty should, under all circumstances, be inviolably maintained.

But the right of property may be violated by *society*. It sometimes happens, that society, or government, which is its agent, though it may prevent the infliction of wrong by individuals upon each other, is by no means averse to inflicting wrong or violating the right of individuals itself. This is done, where governments seize upon the property of individuals by mere arbitrary act, a form of tyranny, with which all the nations of Europe were, of old, too well acquainted. It is also done, by unjust legislation; that is, when legislators, how well soever chosen, enact unjust laws, by which the property of a part, or of the whole, is unjustly taken away, or what is the same thing subjected to oppressive taxation. . . .

It is owing rather to the freedom of her institutions and the equity of her laws, than to her physical advantages, that Great Britain has so far outstripped all other European nations in the accumulation of wealth, and in everything that confers social power. It is almost superfluous, however, to add, that a free constitution is of no value, unless the moral and intellectual character of a people be sufficiently elevated to avail itself of the advantages which it offers. It is merely an *instrument* of good, which will accomplish nothing, unless there exist the moral disposition to use it aright. . . .

II. The second part of the condition mentioned in the beginning of this section is, that the individual be allowed to use his own as he will. . . .

The choice of every man naturally leads him to that employment for which he is best adapted. By allowing every man, therefore, to employ his industry as he chooses, every man will be employed about that for which he is best adapted; and hence, the production of all will be greatly increased, because we thus avail ourselves of the *peculiar* productiveness of every individual. Nor is this all. By allowing every man to labor as he chooses, we very greatly increase the happiness of every individual. And every one knows that a man will labor with better success when his labor is pleasant, than when it is irksome.

The case is the same with respect to *capital*. Every man is more interested in his own success, than any other man can be interested in it. Hence, every man is likely to ascertain more accurately in what manner he can best employ his capital, than any other man can ascertain it for him. If every man, therefore, be allowed to invest his capital as he will, the whole capital of a country will be more profitably invested, than under any other circumstances whatever. And, since, when he is left thus at liberty, there will be the greatest gain to the capitalist, there will also be the greatest stimulus to his industry; for the stimulus to labor is always in proportion to the rewards of labor. And, on the contrary, in just so far as, by any means, this productiveness is diminished, the stimulus to labor is also diminished with it. . . .

Besides, every man feels, instinctively, that he has a *right* to use his capital and his industry as he pleases, provided he interfere not with the rights of another; and that, to restrict him in this use, is injustice. . . .

If this be so, we see the impolicy of several forms of legislative interference, in relation to this subject.

1. We see what must be the effects of monopolies. A monopoly is an exclusive right granted to a man, or to a company of men, to

employ their labor or capital in some particular manner. . . .
Those who hold this exclusive privilege, being liable to no competition, may charge for their commodities whatever they choose. Here
is, therefore, a two-fold injustice; first, the means of the consumer
are diminished; and secondly, the price which he must pay, is enhanced at the mere will of his oppressor.

2. Hence we see the impolicy of obliging an individual, or a
class of individuals, to engage in any labor, or to make any investment, contrary to their wishes. Thus, we are told that during the
French revolution, some individuals were punished capitally, for
raising cattle instead of wheat. Men may call this *legislation*, but the
true name for it is *robbery*. To oblige a man to raise a crop worth
fifteen dollars per acre, when he would otherwise have raised one
worth twenty dollars per acre, is just the same thing as to let him
do as he pleases, and then rob him of five dollars an acre afterwards. The wrong is the more intense, in the former case, inasmuch
as it is done under the semblance of justice, and by men who claim,
as the robber does not, that they have the *right* to do it. Such legislation as this will, in any country, soon produce a famine.

3. Another form of injury under this class, is seen in the restrictions upon industry, formerly, if not now, existing in many of the
countries of Europe. By these regulations, artisans were prohibited
the exercise of more than one trade; they were not allowed to exercise that trade, unless they had served a prescribed apprenticeship;
nor unless they joined a particular trade-society, and bound themselves to comply with certain restrictions, as, for instance, to sell at
particular prices, and never to employ beyond a certain number
of apprentices. The result of all this oppression is most iniquitous.
It reduces the value of skill and industry, the sole estate of the
laborer; and places him in the power of those whose interest it is
to reduce the supply as much as possible, in order to secure to themselves the most exorbitant profit. In such cases, a large amount of
available industry must be kept out of employment; and, of course,
production is, to this whole amount, diminished. The tyranny of
trades-unions, though emanating from the people instead of the
government, produces precisely the same effect.

4. The same effect is partially produced by any mode of legislation, by which, in consequence of favor shown to one party, which

of course another party must pay for, men are obliged to exchange
an employment, for which they have peculiar facilities, for another
which they do not prefer, and for which they have not the same
facilities. . . .

5. Hence, we also see the impolicy of laws regulating consumption. Such are sumptuary laws; or those which limit the degree of
expensiveness in our dress, clothing, or equipage. These were formerly common in Europe. Such also are laws which forbid or restrict
the expenditure of money for the purposes of benevolence, religion,
or any thing of this sort. Every one must see that one of the incitements to industry, is the pleasure which men expect to derive from
expenditure. Now, if this expenditure be innocent, it matters not
what sort of expenditure it is. Society has nothing to do with it; and
it can in no manner interfere with it, without doing injustice, and
taking away one of the strongest inducements to industry.

Section III. Labor Will Be Applied to Capital in Proportion as Every Man Suffers the Inconveniences of Idleness

. . . . men may be relieved from the necessity of labor, by charity.
It will be understood that I here speak of men as poor from indolence, and not by visitation of God. I do not here refer to the
sick, the infirm, the aged, the helpless, the widow, the fatherless,
and the orphan. When God has seen fit to take away the power
to labor, he then calls upon us to bestow liberally, and he always
teaches us, that this mode of expenditure of our property is more
pleasing to him than any other. With this mode of charity I have
now nothing to do. I speak only of provisions for the support of
the poor, simply because he is poor; and of provisions to supply his
wants, without requiring the previous exertion of his labor. Of this
kind are poor laws, as they are established in England, and in some
parts of our own country, and permanent endowments left to particular corporations for the maintenance of the simply indigent.
Now such provisions we suppose to be injurious, for several reasons.

1. They are at variance with the fundamental law of government,
that he who is able to labor, shall enjoy only that for which he
has labored. If such be the law of God for us all, it is best for all,
that all should be subjected to it. If labor be a curse, it is unjust that
one part, and that the industrious part, should suffer it all. If, as is

the fact, it be a blessing, there is no reason why all should not equally enjoy its advantages.

2. They remove from men the fear of want, one of the most natural and universal stimulants to labor. Hence, in just so far as this stimulus is removed, there will be, in a given community, less labor done; that is, less product created.

3. By teaching a man to depend upon others, rather than upon himself, they destroy the healthful feeling of independence. When this has once been impaired, and the confidence of man in the connexion between labor and reward is destroyed, he becomes a pauper for life. It is in evidence, before the committee of the British House of Commons, that, after a family has once applied for assistance from the parish, it rarely ceases to apply regularly, and most frequently, in progress of time, for a larger and larger measure of assistance.

4. Hence, such a system must tend greatly to increase the number of paupers. It is a discouragement to industry, and a bounty upon indolence. With what spirit will a poor man labor, and retrench, to the utmost, his expenses, when he knows that he shall be taxed to support his next-door neighbor, who is as able to work as himself; but who is relieved from the necessity of a portion of labor, merely by applying to the overseer of the poor for aid.

5. They are, in principle, destructive to the right of property, because they must proceed upon the concession, that the rich are under obligation to support the poor. If this be so; if he who labors be under obligation to support him that labors not; then the division of property and the right of property are at an end: for, he who labors has no better right to the result of his labor, than any one else.

6. Hence, they tend to insubordination. For, if the rich are under obligation to support the poor, why not to support them better? nay, why not to support them as well as themselves? Hence the larger provision there is of this kind, the greater will be the liability to collision between the two classes.

If this be so, we see, that in order to accomplish the designs of our Creator in this respect, and thus present the strongest inducement to industry. . . .

That those who are enabled only in part to earn their subsistence, be provided for, to the amount of that deficiency only.

And hence, that all our provisions for the relief of the poor, be so devised as not to interfere with this law of our nature. By so directing our benevolent energies, the poor are better provided for; they are happier themselves; and a great and constantly increasing burden is removed from the community. It has been found that alms-houses, conducted on this plan, will support themselves; and sometimes even yield a small surplus revenue. This surplus, however, should always be given to the paupers, and should never be received by the public. The principle should be carried out, that the laborer is to enjoy the result of his industry.

For the same reason, penitentiaries and State prisons should always be places of assiduous and productive labor. Idleness is a most prolific parent of crime. If the vicious could be accustomed to labor, one half of their reformation would be effected.

Besides, by this means, a great diminution would be effected in the expense to the community. There can be no reason why a hundred able-bodied men, and such are generally the tenants of our prisons, should not both support themselves, and pay for the superintendence necessary to their labor. In a well regulated prison, they will always do this. . . .

Section IV. The Greater the Ratio of Capital to Labor, the Greater Will Be the Stimulus to Labor

. . . . every mode of unnecessary expenditure, whether individual or national, by diminishing the annual accumulation of capital, tends directly to lower the rate of wages, and thus injure the condition of the laboring classes. The millions which are wasted and destroyed by intemperance, if saved, would add to the capital of a country, and thus increase the demand for labor. All unnecessary expenditure, for the maintenance of civil government, has, of course, the same tendency. Hence arises, also, one of the most afflicting consequences of war. Had the almost incalculable sums which Great Britain has expended in wars, for the last hundred years, been added to her operative capital, and, but for these wars, it would have been so added, all her inhabitants would have found, at all times, abundant employment, and, at a rate of wages, which would, by this time, have banished almost the recollection of poverty from her shores.

*Section V. Industry Will Be Applied to Capital, in Proportion
to the Intellectual Improvement of a People*

.... 1. *Intellectual cultivation excites a people to exertion.* Ignorant men are indolent, because they know neither the results that may be accomplished, nor the benefits that may be secured, by industry. This is one of the most common causes of the great indolence of savage nations. An Indian, who knows of no condition better than his own, of no covering better than a skin, of no habitation better than his wigwam, and of no weapon better than his bow and arrow, has no motive to industry, beyond what may be adequate to procure these simple necessaries. Let him know that, by additional effort, he can provide himself with a blanket, and, by a still additional effort, that he can exchange his bow and arrow for a rifle, and his wigwam for a comfortable house, and you present motives to additional labor. His industry will thus expand with the occasion. The case is the same with a nation, at a more advanced period of its history. Hence, the impulse which is always given to industry, by any important improvement in the intellectual character of a people. It was a knowledge of the conveniences and luxuries of the East, which the crusaders brought back to western Europe, that was the precursor and the cause of that dawning of improvement which succeeded the night of the dark ages.

2. *Intellectual cultivation directs to a profitable end, the industry* which it has previously excited. . . . in general, it is evident that, with a given amount of labor and of capital, production will be exactly in proportion to the knowledge which the operator possesses of the laws which govern that department in which he labors, and to the degree in which his labor conforms to his knowledge. If, then, labor will be in proportion to the benefits which it confers; and if, by knowledge, these benefits are increased, we see in what manner labor must be stimulated by intellectual cultivation. Thus we see how it is, that an intelligent people is always industrious, and an ignorant people always indolent. Hence, one of the surest means of banishing indolence, is to banish ignorance from a country.

But, it is evident, that improvement in knowledge, in order to be in any signal degree beneficial, must *be universal.* A single individual can derive but little advantage from his knowledge and industry if he be surrounded by a community both ignorant and indolent. In just so far as other men improve their condition, and become useful to themselves, they become useful to him; and both parties thus become useful to each other. This is specially the case, where a government is, in its character, popular; that is, where laws emanate from the more numerous classes. In such a case, not only is an intelligent man not benefited, but he is positively injured, by the ignorance and indolence of his neighbors. Hence, the reason why every man has a personal interest in the intellectual improvement of every one of his fellow citizens; and why the education of the whole population should be the care of the government; that is, of the whole country.

The efforts of a government may be usefully directed, in this respect, to two objects. 1st. The *increase*; and 2d. The *dissemination* of knowledge.

First. The increase of knowledge. This may be promoted in several ways.

1. By the establishment of colleges, universities, and other seminaries of learning. These, I suppose, should be furnished by the public, with libraries, apparatus, and all the means for instruction, investigation, and discovery. They should be so governed, and the remuneration so adjusted, that teachers should be placed under the strongest stimulus to labor for the promotion of science, and to communicate, most successfully, knowledge to their pupils. Colleges and universities should, at all times, be places of strenuous effort, and vigorous mental discipline, on the part of both instructors and pupils. As soon as they become the places of literary leisure, and intellectual indolence, they are not only useless, but hurtful; inasmuch as they retard, rather than advance, the progress of science.

For this reason, I doubt whether endowments, for the support of professorships, are useful; at least, whenever they render a teacher's support independent of his own exertions. For the same reason, a teacher should not be remunerated by a fixed salary, but by the sale of tickets of admission to his lectures, or by a salary, varying with his ability and success. Large foundations for the support of students in colleges, if under the control of the college itself, so far as they render the number of students in no way dependent upon the ability and faithfulness of the instructor, will have a tendency to remove from him one of the most valuable stimulants to industry.

2. By rewarding those who have been successful in the advancement of science.

1. This may be done, first, *Directly*, as by bestowing premiums, rewards, grants of money, &c., to those who have made discoveries of pre-eminent utility. . . .

2. *Indirectly*, by granting to those who labor in science or invention, the right to derive advantage from their discoveries or inventions. . . .

Secondly. A government may improve the intellectual character of a people, by the *dissemination* of knowledge. This will be done, so far as provision is made for the universal instruction of a people in the elements of a common education. The interest of every man demands that all his fellow citizens should be able to read and write, to keep accounts, to understand geography, and thus possess the means of self-improvement, to whatever degree they may be disposed to carry it. . . .

And now, to sum up what has been said: It will be seen that the inducements to labor, and, hence, of course, the wealth and means of happiness, in any given country, must depend, principally, upon two conditions: 1st. The degree of its intelligence; and 2d. The purity of its moral character.

1. On its intelligence will depend its knowledge of its own advantages, of the laws of nature, and of the means by which it may avail itself of those laws, for the promotion of its own happiness. A nation without knowledge, like a blind man in the garden of Eden, might be surrounded with every thing lovely to the eye or delightful to the taste, without ever being able to ascertain, either where a single object of desire was to be found, or how the possession of it might be secured.

2. On the moral character of a nation depends the justice of its laws, its respect for individual right, security of property, individual and social virtue, together with the industry and frugality which are their invariable attendants.

Of these two, the latter is the more important to national prosperity. For, where virtue, frugality, and respect for right exist, riches will, by natural consequence, accumulate; and intellectual cultivation will, of necessity, succeed. But, intellectual cultivation may easily exist, without the existence of virtue or love of right. In this case, its only effect is, to stimulate desire, and this, unrestrained by the love of right, must eventually overturn the social fabric which it at first erected. Hence, the surest means of promoting the welfare of a country is, to cultivate its intellectual, but especially its moral character. Until this have been done, no permanent foundation for a nation's prosperity has yet been laid. And, if any one will take the pains to examine, he will find, that, other things being equal, the wealth, and happiness, and power of every nation, are in exact proportion to its intellectual and moral character.

And, here, it may not be amiss to add, that all true benevolence may be defended, not less upon principles of political economy, than of philanthropy. The circulation of the Scriptures, the inculcation of moral and religious truth upon the minds of men, by means of Sabbath schools, and the preaching of the Gospel, are of the very greatest importance to the productive energies of a country. The argument is very short, but it seems very conclusive. No nation can rapidly accumulate or long enjoy the means of happiness, except as it is pervaded by the love of individual and social right; but the love of individual and social right will never prevail, without the practical influence of the motives and sanctions of religion; and these motives and sanctions will never influence men, unless they are, by human effort, brought to bear upon the conscience.

The same principles will defend, upon economical grounds, the efforts of benevolence on behalf of foreign nations. Intelligence, virtue, and equitable laws, will have the same effect upon other men, that they have upon us. They will render men industrious, frugal, and consequently rich, and raise them from a savage to a civilized state. Just in proportion as a nation is thus transformed, are its products increased; the riches of the whole world are augmented; the portion of wealth, which falls to the share of each man, is rendered greater; and the ratio of capital to labor is higher. Just as a nation becomes intelligent and rich, its wants are multiplied, and the means for supplying them are provided. Hence, it becomes a better customer to other nations; it gives an additional impulse to their industry; and it repays them for their products, with whatever God has bestowed upon it, which will add to the happiness of others. Can any one doubt that Great Britain and France reap incomparably greater advantages from each other, in their present condition of advanced civilization, than either of them would, if the other were in the condition in which it was found by Julius Caesar? What demand would Great Britain make upon the productions of France, if she were, at this moment, inhabited by half-naked savages? Or again: How much greater benefits does North America confer upon the world, than it would if it were peopled by its aboriginal inhabitants? How great a stimulus would be given to the industry of the world, at this time; and how greatly would the comforts and luxuries of men be increased, if Africa were peopled by civilized and christianized men? Now, if these things be so; and that they are so, I see not that any one can dispute; it seems to me, that civilized nations could in no way so successfully promote their own interests, as by the universal dissemination of the means of education and the principles of religion.

7.

Henry Ward Beecher

"Preaching Christ"

(1861)

Henry Ward Beecher was unquestionably the outstanding popular spokesman of Evangelical religion in nineteenth-century America. Born in 1813, the son of Lyman Beecher, he began life as pastor of a small Presbyterian church in Lawrenceburg, Indiana. From there he moved to Indianapolis, and in 1847 to the pastorate of Plymouth Congregational Church in Brooklyn, New York, one of the most wealthy and prestigious suburban pastorates in the nation. Beecher was pre-eminent for his preaching of "heart religion" based upon "the personality of Christ." Rejecting "the despotisms of doctrine," which had constricted the preaching of his father and Nathaniel W. Taylor, Beecher represents the typical Romantic Evangelicalism of the years 1835–1875. While not an itinerant revivalist, like Finney, Beecher was just as interested in soul winning. But where Finney, who had been a law student prior to his conversion, argued with his auditors "like a lawyer at the bar," Beecher preached always as a poet or artist, appealing to the imagination, the feelings, the "higher sensibilities" of his genteel Victorian congregations. This sermon, preached in Plymouth Congregational Church on September 22, 1861, typifies the Evangelical effort to "melt" the hearts of the middle class by spreading before them "the sufferings and death, as well as the love and everlasting beneficence of the Lord Jesus Christ" in a direct appeal to what Coleridge called "The Reason." The preacher, as poet, paints glowing word pictures which are perceived intuitively or spiritually by the soul as representations of the goodness, the beauty, the sweetness and piety of God in Christ. To make the divine chords within the human heart throb in tune with the divine harmonies of the universe was Beecher's forte. He became the model for Evangelical preachers of his day across the nation.

[This sermon, given complete here, is taken from the second volume of a two-volume edition entitled simply *Sermons* published in New York in 1868.]

PREACHING CHRIST

> "And I, brethren, when I came to you, came not with excellency of speech or of wisdom, declaring unto you the testimony of God. For I determined not to know any thing among you save Jesus Christ, and him crucified."
> —1 Cor., ii., 1, 2.

The New Testament teaches, in the most unequivocal manner, that Jesus Christ is very God. He may therefore be conceived as dwelling in the majesty and supernal glory of heavenly government. Or we may follow faintly in imagination all the rounds of creation, and conceive of his creative acts; for all things were made by him, and without him was not any thing made that is made. Or we may consider his administrative life, and reflect upon his power in renewing, sustaining, and enriching the natural world. Or we may conceive of him as the head of a government over mankind, administered through natural laws, with special divine volitions and purposes which we call providential. In either case our conceptions will be profitable and ennobling; but they will benefit us just in proportion as we are advanced in moral culture, and have begun to be ourselves in some measure like God. "Blessed are the pure in heart, for they shall see God." But ah! how many, then, can see him? Without holiness no man shall see the Lord. But the whole world lieth in wickedness; and how shall we arouse them, inspire hope in them, and bring them, imperfect, sinful, and guilty, to be influenced of God? The reply is already uttered in these words: "The Lamb of God, which taketh away the sin of the world."

Those traits and attributes which lead God to pardon sin and to heal sinners are manifested in Christ Jesus, and it was this pardoning aspect of Christ as God that the apostle so much dwelt upon and so insists upon here. For he does not merely declare, "I determined not to know any thing among you save Jesus Christ." He might know him as Creator, and even as Administrator. He declares, "I determined not to know anything among you save Christ, *and him crucified.*" It is a *crucified* Savior, and not merely the Savior

Christ as God, that the apostle was determined to know. And in the chapter preceding this he says, "The preaching of the cross is to them that perish foolishness; but unto us which are saved, it is the power of God." Not the presentation of Christ as God that is often made, but that peculiar presentation of Christ as God which the cross symbolizes—it is this that the apostle declares to be the foundation of his ministry. The very reliance which he had for success was this—that he believed in such a Savior, and was determined to draw from the consideration of such a Savior all those influences by which he hoped to effect the renovation of men and of society.

This is the reason, then, why Paul so much emphasized the cross, the crucifixion, and the death of Christ. It is God under material conditions, suffering unto bodily death for sinful men, that furnishes the most stimulating and subduing influences that can be brought to bear upon the human soul. Therefore, in going forth upon his apostolic mission, he relied upon the influences that there were in a crucified Savior to revolutionize the human soul and transform the life.

It is said that Christ crucified was unto the Jews a stumbling-block, and unto the Greeks foolishness. The Jew had a conception of the Messiah, but it was an intensely worldly conception. It was altogether sensuous—physical. It contemplated empire; earthly wealth; political power; palaces, and thrones, and armies, and dominions. When, therefore, a broken Jesus was presented to them, humbling himself, and becoming obedient unto death, even the death of the cross, lower than the lowest, and less than the least, he was indeed a stumbling-block to the Jews. He was foolishness to the Greeks. There was no part of their nature that could understand him. There was no part of their nature that could understand the suffering of the Divine Being for the sake of his creatures. In all their mythology there was no record of any gods that had any trait or attribute which would lead them to suffer in behalf of inferior beings.

But Paul had felt the power on his own heart of a broken Christ. The presentation of such a Christ had done its work upon him. He knew what it had done for him. He had seen, too, what influence it had upon others; and it was the very power by which he hoped to change the world.

There is a great scale of motives which influence men, and which may, in their own rank and place, be addressed to men for the production of right conduct. We may attempt to dissuade men from evil by the intrinsic hatefulness of evil. We may attempt to persuade men to a course of holiness on account of the beauty of holiness. We may teach men to leave off things that are wrong, and to revolt from them because they are wrong. We may teach men to follow that which is good because goodness is attractive to every right-minded and noble nature. In this intrinsic hatefulness of evil and attractiveness of good there is a power which we may properly employ. We may appeal to the self-interest of men, and teach that "godliness is profitable in all things, having promise of the life that now is, and of that which is to come." There is a degree of power in that presentation to many minds. There are motives that may in some measure touch every faculty of the soul. But in its nature the soul responds most, not to those collateral motives which are drawn from the things which exist about us, but to those which bring upon us the influence of God's own personal presence. The sense of his being, of his eternity, and of the immortality in which he dwells—this is that to which the soul most responds. It is true that men are so shut out from these views that they are, as a matter of fact, more powerfully influenced by worldly considerations; but the nature of the mind is such that when you can fairly bring to bear upon it these higher motives, they are capable of producing greater changes in it than can any secular, sordid motives whatsoever.

But when divine and infinite things are brought before the mind, some things are more apt to stimulate men than others. Those views which impress the mind with its own weakness, and want, and imperfection, and guilt, and dreadful danger, are very apt to be influential. The impression of these things upon the mind is the result of preaching Christ crucified; of calling attention to the stupendousness of the offering that he made when he gave himself for the world; of pointing out all the steps accompanying his mission on earth, that were afterward declared to be necessary on account of the sinfulness of every human creature, from which sinfulness, without the atonement, men could never have been saved. It is impossible, it seems to me, to produce a rational and realizing sense of man's sinfulness unless you make sin to consist in violations against a living person. When you preach to men that they have broken the law of God, they do not seem to be brought very near to the Divine Majesty; but when you hold up before them not only the justice of God, but his generosity as manifested through Christ, recounting to them the history of his sufferings and the story of his love, you bring them to a sense of their offense against the Most High, which wakes up in the soul, if there is a spark of love in it, a generous sorrow. If you desire to bring to men a view that shall convict them of their sinfulness, you must spread before them the sufferings and death, as well as the love and everlasting beneficence of the Lord Jesus Christ. You may measure human conduct by law, and represent the issues of conduct as wise or foolish; but, after all, though there is a certain measure of truth in this direction, that which seizes the soul, and fills it with enthusiasm of emotion, is that truth which brings before the mind the character of Christ as the Savior of sinners.

Those views which represent God as profoundly concerned for man, as attempting to rescue him, and as willing himself to bear the pains and penalties of sin rather than that we should suffer, have in their very nature a remarkable power and tendency to arouse and affect the whole human soul.

Those views which represent the attractive love of God, burning in his deep soul toward sinful beings while yet in sin, and working out endlessly in endeavors to build them up in beauty and holiness, are admirably adapted to influence the minds of men.

Those views which represent the intimate love of Christ for his disciples, and his familiarity with them, and the spiritual communion which is begun here and is to be consummated hereafter, disclosing the whole economy of God's saving grace as manifested in Christ Jesus, have a constitutional, and, I might almost say, an everlasting relation to the understanding, to the feelings, to the will, to every part of the human soul.

This revelation of God in Christ is a power compared with which there is no other power worth naming. It is the wisdom of God. It is the power of God unto salvation. Above all other known influences it controls the human heart, inspires it with love, and with purity through loving.

Therefore, when the apostle said, "I determined not to know

any thing among you save Jesus Christ, and him crucified," he avowed his faith that in the presentation of the divine nature as represented by Christ, there is more moral power upon the heart and the conscience than in any other thing, and his determination to draw influences from that source in all his work.

In view of this, I remark,

1. The personal influence of Jesus Christ upon the heart is the first requisite for a Christian preacher. We may preach much *about* Christ, but no man will preach *Christ* except so far as Christ is in him. No man can set forth the soul's need of Christ who has not felt that need in his own soul. No man can urgently plead the joy of salvation through Christ who has not experienced that joy in his own heart. It is not enough to have a knowledge of theology, though that is not to be despised. It is not enough to know the mind of man, though the philosophy of the human mind is not to be disregarded, and is, in its place, almost indispensable. The secret of success in the preaching of the Gospel is that the preacher himself shall have felt the power of that Gospel. There are many men that by natural gifts are qualified to stand eminent and pre-eminent above their fellows, who, though they have a certain kind of personal influence, exert but little religious influence; and, on the other hand, there are many men that are comparatively of slender stature and small endowment, whose life is like a rushing, mighty wind in the influence which it exerts. The presence of Christ in them is the secret of their power. The poorest man, the most ignorant man, is mighty through God. If his soul is aroused and inspired by the hope, by the faith, and the love which are in Christ Jesus, he has a power that others can not derive from mere learning, from wisdom, or from any other source.

It is not learning, nor eloquence, nor flow of natural enthusiasm, but that stir and glow which a genuine experience of love, and faith in Christ give, that make a man an efficacious witness and teacher of the Lord Jesus Christ. And I do not mean merely in the pulpit. There is to be professional preaching, but every disciple of the Lord Jesus Christ is, in his own way, to be a preacher. Every parent is to be a preacher to his children. Every schoolmaster or schoolmistress is to be a preacher to his or her pupils. Every man is to be a preacher to those that are subject to his influence. There is not a Christian who has not a parish in which he is bound to preach. Where there is a palpitating love of holiness, where there is a zealous fear of offending God, where the soul yearns and longs for Christ Jesus, it is strange with what a witching power it is endowed.

2. A man's success in preaching will depend upon his power of presenting before men the Lord Jesus Christ. I have said that the experience of Christ's presence in one's own soul was the first requisite. This requisite being possessed, he will have most success in selecting topics for discourses who has power most effectually to present to the minds of his congregation the nature of God as set forth in Christ Jesus. There is a great deal of useful didactic matter that every minister must give to his congregation. There is a great deal of doctrinal matter that he must introduce into his preaching. I do not dissuade from doctrine. It is only the despotisms of doctrine that I would discountenance. No one is fit to instruct his congregation who can not present, with some logical coherence, the great truths of which he speaks. Doctrines have their place in preaching, though not the chiefest place. There is also much of fact, of history, and of description that belongs to the ministerial desk. The Bible is full of material for these things. Ethics should occupy an important place in every minister's teaching. The nature of the human mind; the methods by which it acts; the analysis of character; men's occupations; all the sinuous channels in which our thoughts and feelings run—these are things that it is proper to take up and explain in the pulpit.

But high above all these topics; high above abstract propositions; high above facts of history; above all descriptions; above all teaching of what is right and duty—high above them all is the fountain of influence, Christ, a living person who gave himself a ransom for sinners, and now ever lives to make intercession for them. Though one preaches every other truth, if he leaves this chiefest one out, or abbreviates it, he will come short of the essential work of the Gospel. Put this in, and you have all, as it were, in brief. The power of the Christian ministry is in the presentation, not simply of great truths, but of *the* truth as it is in Christ Jesus. In that will be the measure of its real and lasting influence.

3. There can be no sound and effective method of preaching ethics, even, which does not derive their authority from the Lord

Christ. The motives derivable from the secular and human side of ethics are relatively feeble. Even if one chose to preach the great moralities of life, it were wise to ground them in God. Morality, without spirituality, has no roots. It becomes a thing of custom, changeable, transient, and optional. The dispute sometimes waged between doctrine and practice would never be allowed if high doctrines reached forth to practical results, and if precepts and morality reached back to divine authority. There is no need of controversy any more than between science and art, between pure mathematics and mathematics applied, between analytic chemistry and organic chemistry.

There may be a practical mistake in the proportionate administration of the one or the other element—the abstract or the concrete; but the dynamics and proportions of teaching must be largely left to the judgment and the original nature of each teacher. Men work by different mental instruments. Each man has a right to his own genius; but, whatever method is pursued, the indispensable connection between the spiritual element and the practical development should be maintained. Morality without spirituality is a plant without root, and spirituality without morality is a root without stem and leaves.

The great mistake which men make in regard to the introduction into the pulpit on the Sabbath-day of what are called secular topics, is, that they do not conceive that such topics are to be discussed in the light of higher truths, and that they are to derive their influence and authority from the considerations which flow from the nature of Christ, and his claims upon us. I have a right to speak upon agriculture here—not as agriculture alone, but in the relations which it sustains to religion. "Ye are God's husbandry," saith the apostle. Many men are in that calling. It has an influence upon their thoughts, and feelings, and acts, and is working all the time in one way or another upon their souls, and it is my business to draw from it lessons for their instruction and benefit. Are you called to be a mariner? Then there are a thousand lessons that it is my business to draw from the life of a mariner, because they touch you. Are you called to be a tradesman? Then there are multitudes of lessons that it is my business to draw from the vocation of a tradesman, because it is taking hold of your tastes and habits, and is framing and fashioning something of your immortality. I am bound to discuss financial questions—not for the sake of money, as a banker would discuss them, but because they have an influence upon the life and destiny of those whom they concern. I have a right to introduce into my sermons all secular topics as far as they are connected with man's moral character, and his hopes of immortality. If I discuss them in a merely secular way, I desecrate the pulpit; but if I discuss them in the spirit of Christ, and for Christ's sake, that I may draw men out of their peculiar dangers, and lead them into a course of right living, then I give dignity and nobility to the pulpit.

4. All reformations of evil in society, all civil and social reformations, should spring from this vital centre. It seems to me to be a very dangerous thing to preach Christ so that your preaching shall not be a constant rebuke to all the evil in the community. That man who so preaches Christ, doctrinally or historically, that no one takes offense, no one feels rebuked, no one trembles, is not a legitimate and faithful preacher of Christ. On the other hand, it is a dangerous thing for a man to attack evil in the spirit of only hatred. To arouse evil feelings against evil, to contend against malignant mischief by malignant passions, is surely not Christian! The sublime wisdom of the New Testament is this: "Overcome evil with good." The fundamental rule for a reformer is that he shall not only hate evil, but cleave to that which is good. A man's love of that which is good should be more powerful, if possible, than his hatred of that which is evil; for if a man attempts to reform evil because he hates it, he brings himself into one of the most dangerous states of mind. It is demoralizing to a community to have reforms spring from hatred of evil; but those reforms which spring from the love of Christ are regulated, tempered, restrained. That man only is truly a reformer who is a *Christian* reformer. Was Christ not a reformer? Did he not come to save the world? Did he not come to save the intemperate, the unjust, the dishonest? And when he lived, did he not hate evil? Did he not abhor it? Was he not that God before whose sight no evil could be allowed? And yet with what wondrous pity, and with what sweetness of love did he dwell in the midst of these things, so that the publicans—those men that were debauched and corrupted with the handling of public moneys, learning every trick of iniquity

in consequence of it—so that the publicans and the sinners (for that
is the term by which those fallen creatures that even to this day
swarm our streets are known in Scripture) took heart, became inspired with hope, and drew near to him in strong faith and confidence that there was pity for them in him. Christ reformed men
by inspiring the love of goodness as well as by hatred of evil, and
he drew men from their sin as well as drove them from it. All
hatred of evil is unchristian which is not mingled with compassion
for the evil-doer. The passions are to be controlled by the inspiration of moral sentiments. The sweetness of that which is good, the
beauty of that which is right, the majesty of that which is just and
true, are to work along with the hatred of evil, and to work in
double measure. Evil *is* to be abhorred, but abhorrence must not
overtop benevolence!

The cleansing of the immoral, the liberation of the enslaved,
the restraint of sultry lusts, the detection of criminals and their
punishment, the mitigation of selfishness, the humiliation of pride,
the resistance of greed and avarice, are pre-eminently labors of
love, and not of wrath. Hatred will never reform any thing. It may
destroy, but Love is the only architect.

5. Hence all philanthropies are partial and imperfect that do not
grow out of this same root. As all hatred of evil is dangerous that
is not inspired and accompanied by the love of Christ, so that philanthropy, or the attempt to organize positive good in human life,
is lacking, which does not spring from the same organizing centre,
and which is not inspired by the same influence. But when philanthropy springs from this centre, and is inspired by this influence,
it becomes, not a mere sentimentalism, but a vivid and veritable
power in human society. There are no true philanthropists, it seems
to me, but those that take man in his whole nature; that look upon
him as a creature of God's just government, as a child of immortality, a subject of divine rewards and penalties; and that attempt to
build up in him that which is good, according to the largest pattern
of spiritual truth. Philanthropy without religion becomes meagre.
It is the love of man uninspired by the love of God!

6. All public questions of justice, of liberty, of equity, of purity,
of intelligence, should be vitalized by the power which is in Christ
Jesus. There are other motives that may press men forward a little

way, but there is nothing that has such controlling power as the
personal influence of the Lord Jesus. When, therefore, in such a
time as this, we are crowding along great subjects, or, rather, when
they are crowding us along, and we are swept onward in the current
of great national agitations, let us remember that there is but one
way in which we can deal with all such subjects, and be thorough,
and at the same time certain and safe, namely, by making every
one of them religious subjects, Christian subjects, inspired by direct
contact with the heart of the Lord Jesus Christ. When we bring
secular matters into this relation, there is wholesomeness introduced
into them, as well as into us in the management of them.

And now, my dear Christian friends, are not these views in accordance with the repeated teaching of the whole New Testament
Scriptures—that every thing which belongs to human life must in
some way be connected with the grand redemptive centre of moral
government, Christ Jesus?

"Because we thus judge, that if one died for all, then were all
dead; and that he died for all, that they which live should not
henceforth live unto themselves, but unto him which died for them
and rose again." "Whether we live, we live unto the Lord; and
whether we die, we die unto the Lord: whether we live, therefore,
or die, we are the Lord's." "Whether, therefore, ye eat or drink,
or whatsoever ye do, do all to the glory of God."

In our personal character, in our enthusiasms, in our imaginations, in our enjoyments, in all the amenities of social life, there
is to be the presence of this divine love. In all that we attempt to
do to abate evil, in all that we attempt to do to establish good, in
our sympathy and concurrence with the great movements of the
age in which we live, our power to do good will be in proportion
to the strength and purity of our spiritual life. Jesus Christ, and
him *crucified*, is still the wisdom of God, and the power of God
unto salvation, not only of the individual heart, but of civil societies.

If there be those, then, that are ambitious, and that have felt
with reference to themselves substantially as the mother did respecting her two sons, of whom she said, "Lord, grant that these my
two sons may sit, the one on thy right hand, and the other on
thy left, in thy kingdom;" if there are any that have been desirous
of obtaining influence and power, I would say to them, Beware of

the upswelling of natural pride; beware of an over-active vanity! Remember that the road to power is not through self-elevation and self-aggrandizement, but through humiliation. You are to come to power by the abasement of yourself; by putting on the Lord Jesus Christ; by having your life hid with Christ in God; by learning to look at all things in the light of eternity.

Power and goodness are synonymous. The secret of true power is in self-denial, disinterestedness, an unwearied love, a faith that pierces the invisible, and a hope that appropriates it! But those that go hither and thither, seeking a great name, and place, and influence; wishing to do great things; seeking their own good and not another's, and still less God's glory—all these must needs come short of the highest power. The burying of self; the enthroning of Jesus; the living, not for the visible and the transient, but for the invisible and the eternal; the might of God manifest in Christ, and made known to us through our own experience—these are the ways and methods of power—the secret of power not alone in the individual, but in the ministry, in the Church, in communities, and in the world. Whether we know it or not, God, blessed be his name! is overruling our ignorance, and guiding our very mistakes. He is pressing forward this wonderful moral power to its consummation. The day lingers, but shall not linger forever, when he shall take to himself his almighty power, and come and reign in myriads of now darkened hearts; in churches that are now Christian only in name; in institutions that, though they were established under the benign influences of Christianity, no longer represent it; in civil councils and in warlike camps; and then the whole earth shall see the salvation of our God. Even so, Lord, come quickly!

And now, ye praying, weeping, pleading Christians, that seem to have but a small sphere, remember that every single Christian aspiration which you have, every vital and God-inspired Christian experience that is wrought out in you, no matter when or where, becomes a part of the riches of God in the world. Money is money, and, though locked up in the deepest and darkest vault, every coin is one more coin of the world's wealth. The heart is God's mint, and every single evolution of true Christian feeling is an addition to the greatness of God's power in this world. Do not think that you must be in some public position. Fulfill in secret the will of

Christ Jesus. Let the mind that was in Christ be more and more completely in you. Let the spirit of Christ dwell in you richly in all things; and thus you will be preachers of Christ, and faithful witnesses; and ere long you shall hear that voice, sweeter than all conceivable music, saying, "Well done, thou good and faithful servant, enter thou into the joy of thy Lord."

8.

Horace Bushnell

"Our Obligations to the Dead"

(1865)

Horace Bushnell was too complex and versatile a thinker to be adequately represented by any one selection. Nevertheless he was not so far ahead of his times as some of his disciples liked to think. As Barbara M. Cross has shown in her perceptive biography, Bushnell's thought was molded chiefly by the practical exigencies of his pastorate in the well-to-do North Congregational Church of Hartford, Connecticut, in the years 1833 to 1876. While Bushnell tried in his theological writings to transcend the spirit of this typical urban pastorate, his weekly sermons and occasional addresses embody essentially the same outlook as that of his prosperous parishioners. Eminently conservative in political and economic affairs, he took a cautious stand on the slavery question, and rejected the implications of Darwinian science. This selection exemplifies Bushnell as a Romantic Evangelical in his effort to elicit an emotional response which transcends "the Understanding." It is the more significant because his brilliant mind and comprehensive approach to the meaning of the Civil War lifts this oration out of the common rank of such addresses. Unlike many Evangelicals, Bushnell thought of Christianity always in broad historical and organic perspectives. In this address he captures both the strengths and the weaknesses of the American reaction to the war. His demand for punishment of the rebels is muted; he offers a mild approach to reunion and reconstruction; his principal effort is to emphasize the *national* sacrifice not the Northern sacrifice and to place the struggle within the larger framework of a Providential design for the redemption of the nation from sin by the blood atonement of its best citizens. The Civil War is therefore not a national tragedy, any more than Christ's crucifixion was a tragedy. Rather it is a glorious triumph of good over evil. Nothing could demonstrate more effectively the millennial optimism of the Evangelical faith.

141

[This selection is taken from the collection *Building Eras* (New York, 1881).]

X. OUR OBLIGATIONS TO THE DEAD[1]

BRETHREN OF THE ALUMNI:

To pay fit honors to our dead is one of the fraternal and cus-
tomary offices of these anniversaries; never so nearly an office of
high public duty as now, when we find the roll of our membership
starred with so many names made sacred by the giving up of life
for the Republic. We knew them here in terms of cherished in-
timacy; some of them so lately that we scarcely seem to have been
parted from them; others of them we have met here many times,
returning to renew, with us, their tender and pleasant recollections
of the past; but we meet them here no more: they are gone to
make up the hecatomb offered for their and our great nation's life.
Hence it has been specially desired on this occasion, that we honor
their heroic sacrifice by some fit remembrance. Had the call of
your committee been different, I should certainly not have re-
sponded. . . .

First of all then, we are to see that we give them their due
share of the victory and the honors of victory. For it is one of our
natural infirmities, against which we need to be carefully and even
jealously guarded, that we fall so easily into the impression which
puts them in the class of defeat and failure. Are they not dead? And
who shall count the dead as being in the roll of victory? But the
living return to greet us and be with us, and we listen eagerly to
the story of the scenes in which they bore their part. We enjoy their
exultations and exult with them. Their great leaders also return, to
be crowded by our ovations, and deafened by our applauses. These,
these, we too readily say, are the victors, considering no more the
dead but with a certain feeling close akin to pity. If, sometime, the
story of their fall is told us, the spot described, far in front or on
the rampart's edge, where they left their bodies with the fatal gashes

[1] An oration given at the Commemorative Celebration held in New Haven,
on Wednesday of Commencement Week, July 26, 1865, in honor of the
Alumni of Yale College, who fell in the War of the Rebellion.

at which their souls went out, we listen with sympathy and sad respect, but we do not find how to count them in the lists of victory, and scarcely to include them in the general victory of the cause. All our associations run this way, and before we know it we have them down, most likely, on the losing side of the struggle. They belong, we fancy, to the waste of victory,—sad waste indeed! but not in any sense a part of victory itself. No, no, ye living! It is the ammunition spent that gains the battle, not the ammunition brought off from the field. These dead are the spent ammunition of the war, and theirs above all is the victory. Upon what indeed turned the question of the war itself, but on the dead that could be furnished; or what is no wise different, the life that could be contributed for that kind of expenditure? These grim heroes therefore, dead and dumb, that have strewed so many fields with their bodies,—these are the price and purchase-money of our triumph. A great many of us were ready to live, but these offered themselves, in a sense, to die, and by their cost the victory is won.

Nay, it is not quite enough, if we will know exactly who is entitled to a part in these honors, that we only remember these dead of the war. Buried generations back of them were also present in it, almost as truly as they. Thus, if we take the two most honored leaders, Grant and Sherman, who, besides the general victory they have gained for the cause, have won their sublime distinction as the greatest living commanders of the world, it will be impossible to think of them as having made or begotten their own lofty endowments. All great heroic men have seeds and roots, far back it may be, out of which they spring, and apart from which they could not spring at all; a sublime fatherhood and motherhood, in whose blood and life, however undistinguished, victory was long ago distilling for the great day to come of their people and nation. They knew it not; they sleep in graves, it may be, now forgot. But their huge-grown, manful temperament, the fights they waged and won in life's private battle, the lofty prayer-impulse which made inspirations their element, their brave self-retaining patience, and the orderly vigor of their household command were breeding in and in, to be issued finally in a hero sonship, and by that fight themselves out into the grandest victory for right and law the future ages shall know. So that if we ask who are the dead that are to be counted in our victory, we must pierce the sod of Wethersfield and Stratford, of Woodbury and Norwalk, and find where the Honorable Sherman, the Deacon Sherman, the Judge Sherman, and all the line of the Shermans and their victor wives and mothers lie; and then, if we can guess what they were and how they lived, we shall know who fought the great campaigns at Atlanta, Savannah and Raleigh. So again, if we begin at the good Deacon Grant in Mr. Warham's church at Windsor; descending to the historic Matthew Grant of Tolland, fellow-scout with Putnam and captain of a French war company; then to the now living Joel Root Grant, who removed to Pennsylvania, afterwards also to Ohio, afterwards finally, I believe, to Illinois, whose wanderings appear to be commemorated in the classic name of Ulysses; we shall see by what tough flanking processes of life and family the great Lieutenant-General was preparing, who should turn the front of Vicksburg, and march by Lee and Richmond, and cut off, by the rear, even the Great Rebellion itself. O, if we could see it, how long and grandly were the victories of these great souls preparing! The chief thing was the making of the souls themselves, and when that was done the successes came of course.

And from these two examples you may see by what lines of private worth, and public virtue, and more than noble blood, the stock of our great patriotic armies has been furnished. For how grand a pitch of devotion has been often shown by the private soldiers of these armies! There was never embodied, in all the armies of the world, a public inspiration so remarkable. Really the grandest heroes are these, who have neither had, nor wanted, any motive but the salvation of the Republic. And do you think there was nothing back of them to make them what they were? What but an immense outgrowth were they of whole ages of worth, intelligence, and public devotion? And for what more honorable distinction should we here and always pay our thanks to God? O, it is these generations of buried worth that have been fighting in our battles, and if we will pay our obligations to the dead, it is this nameless fatherhood and motherhood, before whose memory we shall bare our head in the deepest homage and tenderest reverence. . . .

But I pass to a point where the dead obtain a right of honor that is more distinctive, and belongs not to the living at all; or if in certain things partly to the living, yet only to them in some less sacred and prominent way. I speak here of the fact that, according to the true economy of the world, so many of its grandest and most noble benefits have and are to have a tragic origin, and to come as outgrowths only of blood. Whether it be that sin is in the world, and the whole creation groaneth in the necessary throes of its demonized life, we need not stay to inquire; for sin would be in the world and the demonizing spell would be upon it. Such was, and was to be, and is, the economy of it. Common life, the world's great life, is in the large way tragic. As the mild benignity and peaceful reign of Christ begins at the principle: "without shedding of blood, there is no remission," so without shedding of blood, there is almost nothing great in the world, or to be expected for it. For the life is in the blood,—all life; and it is put flowing within, partly for the serving of a nobler use in flowing out on fit occasion, to quicken and consecrate whatever it touches. God could not plan a Peace-Society world, to live in the sweet amenities, and grow great and happy by simply thriving and feeding. There must be bleeding also. Sentiments must be born that are children of thunder; there must be heroes and heroic nationalities, and martyr testimonies, else there will be only mediocrities, insipidities, common-place men, and common-place writings,—a sordid and mean peace, liberties without a pulse, and epics that are only eclogues.

And here it is that the dead of our war have done for us a work so precious, which is all their own,—they have bled for us; and by this simple sacrifice of blood they have opened for us a new great chapter of life. We were living before in trade and commerce, bragging of our new cities and our census reports, and our liberties that were also consciously mocked by our hypocrisies; having only the possibilities of great inspirations and not the fact, materialized more and more evidently in our habits and sentiments, strong principally in our discords and the impetuosity of our projects for money. But the blood of our dead has touched our souls with thoughts more serious and deeper, and begotten, as I trust, somewhat of that high-bred inspiration which is itself the possibility of genius, and of a true public greatness. Saying nothing then for the

present of our victors and victories, let us see what we have gotten
by the blood of our slain.

And first of all, in this blood our unity is cemented and forever
sanctified. Something was gained for us here, at the beginning, by
our sacrifices in the fields of our Revolution,—something, but not
all. Had it not been for this common bleeding of the States in
their common cause, it is doubtful whether our Constitution could
ever have been carried. The discords of the Convention were imminent, as we know, and were only surmounted by compromises
that left them still existing. They were simply kenneled under the
Constitution and not reconciled, as began to be evident shortly in
the doctrines of state sovereignty, and state nullification, here and
there asserted. We had not bled enough, as yet, to merge our
colonial distinctions and make us a proper nation. Our battles had
not been upon a scale to thoroughly mass our feeling, or gulf us
in a common cause and life. Against the state-rights doctrines, the
logic of our Constitution was decisive, and they were refuted a
thousand times over. But such things do not go by argument. No
argument transmutes a discord, or composes a unity where there
was none. The matter wanted here was blood, not logic, and this
we now have on a scale large enough to meet our necessity. True
it is blood on one side, and blood on the other,—all the better for
that; for bad bleeding kills, and righteous bleeding sanctifies and
quickens. The state-rights doctrine is now fairly bled away, and the
unity died for, in a way of such prodigious devotion, is forever
sealed and glorified.

Nor let any one be concerned for the sectional relations of defeat
and victory. For there has all the while been a grand, suppressed
sentiment of country in the general field of the rebellion, which is
bursting up already into sovereignty out of the soil itself. There is
even a chance that this sentiment may blaze into a passion hot
enough to utterly burn up whatever fire itself can master. At all
events it will put under the ban, from this time forth, all such
instigators of treason as could turn their peaceful States into hells
of desolation, and force even patriotic citizens to fight against the
homage they bore their country. However this may be, the seeds
of a true public life are in the soil, waiting to grow apace. It will be

as when the flood of Noah receded. For the righteous man perchance began to bethink himself shortly, and to be troubled, that he took no seeds into the ark; but no sooner were the waters down, than the oaks and palms and all great trees sprung into life, under the dead old trunks of the forest, and the green world reappeared even greener than before; only the sections had all received new seeds, by a floating exchange, and put them forthwith into growth together with their own. So the unity now to be developed, after this war-deluge is over, is even like to be more cordial than it ever could have been. It will be no more thought of as a mere human compact, or composition, always to be debated by the letter, but it will be that bond of common life which God has touched with blood; a sacredly heroic, Providentially tragic unity, where God's cherubim stand guard over grudges and hates and remembered jealousies, and the sense of nationality becomes even a kind of religion. How many would have said that the Saxon Heptarchy, tormented by so many intrigues and feuds of war, could never be a nation! But their formal combination under Egbert, followed by their wars against the Danes under Alfred, set them in a solid, sanctified unity, and made them, as a people, one true England, instead of the seven Englands that were; which seven were never again to be more than historically remembered. And so, bleeding on together from that time to this in all sorts of wars; wars civil and wars abroad, drenching the land and coloring the sea with their blood; gaining all sorts of victories and suffering all kinds of defeats; their parties and intestine strifes are no more able now to so much as raise a thought that is not in allegiance to their country. In like manner,—let no one doubt of it,—these United States, having dissolved the intractable matter of so many infallible theories and bones of contention in the dreadful menstruum of their blood, are to settle into fixed unity, and finally into a nearly homogeneous life.

Passing to another point of view, we owe it to our dead in this terrible war, that they have given us the possibility of a great consciousness and great public sentiments. There must needs be something lofty in a people's action, and above all something heroic in their sacrifices for a cause, to sustain a great sentiment in them. They will try, in the smooth days of peace and golden thriftiness and wide-spreading growth, to have it, and perhaps will think they really have it, but they will only have semblances and counterfeits; patriotic professions that are showy and thin, swells and protestations that are only oratorical and have no true fire. All the worse if they have interests and institutions that are all the while mocking their principles; breeding factions that can be quieted only by connivances and compromises and political bargains, that sell out their muniments of right and nationality. Then you shall see all high devotion going down as by a law, till nothing is left but the dastard picture of a spent magistracy that, when everything is falling into wreck, can only whimper that it sees not anything it can do! Great sentiments go when they are not dismissed, and will not come when they are sent for. We cannot keep them by much talk, nor have them because we have heard of them and seen them in a classic halo. A lofty public consciousness arises only when things are loftily and nobly done. It is only when we are rallied by a cause, in that cause receive a great inspiration, in that inspiration give our bodies to the death, that at last, out of many such heroes dead, comes the possibility of great thoughts, fired by sacrifice, and a true public magnanimity.

In this view, we are not the same people that we were, and never can be again. Our young scholars, that before could only find the forms of great feeling in their classic studies, now catch the fire of it unsought. Emulous before of saying fine things for their country, they now choke for the impossibility of saying what they truly feel. The pitch of their life is raised. The tragic blood of the war is a kind of new capacity for them. They perceive what it is to have a country and a public devotion. Great aims are close at hand, and in such aims a finer type of manners. And what shall follow, but that, in their more invigorated, nobler life, they are seen hereafter to be manlier in thought and scholarship, and closer to genius in action.

I must also speak of the new great history sanctified by this war, and the blood of its fearfully bloody sacrifices. So much worth and character were never sacrificed in a human war before. And by this mournful offering, we have bought a really stupendous chapter of history. We had a little very beautiful history before, which we were beginning to cherish and fondly cultivate. But we had not enough of it to beget a full historic consciousness. As was just now intimated in a different way, no people ever become vigorously conscious, till they mightily do, and heroically suffer. The historic sense is close akin to tragedy. We say it accusingly often,—and foolishly,—that history cannot live on peace, but must feed itself on blood. The reason is that, without the blood, there is really nothing great enough in motive and action, taking the world as it is, to create a great people or story. If a gospel can be executed only in blood, if there is no power of salvation strong enough to carry the world's feeling which is not gained by dying for it, how shall a selfish race get far enough above itself, to be kindled by the story of its action in the dull routine of its common arts of peace? Doubtless it should be otherwise, even as goodness should be universal; but so it never has been, and upon the present footing of evil never can be. The great cause must be great as in the clashing of evil; and heroic inspirations, and the bleeding of heroic worth must be the zest of the story. Nations can sufficiently live only as they find how to energetically die. In this view, some of us have felt, for a long time, the want of a more historic life, to make us a truly great people. This want is now supplied; for now, at last, we may be said to have gotten a history. The story of this four years' war is the grandest chapter, I think, of heroic fact, and tragic devotion, and spontaneous public sacrifice, that has ever been made in our world. The great epic story of Troy is but a song in comparison. There was never a better, and never so great a cause; order against faction, law against conspiracy, liberty and right against the madness and defiant wrong of slavery, the unity and salvation of the greatest future nationality and freest government of the world, a perpetual state of war to be averted, and the preservation for mankind of an example of popular government and free society that is a token of promise for true manhood, and an omen of death to old abuse and prescriptive wrong the world over; this has been our cause, and it is something to say that we have borne ourselves worthily in it. Our noblest and best sons have given their life to it. We have dotted whole regions with battle-fields. We have stained how many rivers, and bays, and how many hundred leagues of railroad, with our blood! We have suffered appalling defeats; twice

at Bull Run, at Wilson's Creek, in the great campaign of the
Peninsula, at Cedar Mountain, at Fredericksburg, at Chancellors-
ville, at Chickamauga, and upon the Red River, leaving our acres
of dead on all these fields and many others less conspicuous; yet,
abating no jot of courage and returning with resolve unbroken, we
have converted these defeats into only more impressive victories.
In this manner too, with a better fortune nobly earned, we have
hallowed, as names of glory and high victory, Pea Ridge, Donel-
son, Shiloh, Hilton Head, New Orleans, Vicksburg, Port Hudson,
Stone River, Lookout Mountain, Resaca, Atlanta, Fort Fisher, Gettys-
burg, Nashville, Wilmington, Petersburg and Richmond, Benton-
ville, Mobile Bay, and, last of all, the forts of Mobile city. All these
and a hundred others are now become, and in all future time are
to be, names grandly historic. And to have them is to be how great
a gift for the ages to come! By how many of the future children
of the Republic will these spots be visited, and how many will
return from their pilgrimages thither, blest in remembrances of the
dead, to whom they owe their country! . . . God forbid that any
prudishness of modesty should here detain us. Let us fear no more
to say that we have won a history and the right to be a consciously
historic people. Henceforth our new world even heads the old,
having in this single chapter risen clean above it. The wars of
Caesar, and Frederic, and Napoleon, were grand enough in their
leadership, but there is no grand people or popular greatness in
them, consequently no true dignity. In this war of ours it is the
people, moving by their own decisive motion, in the sense of their
own great cause. For this cause we have volunteered by the million,
and in three thousand millions of money, and by the resolute bleeding of our self-taxation, we have bought and sanctified consentingly
all these fields, all that is grand in this thoroughly principled history.

Again, it is not a new age of history only that we owe to the
bloody sacrifices of this war, but in much the same manner the
confidence of a new literary age; a benefit that we are specially
called, in such a place as this, and on such an occasion, to remember and fitly acknowledge. Great public throes are, mentally speaking, changes of base for some new thought-campaign in a people.
Hence the brilliant new literature of the age of Queen Elizabeth;

then of another golden era under Anne; and then still again, as in the arrival of another birth-time, after the Napoleonic wars of George the Fourth. The same thing has been noted, I believe, in respect to the wars of Greece and Germany. Only it is in such wars as raise the public sense and majesty of a people that the result is seen to follow. For it is the high-souled feeling raised that quickens high-souled thought, and puts the life of genius in the glow of new-born liberty. This we are now to expect, for the special reason also that we have here, for the first time, conquered a position. Thus it will be seen that no great writer becomes himself, in his full power, till he has gotten the sense of position. Much more true is this of a people. And here has been our weakness until now. We have held the place of cliency, we have taken our models and laws of criticism, and to a great extent our opinions, from the English motherhood of our language and mind. Under that kind of pupilage we live no longer; we are thoroughly weaned from it, and become a people in no secondary right. Henceforth we are not going to write English, but American. As we have gotten our position, we are now to have our own civilization, think our own thoughts, rhyme in our own measures, kindle our own fires, and make our own canons of criticism, even as we settle the proprieties of punishment for our own traitors. We are not henceforth to live as by cotton and corn and trade, keeping the downward slope of thrifty mediocrity. Our young men are not going out of college, staled, in the name of discipline, by their carefully conned lessons, to be launched on the voyage of life as ships without wind, but they are to have great sentiments, and mighty impulsions, and souls alive all through in fires of high devotion.

We have gotten also now the historic matter of a true oratoric inspiration, and the great orators are coming after. In the place of politicians we are going to have, at least, some statesmen; for we have gotten the pitch of a grand, new, Abrahamic statesmanship, unsophisticated, honest and real; no cringing sycophancy, or cunning art of demagogy. We have also facts, adventures, characters enough now in store, to feed five hundred years of fiction. We have also plots, and lies, and honorable perjuries, false heroics, barbaric murders and assassinations, conspiracies of fire and poison,—enough of them, and wicked enough, to furnish the Satanic side of tragedy for long ages to come; coupled also with such grandeurs of public valor and principle, such beauty of heroic sacrifice, in womanhood and boyhood, as tragedy has scarcely yet been able to find. As to poetry, our battle-fields are henceforth names poetic, and our very soil is touched with a mighty poetic life. In the rustle of our winds, what shall the waking soul of our poets think of, but of brave souls riding by? In our thunders they may hear the shocks of charges, and the red of the sunset shall take a tinge in their feeling from the summits where our heroes fell. A new sense comes upon everything, and the higher soul of mind, quickened by new possibilities, finds inspirations where before it found only rocks, and ploughlands, and much timber for the saw. Are there no great singers to rise in this new time? Are there no unwonted fires to be kindled in imaginations fanned by these new glows of devotion? We seem, as it were in a day, to be set in loftier ranges of thought, by this huge flood-tide that has lifted our nationality, gifted with new sentiments and finer possibilities, commissioned to create, and write, and sing, and, in the sense of a more poetic feeling at least, to be all poets. . . .

I might also speak at large, if I had time, of the immense benefit these dead have conferred upon our free institutions themselves, by the consecrating blood of their sacrifice. But I can only say that having taken the sword to be God's ministers, and to vindicate the law as his ordinance, they have done it even the more effectively in that they have died for it. It has been a wretched fault of our people that we have so nearly ignored the moral foundations of our government. Regarding it as a merely human creation, we have held it only by the tenure of convenience. Hence came the secession. For what we create by our will, may we not dissolve by the same? Bitter has been the cost of our pitifully weak philosophy. In these rivers of blood we have now bathed our institutions, and they are henceforth to be hallowed in our sight. Government is now become Providential,—no more a mere creature of our human will, but a grandly moral affair. The awful stains of sacrifice are upon it, as upon the fields where our dead battled for it, and it is sacred for their sakes. The stamp of God's sovereignty is also upon it; for he has beheld their blood upon its gate-posts and made it the sign of his passover. Henceforth we are not to be manufacturing government, and defying in turn its sovereignty because we have made it ourselves; but we are to revere its sacred rights, rest in its sacred immunities, and have it even as the Caesar whom our Christ himself requires us to obey. Have we not also proved, written it down for all the ages to come, that the most horrible, God-defying crime of this world is unnecessary rebellion?

I might also speak of the immense contribution made for religion, by the sacrifices of these bleeding years. Religion, at the first, gave impulse, and, by a sublime recompense of reaction, it will also receive impulse. What then shall we look for but for a new era now to break forth, a day of new gifts and powers and holy endowments from on high, wherein great communities and friendly nations shall be girded in sacrifice, for the cause of Christ their Master? . . . Who of you does not ache with me for the impossibility of doing justice to these glorious obscure, these private heroes of the war? What ghostly troops of them had our good father and martyr President sent on before him, from all his fields of battle! And as our Abraham's bosom was never shut to such on earth, much more tenderly open will it be now! How paternally has he greeted them! How eagerly caught the sublime story of their soldiership! And if he could return again to his office, it would not be strange if he should send in a new batch of Major-Generals to be passed, whom the Senate never before heard of! Really this wonderful massing of private worth and public valor in our armies, is the proudest fact of the war, and we owe it to ourselves to say it, and to make our account of it, in whatever way we are able.

But there is one other and yet higher duty that we owe to these dead; viz., that we take their places and stand in their cause. It is even a great law of natural duty that the living shall come into the places and works of the dead. The same also is accepted and honored by Christianity, when it shows the Christian son, and brother, and friend, stepping into the places made vacant by the dead, to assume their blessed and great work unaccomplished, and die, if need be, in the testimony of a common martyrdom. They challenged, in this manner, if the commentators will suffer it, the vows of baptism, and "were baptized for the dead,"—consecrated upon the dead, for the work of the dead. God lays it upon us in the same way now, to own the bond of fealty that connects us with

the fallen, in the conscious community and righteous kinship of
their cause. And then, as brothers baptized for the dead,—Alumni,
so to speak, of the Republic,—we are to execute their purpose and
fulfill the idea that inspired them. Neither is it enough at this
point to go off in a general heroic, promising, in high rhetoric, to
give our life for the country in like manner. There is no present
likelihood that we shall be called to do any such thing. No, but we
have duties upon us that are closer at hand; viz., to wind up and
settle this great tragedy in a way to exactly justify every drop of
blood that has been shed in it. Like the blood of righteous Abel it
cries both to us and to God, from every field, and river, and wood,
and road, dotted by our pickets and swept by the march of our
armies.

First of all we are sworn to see that no vestige of state sovereignty
is left, and the perpetual, supreme sovereignty of the nation established. For what but this have our heroes died? Not one of them
would have died for a government of mere optional continuance;
not one for a government fit to be rebelled against. But they volunteered for a government in perfect right, and one to be perpetual
as the stars, and they went to the death as against the crime of hell.
Tell me also this,—if a government is good enough to die *for*,
is it not good enough to die *by*, when it is violated? Not that every
traitor is, of course, to be visited by the punishment of treason. It
is not for me to say who, or how many or few, shall suffer that
punishment. But I would willingly take the question to the dead
victims of Belle Isle, and Salisbury, and Andersonville, and let
them be the judges. There is no revenge in them now. The wild
storms of their agony are laid, and the thoughts which bear sway
in the world where they are gathered are those of the merciful
Christ, and Christ is the judge before whose bar they know full
well that their redress is sure. And yet I think it will be none the
less their judgment that something is due to law and justice here.
As, too, it was something for them to die for the law, I can imagine
them to ask whether it is not something for the law to prove its
vindicated honor in the fit punishment of such barbarities? May
it not occur to them also to ask, whether proportion is not an
everlasting attribute of justice? And if punctual retribution is to
follow the sudden taking off of one, whether the deliberate and

slow starvation of so many thousands is to be fitly ignored and raise no sword of judgment? Neither is it any thing to say, that the awful ruin of the rebellious country is itself a punishment upon the grandest scale, and ought to be sufficient; for the misery of it is, that it falls on the innocent and not on the leaders and projectors, who are the chief criminals. . . . We are driven in thus on every side, upon the conclusion that examples ought to be and must be made. Only they must be few and such as can be taken apart from all sectional conditions; for we have sections to compose, and the ordinary uses of punishment in cases of private treason do not pertain where the crime is nearly geographic, and is scarcely different from public war.

One thing more we are also sworn upon the dead to do; viz., to see that every vestige of slavery is swept clean. We did not begin the war to extirpate slavery; but the war itself took hold of slavery on its way, and as this had been the gangrene of our wound from the first, we shortly put ourselves heartily to the cleansing, and shall not, as good surgeons, leave a part of the virus in it. We are not to extirpate the form and leave the fact. The whole black code must go; the law of passes, and the law of evidence, and the unequal laws of suit and impeachment for crime. We are bound, if possible, to make the emancipation work well; as it never can, till the old habit of domination, and the new grudges of exasperated pride and passion, are qualified by gentleness and consideration. Otherwise there will be no industry but only jangle; society in fact will be turned into a hell of poverty and confusion. And this kind relationship never can be secured, till the dejected and despised race are put upon the footing of men, and allowed to assert themselves somehow in the laws. Putting aside all theoretic notions of equality, and regarding nothing but the practical want of the emancipation, negro suffrage appears to be indispensable. But the want is one thing, and the right of compelling it another. Our States have always made their own laws of suffrage, and if we want to resuscitate the state-rights doctrine, there is no so ready way as to rouse it by state wrongs. But there is always a way of doing what wants to be done,—pardon me if I name it even here; for our dead are not asking mere rhetoric of us, but duty. They call us to no whimpering over them, no sad weeping, or doling of soft sympathy, but to counsel and true action. I remember too, that we have taken more than a hundred thousand of these freedmen of the war to fight our common battle. I remember the massacre of Fort Pillow. I remember the fatal assault of Fort Wagner and the gallant Shaw sleeping there in the pile of his black followers. I remember the bloody fight and victory on the James, where the ground itself was black with dead. Ah, there is a debt of honor here! And honor is never so sacred as when it is due to the weak. Blasted and accursed be the soul that will forget these dead! If they had no offices or honors, if they fought and died in the plane of their humility,—Thou just God, forbid that we suffer them now to be robbed of the hope that inspired them!

Do then simply this, which we have a perfect constitutional right to do,—pass this very simple amendment, that the basis of representation in Congress shall hereafter be the number, in all the States alike, of the free male voters therein. Then the work is done; a general free suffrage follows by consent, and as soon as it probably ought. For these returning States will not be long content with half the offices they want, and half the power allowed them in the Republic. Negro suffrage is thus carried without even naming the word.

Need I add, that now, by these strange fortunes of the rebellion rushing on its Providential overthrow, immense responsibilities are put upon us, that are new. A new style of industry is to be inaugurated. The soil is to be distributed over again, villages are to be created, schools established, churches erected, preachers and teachers provided, and money for these purposes to be poured out in rivers of benefaction, even as it has been in the war. A whole hundred years of new creation will be needed to repair these wastes and regenerate these habits of wrong; and we are baptized for the dead, to go forth in God's name, ceasing not, and putting it upon our children never to cease, till the work is done.

My task is now finished; only, alas! too feebly. There are many things I might say, addressing you as Alumni, as professors and teachers, and as scholars training here for the new age to come. But you will anticipate my suggestions, and pass on by me, to conceive a better wisdom for yourselves. One thing only I will name, which is fitting, as we part, for us all; viz., that without any particle of vain assumption, we swear by our dead to be Americans. Our position is gained! Our die of history is struck! Thank God we have a country, and that country has the chance of a future! Ours be it henceforth to cherish that country, and assert that future; also, to invigorate both by our own civilization, adorn them by our literature, consolidate them in our religion. Ours be it also, in God's own time, to champion, by land and sea, the right of this whole continent to be an American world, and to have its own American laws, and liberties, and institutions.

9.

Phillips Brooks

"The Law of Growth"

(1877)

In the nineteenth century, when Boston was "the hub of the universe,"
Bishop Phillips Brooks was one of its stellar figures. Himself a native
Bostonian, a graduate of Harvard, and a descendant of the Puritans,
Brooks was rector of Trinity Episcopal Church from 1869 to 1895.
Here he preached to some of the most cultured, influential, and wealthy
Americans in the nation. But although they represented the opposite
pole of Evangelicalism from the crude frontier folk to whom Peter
Cartwright spoke, their fundamental philosophical and theological
beliefs were the same. Brooks was one of the most ecumenical of
Evangelicals, willing to share fellowship with all denominations and
all social levels of Christianity. He even participated in the brusque
enthusiasm of Dwight L. Moody's revival campaign in Boston in 1877
because he believed that Moody's preaching of Evangelical truth would
"reach the masses" as his own reached the classes. Although he made
Romantic Evangelicalism more mellow, refined, and cultivated than
Henry Ward Beecher, Brooks differed little from him in his desire to
save souls by melting the heart—except perhaps that he preferred conversion by cultivation to conversion by titillation. Brooks was just
as wedded to Wayland's theories of moral science and political economy
as Beecher and just as conservative and complacent about the manifest
destiny of the Anglo-Saxon race and institutions. In this selection,
preached to his congregation on March 11, 1877, Brooks stresses the
Evangelical belief in development of individual Christian character,
the importance of moral uplift, the reform of the individual not of
the social system, and the sublimation of earthly concerns to the growth
of the spirit.
[This sermon, given here in its entirety, is from the collection *The
Law of Growth* (New York, 1902).]

I. LAW OF GROWTH

"For whosoever hath, to him shall be given; and whosoever hath not, from him shall be taken even that which he seemeth to have."—Luke viii. 18.

It is interesting to know, of any one whose character and ways of thought we are studying, what words are oftenest upon his tongue. And it would seem as if this proverb, which I have just quoted from Him, were a favorite utterance of Jesus. Three of the Evangelists record it, and the circumstances with which they connect it are different. St. Matthew mentions two occasions on which Christ used the words.

It would seem, then, as if the truth which these words record seemed to Christ very impressive and important. He found in it the occasion for the most earnest exhortation to faithfulness. Such a fact must deserve our best study and come very close to our life. Let us try to see what it is.

"To him that hath shall be given, and from him that hath not shall be taken even that which he seemeth to have." In one case when Jesus used the proverb the parable of the talents had come just before. The immortal picture was just fresh in the Disciples' minds,—the careful, prudent, faithful merchant, whose five talents had attracted five others, and turned themselves to ten; the poor, timid, helpless creature who brought his one talent, all caked and useless with the earth in which it had been lying. And while the people were listening with that suspicion of injustice, that uneasy sense of something wrong, which almost always comes when prosperity and misery, success and unsuccess, stand side by side, Jesus went on frankly to declare that the truth of the parable was a truth everywhere; that everywhere there was a law of growth, a law of accumulation and of loss, which drew more blessing where blessing was already, and condemned to decay that which had no real vitality. It was a sort of "survival of the fittest" declared to be existing throughout the world.

And, just as soon as such a truth is announced, there are a multitude of voices which proclaim how true it is. Many of them speak in bitterness and anger. Indeed, it is the taunt of every disappointed soul. "Look," he who has failed says, "look and see how everywhere the prosperous prosper and the unhappy attract unhappiness by a terrible affinity. Behold how, when a man is rich, riches fly to his overloaded coffers of their own accord, while the poor man by his side grows poorer every day. Yes, it is true enough; let a man be going up and all the world hurries to help him; let him begin to go down, and where is the friend that will not push him lower?" So men speak with all the exaggeration of bitterness. Now, we want to leave out all the bitterness, for that is an element that never helps men to the truth. We shall see by and by whether the truth is one that ought to make us bitter. We want to stand now calmly and look over all the broad world, and see how true it is,—this centralization of blessing, this tendency of all privilege to attract other privilege.

It appears in the distributions of business. He who is fullest of work, he to whom the multitude are resorting to buy their goods, or to secure the building of their houses, is the man whom each new customer seeks out, while his neighbor sits with his tools around him, waiting for work which flows in a full stream past his doors, and lets no drop free to trickle in. It is true in learning. The more a man knows, the more the sources of learning open to him on every side. All the mouths of the world seem to be opened to tell him everything they know. The same is true of wealth. When a man reaches a certain point of wealth, his money reduplicates itself almost without his efforts, even drawing into itself the hard-earned profits of the toil of poorer men. And it is true of public favor. The man whom all are praising is the man whom all men praise. Popularity draws the eyes and voices of the crowd, and gathers with most unneeded profusion about some one or two people in the town. And of that far more sacred thing, Friendship, see how true it is. To him who has friends, friends are given. They come crowding up to claim some little fragment of the kindness of the much-loved man, leaving the other man, who has a whole heart to give away, with no one to ask him for it.

Or think of usefulness. One man cannot walk anywhere but at his feet there start innumerable opportunities to help his fellow-men. Need flies to him, and if he had a hundred hands, and each day were a hundred hours long, he could not satisfy the opportun-

ities for doing good which crowd themselves tumultuously upon
him. And then, right in the resounding echoes of his busy work,
you will find that other sight—always so sad!—of one who wants
to help his brethren, and round whose life there shuts a wall of
uselessness, within which he can only sit and feed upon himself.

Or think of health. The well man breathes it in from every
breeze. The sick man feels every touch of the life-giving nature
stealing what little life he has away. And so of healthiness of soul,
—that cordial, fresh, and kindly interest in things which makes
the joy of living. All the complications of life, all the touchings of
life on life, are always pouring more of this red wine into the cup
that is already full, while they make more morbid the soul that is
filled with suspicion and discontent already. And so of enthusiasms
and devotions. Your mind is full of an idea, your soul is given to
a cause, and inspiration and encouragement flow in to you from
every side. You find assurances that you are right and will succeed
everywhere. Nature and man both become the prophets of your
strong belief. But to your friend who, working with you, has no
such faith as yours, all nature and all men have only voices of discouragement. All that comes to him frightens him.

We might go on and catalogue everything that there is good
and fine in human life. We make our theories of compensation and
of equal distribution. We go on expecting that somehow, some
time, everything will be adjusted and equality proclaimed: the
conditions are to be reversed; the outs are to come in and the ins
are to go out. We try to make it appear that everything is mechan-
ically adjusted by what we call "impartial justice" every Saturday
night, or at that great Saturday night of all which we call death.
And all the time, underneath all our theories and expectations,
breaking up through them constantly with its contradictions, there
runs this vast law with its countless illustrations,—the law that
the happy always tend to become happier, and the good better, and
the wise wiser, and the rich richer, and the bad wickeder, and the
fools more foolish, and the poor poorer. All the while to him that
hath it is being given, and from him that hath not is being taken
away that which he seemeth to have.

And now what shall we say about this law? In the first place,
there can be no doubt that in the operation of the law there is

wrought out the greater part of the picturesqueness and interest of human life. That which some amiable theorists delineate, and try to establish as the actual condition of things, would certainly make a very tame and monotonous world. The strong, emphatic characters and careers which, having much, are always drawing to themselves more and more of the things which make life rich,—these certainly give to humanity a various strength and beauty which none of us, not even the humblest and the least endowed, would really be content to lose. Do you suppose that the obscure man who finds that everything like fame or notice drifts away from his life and gathers about the lives of one or two preëminent men of his time would really wish, in all his discontent, that all the world of reputation could be rolled level and no man be thought more of than any other man in the great, flat expanse of average existence? I think not. There are—and it is one of the signs of goodness that there are—new emotions and sources of pleasure which come out and exercise themselves when a man finds that his is not to be one of the privileged points of human life. The pleasure and growth which come by admiration of what is greater than himself; the unselfish joy in helping to complete the good work of some one who is supremely qualified to do it; the growing conviction that the world is richer for these concentrations of power which at first only excited jealousy,—all of these, which are among the truest and most cultivating pleasures which a man can have, become available to him who accepts and rejoices in the law which makes some lives supremely rich, even though his be not one of the rich but of the poor. The valley may wish it were the mountain up to which it gazes from its humble depth, but it would rather be the valley with the glorious mountain towering above it, and drinking in its sustenance from the mountain's side, than to have the whole earth rolled smooth, mountain and valley obliterated together in one indistinguishable level of dreary, barren plain.

Believe me, my friends, there is something better for you to do than to accept the patent inequalities of life with forlorn resignation. There was never any champion of individuality like Jesus, and yet He recognized and found no fault with the law of privilege, the law by which wealth and culture and the patent forms of happiness flow together and collect in the rich lives of certain men. It is possible for you, though a poor man, to take so wide a view of the world, and of your race, that you shall be thoroughly glad that some other men are rich. In conscious ignorance and inability to learn, you may delight to know that some man whom you see is very learned, and learns more and more every day. Nay, you may be very wretched, and yet have your wretchedness not deepened, but lightened, by the sight of some brother's life, into which happiness seems to have poured its most profuse abundance, and who goes singing under the windows of your sorrow.

You have anticipated me, I know, in thinking that the perplexity and difficulty come when we apply our law to moral life, and find that goodness and badness also have the same principle of accumulation. Then it is often very bewildering. There is a man who has the love of goodness in him. Something of the divine passion of holiness has touched him. He is very far indeed from perfect, but he is a good man as distinct from a bad man. The direction of his life is set toward righteousness. To him come trooping all good influences from all regions of the earth. Everything he reads and sees and does, everything that other people do to him or around him, seems to give him some new opportunity of good. The very temptations that beset him seem compelled to render up to him their strength, and help him to grow better. The world of things seems to have taken his goodness into its charge, to bring it to completeness.

Close by his side, it may be, is another man, whom all the world calls bad. He does a good thing here and there, but the choice of his life is wickedness. The deeper dispositions which run under all the casual events are deliberately set toward sin. What is it that makes that man's life terrible to watch? What is it that makes gradually gather in his own eyes a hopelessness that sometimes enrages him, and sometimes only serves him for an excuse? Is it not the way in which everything that happens to him seems to increase his wickedness? The evil element in everything seems to fly to him. Out of the quietest scenes there rise up voices calling him to sin. If there is a bad man, he meets him. If there is a combination of circumstances which can bewilder faith and shake responsibility, it seems to gather around him. This is the way in which life easily comes to look to us like a great machine for making good people better

and making bad people worse. It matters not that round the good
man there do gather manifold temptations to be wicked, and round
the wicked man come crowding the persuasions to be good,—nay,
the very subtlety with which goodness draws out of the worst temptation some ministry of grace, the dreadful ingenuity with which sin
draws out of the best influences some provocation of evil, only
makes the truth more manifest of how easy it is for the good to
grow better and for the wicked to grow worse in this great, mysterious, fertile world.

You wonder sometimes how men can believe in heaven and hell.
My friends, the wonder is how, with this sight before them which
I have described, men can help it. The belief in heaven and hell is
but the carrying out into the long vista of eternity of what men see
about them every day,—the law of spiritual accumulation and ac-
celeration, the law by which sin and goodness increase each after
its kind. The more clearly a man believes in the life to come, and
thinks of it as under the same great moral forces that pervade this
life, the more impressive grow to him its spiritual necessities. He
believes in a mercy which runs beyond the grave; but unless it be
a mercy which does what mercy never does now, and *compels* to
goodness the soul refusing to be good, there still stretches out the
possibility of a wickedness forever obstinate, and so forever wretched.

But think of it, if you will, only as it concerns this present life.
It would be impressive enough even if there were no life to come,
this tendency of everything to make the good grow better and the
evil worse. If the fact is as clear as I have stated it, then it must
stand as one of those things, like the wind or the sunshine, of which
it is quite unnecessary that we should spend our time in asking
whether it ought to be, as we can see very plainly that it is. What
we do need to ask is the value of such a truth, so fundamental, so
pervasive, set right into the midst of our life. How will it affect our
living? What good effects is it intended to produce? The answer to
that question seems to me to be twofold. It will emphasize individuality; and it will keep ever vivid the difference between right
and wrong. Let us look at these, and see if they are not what the
world very much needs.

The emphasis of individuality, the conviction of a man's self as
having a personal character and living a personal life, is not this

the thing the lack of which has made the weakest moments of all
our lives? There are two classes of sins,—those that come from
our feeble yielding and those that come of our wanton obstinacy.
Of the latter class we may say sometimes that they result from our
exaggerated individuality. Really they come of our distorted and
diseased individuality. But the other class comes surely from the
absence of any strong sense of individual life at all. From the boy
who catches his first oath from the lips of the boy three years older
than himself, whose impressive age and experience swallow up the
personal responsibility of the admiring youngster by his side, on to
the old man who dies rich, with a fortune that he has made by
some of the conventional unrighteousnesses—where is the trouble
in it all? Is it not in the feebleness of the boy's and the man's conception of *himself?* Duty, duty, that great, personal idea, something
that he owes to God, something that he must do, whatever anybody
or everybody beside him in the world may do,—that has not taken
hold of him. He knows nothing about it. If he gets deep enough
to have any philosophy about it all, his whole philosophy will be
this,—that goodness and wickedness, like happiness or unhappiness,
come by chance, that neither is to be struggled after or avoided.

Oh, it is terrible to think how full our streets and houses are of
that philosophy! The man you do your business with, the friend
you take your pleasure with, the brother or sister with whom you
live in the same house, it is terrible to think how all moral life
seems to him an accident, that it is as perfectly uncertain whether
he will be noble or base to-morrow as whether the wind will blow
east or blow west. There can be no strong sense of personality
there. There personal life resolves itself into a bundle of tastes,
and the man recognizes himself only by what he likes or hates.
But now suppose that man can come into our law. Growing cogni-
zant of moral life, trying to be a good man or coming to know
himself a bad man, he finds all the world declaring a disposition
towards him, helping him on in the way which he has chosen.
He has called it a world of accidents, and thought himself its
puppet. But the minute he makes any moral declaration of himself
he finds the world all devoting itself to the fulfilment of that
declaration, all tending to make him more and more what he has
set out to be. He has been floating on the waves, tossed where they

pleased to toss him, but the minute that he says, "I will go thither," and begins to swim, the water under him becomes his helper; it lifts him up and floats him; it answers to the beating of his hands; it bears him on and lands him where he wants to be. Now that is thoroughly personal. It cannot be anything else. A man setting a moral destiny before himself, and feeling the whole current and power of things immediately bearing him on to it, *must* come to the certainty that he is a self-determined being and that God helps his self-determination.

Oh, my dear friend, this is what you want. In your parlor, at your club, you are losing yourself, you are losing your soul, you are getting to seem to yourself the mere creature of accidents. What do you need? Go and undertake some duty. Go and be moral. Go and be good. Go and find the soul that you have lost. Go, and in the midst of your self-indulgent life surprise yourself by doing what perhaps you have not done for years,—by doing *something that you ought to do because you ought to do it.* As you enter that moral region you have no idea of the revolution that will come in all these accidents and their relation to your life. It will be as if a general had forgotten his generalship, and gone to playing games and running races with his soldiers, who have forgotten it, too. But by and by the bugle sounds, and he recalls himself. He flings his play aside, and arms him for the battle. And then they, too, reverence him again, and cry, "Oh, let us help you, for we are only your servants as soon as you have really undertaken to be worthy of yourself." So all the world will help you as soon as you try to do your duty. When you claim your manhood it will own your manhood, and you, who have counted yourself a mere playfellow of the blind chances of the world, will find yourself recognized by the world as a true moral creature, to whom it is commissioned, by the God who made it, to render its humble help in working out your moral life.

I said, again, that the truth which Jesus emphasizes so, and on which we have been dwelling, is of value because it keeps ever vivid the difference between right and wrong. The idea that out of the mass of influences about us the good character appropriates the elements which belong to it, so that it grows ever better, and the bad character appropriates its own elements and grows ever worse

—that seems to me to be one of the most profoundly impressive declarations of what essentially different things the good and evil are. I take two seeds which look so much alike that only the skilled eye can tell the difference between them. I plant them side by side in the same soil. Immediately each of them sends out its summons. Each demands of the ground the elements of growth which its peculiar nature craves. The earth hears and acknowledges the summons, and renders up to each what it demands. So two men, who seem just alike, are set down in the same city. Instantly to one there fly all the influences of good; to the other there gather all the powers of evil that pervade that city's life. Or, into a man's life is dropped a purpose. That purpose instantly declares its character by the way in which it divides the forces of his life. If it is good, it calls all that is good within him or around him to its aid. All that is noble gives its strength willingly to this new, feeble plan. All that is sluggish, base, selfish, in his nature or his circumstances sets itself against his new desire.

It is in such discriminations that the essential differences of the qualities of the good and bad display themselves. In the least atom of good there lies a power to attract goodness and repel wickedness. In the least atom of wickedness there lies a power to repel the good and to attract the bad. That is the qualitative power of moral natures. Ah, when we think how everywhere we are imposed upon by *quantities*, do we not need, do we not welcome, this strong statement, that the real power of things lies in their *qualities*—in what they really are, whether there be much of them or little? See how we are deluded. We take some vice which, in its larger manifestations, we know is flagrant and destructive. We make it small. Without changing its character in the least, we bring down its dimensions. We turn the great public cheat into the little personal deception; we transform the large, insulting slander into base, personal, gossiping detraction; and what was acknowledgedly bad on the large scale is accepted as graceful and venial in its smallness. Or, just the opposite: we take some action which in its petty forms everybody owns to be bad and mean, like the bullying of the weaker by the stronger, and, lifting it to a higher degree, we crown it with dignity and honor, as when we glorify the oppressor and the tyrant. Oh, we do need everywhere more of that conscientiousness which looks at the qualities, less of that superficialness which is overcome by the mere quantities of things.

The other side of this is to me even more impressive. If we lose sight of the essential nature of evil very often by dwelling upon the increase or diminution of its size, so that the very great or the very little evil seems to us to be almost absolutely good, the same is true about the quality of goodness. There, too, we are imposed upon by quantity till we forget that quality alone is vital. If we could all see, and always see, the essential force which is in every good act, however slight it is, and in every true belief, however meagre it is, how different our lives would be! But our goodness and our faith grow very small; and, instead of valuing all the more intensely what is left, our ordinary impulse is to throw the remnant away. It is so little, we think, that it is not worth the keeping.

Suppose that out of the world there should be slowly or suddenly destroyed all the seed of corn except one handful, just so much as one man could hold in his palm. Can you picture to yourself the care with which that handful would be guarded? Can you imagine the interest that would gather about it, the poetry and dearness that would be in it; how men, looking at it and knowing it to be the real thing,—true, real corn,—would see in it the assurance of days yet to come when all the fields should wave once more with harvests? That is the way in which you ought to treasure your faith if there is not much of it, if little by little it has slipped away from you. You say it has grown to be very little. You say that many things which you used to believe seem to you no longer to be true. You stand holding in your hand the remnant of a faith. When then? Is it real? Is it true faith? Whether it be little or great, do you really believe it? If you do, then surely that belief ought to be very precious to you. A little, a very little belief it may be,—nevertheless treasure it because it is belief, instead of despising it because it is little. Value it for its quality, instead of dishonoring it for its quantity. As you look into it behold its possibilities. See in its meagreness the promise and power of a great and manifold belief that may yet some day cover your whole life with verdure. Put it where it will be safe; and the only place where a faith ever can be safe is in the shrine of an action. Put it there. Do what that

belief would tempt you and command you to do; and trust to its
true quality to grow under the care of God, who knows in heaven
every particle of true faith that there is scattered about the earth.
In His sight it is all too precious to forget.

What a great many people need to-day is to forget for a while
their care about the quantity of their belief, and to give their anxious
attention to its quality. Not, *how much* do I believe? but, *how* do
I believe? It is well worth while for you to learn to ask that deeper
question. Seek reality, even though it be by casting aside much that
you have carried about with you that was unreal. It is a glad day
for a true man when at least he plucks off and casts away a faith
which he has not believed, or a hypocritical habit which has not
been truly his. "Coming down to reality," he calls it. It really is
coming *up* to reality. The fresh, strong, hopeful future opens before him.

Of every other experience that is true which I have been stating
thus about belief. You need to learn, when you hear Christ your
Master insisting on repentance, on love for Himself, on love for
fellow-man, on devoted work, that His desire is, first of all and
deepest of all, for the qualities of those things. He wants a real
repentance, a real love, a real devotion. If He sees reality, we can
well understand how He can be infinitely patient with littleness;
for where He stands eternity is all in sight. He sees forever. He
knows through what summer of cloudless sunshine the least grace
will have time to ripen to the richest. He knows in what rich fields
the seed will find eternal lodgment. So there is time enough, if only
the seed is real. If it is not real, eternity is not long enough and
heaven is not rich enough to bring it to anything.

How impressive this is in the story of Christ's earthly life! How
patient He was with imperfection! How intolerant He always was
of unreality! He could wait for a publican while he unsnarled
himself out of the meshes of his low vocation, but He cut with a
word like a sword through the solemn trifling of the Pharisees.
He never was impatient with His disciples. Their graces were very
small, but they were real. Eternity was long, and He could wait
till the graces which He saw to be real opened into all the possibility which He discerned in them; till the Peter who paraded
his genuine but feeble resolution of devotion at the Supper grew

to the Peter who could die for Him at Rome, and live with Him in some high doing of His will in heaven.

It is good for us if we can treat ourselves as our Lord treats us. Try to find out whether your repentance for sin is real—a genuine sorrow for a wrong life. If it is, no matter if it falls far short of the complete contrition which you picture to yourself, still keep it, hold it fast. Do not let it slip away and drop back into the placid content which you felt before you were penitent at all. So with your love to your Saviour,—do not throw it away because it is not that large-winged devotion which soars up into the very sunshine of His closest company. Keep it. Feed it on all you know of Him. Never trifle with it, or surround it with any unreality of profession merely to make it seem larger than it is. Reverence it, not because it is great enough to be worthy of Him, but because for such a being as you are to love at all such a being as He is, is a sublime act,—the glorification of your nature, and the promise of infinite growth.

I long for every Christian, especially for every young Christian, to see this first Christian truth of the value of the essential qualities of things set deep into his life. Christ was full of it. Christ showed us how full God is of it. In it is the secret of endless patience. In it is the power of enthusiasm at every stage of growth. Can the soul just come to Christ, just trembling with its first love, its first hope, lift up itself and sing enthusiastically? Yes, if it can know indeed that "to him which hath shall be given," that it is in the very essential nature of the life it has begun to go on, and never stop, until it stands in the glory which is before the Throne of God.

In the truth which Jesus taught, then, in the proverb which was so often on His lips, there lie still the warning and the inspiration which He put there. It is the truth of a live world, a world so full of life that into it nothing can fall without partaking of its life, a world that makes the good grow better and the bad grow worse always. If the world is making us worse, then not to change the world, but to be changed ourselves, is what we need. We must be regenerate by Christ, and then the world shall become His school-room, by all its ministries bringing us more and more perfectly to Him. May He give us His new life, that the world may become new to us!

10.

Dwight L. Moody

"How Can Non-Church-Goers Be Reached?,"
"To Reformed Men,"
and "The Return of Our Lord"
(1877)

The fact that Dwight L. Moody was never ordained indicates both the decline of denominational orthodoxy, the measurement of divine calling by the pragmatic test of soul saving, and the rise of the laity to positions of prominence in American religious life—all outstanding aspects of the later Evangelical movement. But Moody's prime importance lay in transforming the revival techniques of Finney and the pre-Civil War evangelists to the problems of postwar urbanism. The rise of the city brought with it the rise of a large unchurched urban proletariat part of which came from the rural areas of America and part from European immigration. Moody learned from industrialists how to make revivalism a big business; he learned from his work as an urban missionary and from Y.M.C.A. workers in Chicago how to "reach the masses." Partly out of conservative fears about the dangers of an unconverted proletariat but more out of a sincere belief that the Christianization and Americanization of the masses was the best way to promote their own and the nation's prosperity, the big businessmen of the era from J. P. Morgan to the Fricks, Wanamakers, Armours, Drexels, Biddles, and McCormicks, gave their money, time, and moral support to Moody's revival crusades. From his initial success in the largest cities of the British Isles during 1873–1875, Moody went on to conduct what he called "preaching missions" in the largest cities of the United States over the last quarter of the century. It is impossible to capture the color, the variety, and the spirit of these revivals in any one sermon; the first selections here represent his ap-

proach to converting the masses. But equally important for an understanding of the changing mood of Evangelicalism was Moody's emphasis upon the pre-millennial theory of the Second Coming of Christ. Concern with biblical prophecy, dispensationalism, biblical literalism were to become characteristic of the Fundamentalist movement after Moody's death. Moody gave them new emphasis partly in reaction to the higher criticism and social Darwinism but also out of his recognition that the cultivated gentility of Romantic Evangelicalism was not effective among the lower middle class to which and for which he spoke.
[The first two selections are taken from the collection *To All People* (New York, 1877) and the third from W. H. Daniels, ed., *Moody, His Words, Work and Workers* (New York, 1877).]

HOW CAN NON-CHURCH-GOERS BE REACHED?

I would like to say one word before we close this question. I don't believe there is a minister in this congregation but would have a full house if he would just work for it. A few years ago, before I thought I could preach, we built a hall in Chicago for the Young Men's Christian Association, and our plan was to get the different ministers to go there every Sunday night and preach, but we failed in that; we couldn't get many to come, and the ministers didn't like to go there to preach, and so one night they came to me and wanted me to go down there and preach. It was pretty hard to preach to empty chairs. But I got a few interested in the meeting and then we got out some hand-bills that cost about sixty cents a thousand, and then we took some of the young men and got them to come together every night in the hall, and we gave them some tea and they prayed together; and they took these handbills and went out on the street, and every man had a district, and they visited every saloon and billiard hall and bowling alley, and there was not a man who came within a mile of the building but got from one to half a dozen of these invitations to come to that meeting. And when a man was converted we yoked him up with another, two and two, and sent them out to bring others, and that is the way we did it, and we have always had an audience ever since. Now if people won't come to our churches, let us go for them in that way and keep the church awake. If a man goes out on the street trying to get people to come into the church and he gets another man to come in, he will not go to sleep. He will try to have that man interested in the exercises; and if he does not like the sermon, he will go to the minister afterwards and say, "You must make that sermon plainer; that man that I brought didn't understand it." There was a man we converted in Chicago who couldn't speak a word of English, and we had to make use of an interpreter, and what to do with that man after he became a Christian I didn't know. He wanted to do something for the Lord, and, finally, I stationed him at the corner of Clark and Madison streets to give out these handbills. And when the Lord converted him the man was so happy! His face was just lit up, and to every man that went by—and there were some pretty hard cases—he just gave a handbill. And some thanked him and some swore at him, but he kept smiling all the time. He couldn't tell the difference between thanks and curses. And for two months he stood there, without a hat part of the time, and every night he was there; when it got to be dark in the short days he would have a transparency all lighted up right there on the corner; and there he would stand, and he stood there months and months, and the Lord gave him a good many souls. You can say that may be done in the cities, but what can we do in the country towns? Well, we can try something else in the country towns. I remember in one country town where the people did not attend the meetings, they went out into the mountains and fields and had meetings there, and the church soon became four or five times larger than it was. That gave them an interest. If people will not come to the churches, why not send others out after them, and why not have meetings outside? That will soon give them an interest so that they will come to the house of God. Another way is to have prayer-meetings in the homes. A good many mothers cannot come out to church; but we can go down to their homes, and have four or five families come together, and pray with them and get them interested. Many a mother cannot go to the house of God for years, they have no servants to take care of their children, and they have to stay at home and look after their families, and the only way to reach them is to have cottage prayer-meetings. There must be a personal interest taken in them. These young converts coming to Christ want something to do. Let them have the privilege, the glorious luxury of carrying the water of life to them that are perishing. Another thing —have good singing. In some of these churches they have been

singing the same old hymns for the last twenty years, and instead
of the organ being up in the gallery with two or three singers about
it doing all the singing, bring the organ right down among the
people and let them gather right round it and sing themselves.
And if some of the people don't know how to sing, have a meeting
once a week, where the people can go and learn. If the church will
only set the young converts to work, why we can reach a great many
homes; but if we just take them into the church and leave them
there, and not teach them how to work, the homes are never going
to be reached. Some young converts during the past weeks have
been to work, and they have already brought, some eight, some ten,
and some twelve of their friends to Christ. If we keep on in that
way how long will it be before we have hundreds and thousands of
converts in this city? The church makes a woful mistake in not
setting these young converts to work. Those men who have been
drunkards, let them just set out and work among their old friends.
No man can reach a drunkard better than one who has been a
drunkard himself. I don't know any work so blessed in Chicago
as the going out into the billiard saloons and preaching the gospel
there. If they will not come to church, go down where they are, in
the name of our God, and you will reach them. If you say, "Oh,
they will put you out," I say, "No, I have never been turned out
of a saloon in my life." Go down in a saloon where there are thirty
or forty men playing, and ask them if they don't want a little
singing. They say, "Yes, we don't mind your singing." "Well, what
will you have?" And perhaps they ask you to sing a comic song.
"But we don't know any. We don't know how to sing comic songs.
Wouldn't you like to have us sing the 'Star Spangled Banner,' or
'My Country, 'tis of Thee.' " And so you sing "My Country, 'tis of
Thee," and they stop playing cards. "Now boys, wouldn't you like
to have us sing a hymn our mothers taught us when we were boys?"
And then you can sing

> "There is a fountain filled with blood,
> Drawn from Immanuel's veins;
> And sinners plunged beneath that flood
> Lose all their guilty stains."

Or give out "Rock of Ages, Cleft for Me," and it won't be long before the hats will be coming off, and they will remember how their mothers sung that to them once when they were in bed, and the tears will begin to run down their cheeks, and it won't be long before they will want you to read a few verses out of the Bible, and then they will ask you to pray with them, and you will be having a prayer-meeting there before you know it. We took sixteen out of a saloon in that way one night, and nine of them went into the inquiry-room; what we need in Boston is to go out and get these men. If men will not come out to hear the glorious Gospel of the Son of God, let us take and carry it into these attic homes and saloons. Thank God! Boston is going to be visited. Let every man, woman and child help us a little and we pray that as they go into these attics and these households, the Holy Spirit may help them to present Christ in all His glory and loveliness. Let all take hold and help; and then religion will be like a red-hot ball rolling over the earth and nothing can stand against it. The churches can be crowded full and the masses reached if we go about it in the Spirit of the Master.

TO REFORMED MEN

Last Friday I was to have a question drawer to receive questions which I was to answer, and some of these questions are constantly arising now. As to this question that has been before us every Friday since we have been in this city, "Ought a reformed drunkard, whose family is in want, give any of his money for charitable purposes outside of his own family?" perhaps some were here last night and felt as if they would like to give, because they have been so blessed by this Tabernacle, and perhaps they felt as if they did not show true gratitude if they did not give. Let me say right here that your first work is to take care of your family. Your money belongs at home. If your wife has had a hard struggle, and you have been squandering your money in saloons and billiard halls and rum shops, you want to take it home now; your aim should be to make your home just as comfortable for your dear ones as you possibly can. We read in the fifth chapter of Timothy and the eighth verse:

> "If any provide not for his own, and especially for those of his
> own house he hath denied the faith, and is worse than an infidel."

There is what Paul says to you upon that subject. "He is worse than an infidel."

Let your first earnings go to that home. Clothe your children, and don't let them be hooted at on the street as sons and daughters of a drunkard. Give them comfortable clothes and a comfortable home, that is where you want to put your money. Now, here is another question that has been asked: "Ought a man to pay his liquor bills after he is converted?" "Render unto Caesar the things that belong to Caesar." If you want to have any influence with these rumsellers go and pay up your bills. The mistake is made; you never ought to have contracted the bill or run into debt, but if you have, go and pay your debt.

In the thirteenth chapter of Romans and in the seventh and eighth verses we read:

> "Render therefore to all their dues; tribute to whom tribute is due; custom to whom custom; fear to whom fear; honor to whom honor."
> "Owe no man anything, but to love one another; for he that loveth another hath fulfilled the law."

We have a right to go into debt for one thing, that is love. I believe that a great many people are now suffering, and are suffering a thousand times more than they would if they had not run into debt, not only for liquor, but for other things. And I want to say to you young converts, that if you will take my advice, you will keep out of debt. If friends want to advance you money to help you up, tell them you won't have it. Don't you take it. I would rather have twenty-five cents that I have earned by the sweat of my brow than twenty-five dollars that I have borrowed, and that I will have to pay back. Work your way up to the top of the ladder and you will like to stay up there; but if you are lifted up there by somebody you will be all the time tumbling back and you will get disheartened and discouraged. There are a great many of these men that cannot make restitution, and because they have not paid their debts there may be a good many of these enemies of religion that will say that they have not been truly born again; that they have not been truly regenerated. It may be that it will take years for some of these men to pay their debts. They have been running up a pretty good account, but that is not going to keep them from Christ. If their hearts are right and their purpose right, and they mean to pay their bills, and they pay them just as soon as they can, that is just as acceptable to God as if they paid them all at once. If any of these reformed men are hundreds of dollars in debt, and they have not a penny to pay them with, their creditors must wait. That ought to be your first aim, to pay off those debts and get out of it as quickly as possible. I have great confidence in those men that profess to be reclaimed, if they go to work. If you cannot get what you want, get what you can. If you cannot get as much for your work as you think you ought to get, get whatever you can. One of these men that had been reclaimed wanted to find work right off, and that was a very good sign of his conversion. But some of these men have not done anything for years but drink liquor, and they are not adapted to hardly anything, and they are not fit for much at first. It is difficult to get them situations, and if we do succeed in getting them work they ought to take it and thank God for it. If it is not what you like, thank God that it is something. Something is a good deal better than nothing. There was one of these converted men in Chicago that could not get what he wanted to do, but he got a man that would board him and give him twenty-five cents a week. He took up the offer and went to work. Twenty-five cents a week! Well, that wasn't much, but he got his board, and that was a good deal. Pretty soon a business man heard of it, and he said, "That is the man for me; that is just the man I want;" and he hired him and gave him $4 a day. There is many a man that will help you up if you will show a disposition to help yourself. There is a man upon this platform who is going to speak to you that I admire very much, because he went to work for $3 a week, and boarded himself. You say that $3 a week won't pay your board, but it will help, and it is a good deal better than nothing.

Nothing won't if three dollars don't. That is better than running up and down the street idle and getting into debt. If you do this and work faithfully for three dollars a week, it won't be long before you have six dollars, and then you will get ten dollars, and then twelve dollars a week. You want to get these employers always under an obligation to you. You must be such true men and be so helpful to your employers that they cannot get along without you, and then you will work up, and your employer will increase your wages. If a man works in the interest of his employer he will be sure to keep him and treat him well, but if he only works for money and don't take any interest in his employer's business, he will let him go at any time. They can get any quantity of such men. But if they get a man that takes an interest in his work they cannot spare him, for such men are scarce. Let me say to these reformed men that, if you will take my advice, you will get something to do. If you cannot earn more than a dollar a week, earn that. That is better than nothing, and you can pray to God for more. . . .

These are hard times, I know, and it is hard to get work, but spring has come, and if you cannot get work in the city, strike out into the country. A great many farmers want men now. It is not degrading to go out and hoe and shovel in the field. It is noble, I think. I do not believe there is a man in this city that really wants work but can get it in the country. If you haven't money to ride, walk out. You can foot it on a good pleasant day like this, ten or fifteen miles a day. Besides, you will have a better chance walking than if you passed the farmers' places on a train. If you are looking for work do not beg. Ask for something to do. If you are offered anything without work do not take it. They will give you some wood to saw, or some work to do that will pay for what you get. Your meals will taste a good deal sweeter, when you have earned them by the sweat of your brow. There was one good thing about that prodigal, he would not beg, and he would not steal. He would not even steal the swine's food. That is the kind of men we want now. If you will not beg or steal, men will respect and help you. What we want to-day is true men, and if people find that you are a true man, they will make room for you. It may be a hard chance to get the first footing, but if you hold right on, God will open a way for you, and if need be send down a legion of angels to help you. "What would you do with a man that would not work?" There is the same thing. I think Paul has it right.

If a man will not work, he shall not eat. I think we are doing these men a great injury if we help them when they won't work. Some of these men have professed, but there is a difference between conversion and being born of God; being regenerated. We are living in days of sham—and they see others come out, and that they are getting fed, and getting new clothes, and they say: "These men are making a good thing out of it; I guess I'll reform too." But it is easy to tell them. They are a blight in the hollow; they are not whole in the root. And if they will not work, that is a pretty good sign that they have not been born of God. When I was President of the Young Men's Christian Association in Chicago we used to have those men coming in all the time. They would tell about their suffering, and how they had no work and wanted help. At last I got two or three hundred cords of wood and put it in a vacant lot, and got some saws and sawbucks and kept them out of sight. A man would come and ask for help. "Why don't you work?" "I can't get any." "Would you do it if you could get any?" "Oh, yes, anything." "Would you really work in the street?" "Yes." "Would you saw wood?" "Yes." "All right," and then we would bring out the saw and sawbuck and send them out, but we would have a boy to watch and see that they did not steal the saw. Then the fellow would say, "I will go home and tell my wife I have got some work," and that would be the last we would see of him. Out of the whole winter I never got more than three or four cords of wood sawed. We heard from our friend Dr. Tyng last week that we want a good deal of mother in this work; yes, and we want some father, too. If you are always showering money on these men, and giving them clothing and raiment, they will live in idleness, and not only ruin themselves, but their children. It is not charity at all to help them when they will not work. If a man will not work, let him starve. They never die. I never heard of them really starving to death. You may say that is harsh, but we need a little of that now. . . . You cannot keep the body healthy without work. "By much slothfulness the building decayeth, and through idleness of the hands the house droppeth through." If you want to keep the body in a good, healthy state, you have got to work. We are commanded to earn our bread by the sweat of our brows. Get something to do. If it is for fifteen hours a day, all the better, for while you are at work Satan does not have so much chance to tempt you. It is these men that are out of work that Satan tempts.

"Do you think it best for a reformed man to give up tobacco?" Yes; I would let that go with the whiskey; it is part of the old nature. "Have you any passage of Scripture against this?" I think it is clearly taught that these bodies are the temples for the Holy Ghost, and we ought to be careful to keep them pure. I do not think it is becoming for a son of the Most High to be using that filthy weed. I don't know how it is, for I never used it, but I have an idea that it whets up the appetite for strong drink. It belongs to the old creation. How is it with men who have no work, using tobacco? I don't see how they can afford it, put it on that ground. I do not think it keeps the body in a healthy state. I think we ought to be very careful about the body because it is so identified with the soul. "I am so poor that I cannot afford to go to church; what shall I do?" Give up your tobacco. There are plenty of churches in this city that are perfectly free. You are welcomed, you are invited, you are urged to come, and there is not a minister in this town but would like to see his church filled. There may be some fashionable churches that are crowded without you, where you would not receive so warm a welcome as at others. If you cannot afford to pay a pew rent, tell them so, and you will find scores of churches in this city of Boston that will be glad to welcome you. I hope you reformed men will find homes in churches soon, where the godly people will gather around you. You will find many of the very best friends in these churches, and they will be more than glad to have you come. Let all these reformed men find some church at once, and in that way others will be of great good to you and you to them. . . .

THE RETURN OF OUR LORD

In 2 Timothy iii, 16, Paul declares: "All Scripture is given by inspiration of God, and is profitable for doctrine, for reproof, for correction, for instruction in righteousness"; but there are some people who tell us when we take up prophecy that it is all very well to be believed, but that there is no use in trying to understand it: these future events are things that the Church doesn't agree about, and it is better to let them alone, and deal only with those prophecies which have already been fulfilled. But Paul doesn't talk that way; he says: "All Scripture is . . . profitable for doctrine." If these people are right, he ought to have said: "*Some* Scripture is profitable; but you can't understand the prophecies, so you had

better let them alone." If God didn't mean to have us study the
prophecies he wouldn't have put them into the Bible. Some of them
are fulfilled, and he is at work fulfilling the rest, so that if we do
not see them all completed in this life, we shall in the world to come.

I don't want to teach any thing to-day, dogmatically, on my
own authority; but to my mind this precious doctrine—for such I
must call it—of the return of the Lord to this earth is taught in the
New Testament as clearly as any other doctrine in it; yet I was in
the Church fifteen or sixteen years before I ever heard a sermon
on it. There is hardly any Church that doesn't make a great deal
of baptism, but the New Testament only speaks about baptism thir-
teen times, while it speaks of the return of our Lord fifty times; and
yet the Church has had very little to say about it.

Now I can see a reason for this: the devil does not want us to
see this truth, for nothing would wake up the Church so much.
The moment a man takes hold of the truth that Jesus Christ is
coming back again to receive his friends to himself, this world
loses its hold upon him; gas-stocks, and water-stocks, and stocks in
banks and in horse railroads, are of very much less consequence to
him then. His heart is free, and he looks for the blessed appearing
of his Lord, who at his coming will take him into his blessed
kingdom. . . .

I don't know why people shouldn't like to study the Bible, and
find out all about this precious doctrine of our Lord's return. Some
have gone beyond prophecy, and tried to tell the very day he would
come. Perhaps that is one reason why people don't believe this
doctrine. That he is coming, we know; but just when he will come
we don't know. Matthew xxiv, 36, settles that. The angels don't
know, and Christ says that even he doesn't know; that is something
the Father keeps to himself.

If Christ had said, "I will not come back for two thousand years,
none of his disciples would have begun to watch for him; but it is
the proper attitude of a Christian to be always looking for his
Lord's return. So God does not tell us when he is to come, but
Christ tells us to watch. In this same chapter we find that he is
to come unexpectedly and suddenly. In the twenty-seventh verse
we have these words: "For as the lightning cometh out of the east,
and shineth even unto the west; so shall also the coming of the

Son of man be." And again in the forty-fourth verse: "Therefore
be ye also ready; for in such an hour as ye think not the Son of
man cometh." Some people say that means death; but the word of
God doesn't say it means death. Death is our enemy, but our Lord
hath the keys of death; he has conquered death, hell, and the grave,
and at any moment he may come to set us free from death, and
destroy our last enemy for us; so the proper state for a believer
in Christ is waiting and watching for his Lord's return.

In the last chapter of John there is a text that seems to settle
this matter. Peter asks the question about John, "Lord, and what
shall this man do? Jesus said unto him, If I will that he tarry till
I come, what is that to thee? Follow thou me. Then went this
saying abroad among the brethren, that that disciple should not
die." They didn't think that the coming of the Lord meant death;
there was a great difference between these two things in their
minds. Christ is the prince of life; there is no death where he is;
death flees at his coming; dead bodies sprang to life when he
touched them or spoke to them. His coming is not death: he is
the resurrection and the life, and when he sets up his kingdom
there is to be no death, but life for evermore.

There is another mistake, you will find, if you read your Bibles
carefully. Some people think that at the coming of Christ every
thing is to be all done up in a few minutes; but I do not so understand it. The first thing he is to do is to take his Church out of the
world. He calls the Church his bride, and he says he is going to
prepare a place for her. "We may judge," says one, "what a glorious
place it will be from the length of time he is in preparing it; and
when the place is ready he will come and take the Church to
himself."

Toward the close of the fourth chapter of First Thessalonians
Paul says: "If we believe that Jesus died and rose again, even so
them also which sleep in Jesus will God bring with him. . . . We
which are alive and remain unto the coming of the Lord shall
not prevent them which are asleep. For the Lord himself shall
descend from heaven with a shout, with the voice of the archangel,
and with the trump of God: and the dead in Christ shall rise first:
then we which are alive and remain shall be caught up together
with them in the clouds to meet the Lord in the air: and so shall
we ever be with the Lord. Wherefore, comfort one another with

these words." That is the comfort of the Church. There was a time when I used to mourn that I should not be alive in the millennium; but now I expect to be in the millennium. Dean Alford says—almost every body bows to him in the matter of interpretation—that he must insist that this coming of Christ to take his Church to himself in the clouds is not the same event as his coming to judge the world at the last day. The deliverance of the Church is one thing, judgment is another. Now, I can't find any place in the Bible where it tells me to wait for signs of the coming of the millennium, as the return of the Jews, and such like; but it tells me to look for the coming of the Lord; to watch for it; to be ready at midnight to meet him, like those five wise virgins. The trump of God may be sounded, for anything we know, before I finish this sermon; at any rate we are told that he will come as a thief in the night, and at an hour when many look not for him. . . .

There are three great facts foretold in the word of God: First, that Christ should come; that has been fulfilled. Second, that the Holy Ghost should come; that was fulfilled at Pentecost, and the Church is able to testify to it by its experience of his saving grace. Third, the return of our Lord again from heaven: for this we are told to watch and wait "till he come." Look at the account of the last hours of Christ with his disciples. What does Christ say to them? If I go away I will send death after you to bring you to me? Not at all. He says, "I will come again and receive you unto myself." If my wife were in a foreign country, and I had a beautiful mansion all ready for her, she would a good deal rather I should come and take her unto it than to have me send someone else to bring her. So the Church is the Lamb's wife; he has prepared a mansion for his bride, and he promises for our joy and comfort that he will come himself and take us to the place he has been all this while preparing.

My friends, it is perfectly safe to take the word of God just as we find it. If he tells us to watch, then watch. If he tells us to pray, then pray. If he tells us he will come again, wait for him. Let the Church bow to the word of God, rather than be trying to find out how these things can be. "Behold, I come quickly," said Christ. "Even so; come, Lord Jesus," should be the prayer of the Church.

Take the account of the words of Christ at the communion table.

It seems to me the devil has covered up the most precious thing about it. "For as often as ye eat this bread, and drink this cup, ye do show the Lord's death *till he come*." Most people seem to think that the Lord's table is the place for self-examination and repentance, and making good resolutions. Not at all; you spoil it that way; it is to show forth the Lord's death; and we are to keep it up till he comes.

Some people say, "I believe Christ will come on the other side of the millennium." Where do you get it? I can't find it. The word of God nowhere tells me to watch and wait for the coming of the millennium, but for the coming of the Lord. I don't find any place where God says the world is to grow better and better, and that Christ is to have a spiritual reign on earth of a thousand years. I find that the earth is to grow worse and worse, and that at length there is going to be a separation. "Two women grinding at a mill; one taken and the other left; two men in one bed, one taken and the other left." The Church is to be translated out of the world; and of this we have two examples already, two representatives, as we might say, in Christ's kingdom, of what is to be done for all his true believers. Enoch is the representative of the first dispensation, Elijah of the second, and as the representative of the third dispensation we have the Saviour himself, who is entered into the heavens for us, and become the first-fruits of them that slept. We are not to wait for the great white-throne judgment, but the glorified Church is sit on the throne with Christ, and help to judge the world.

Now, some of you think this is a new and strange doctrine, and that they who preach it are speckled birds; but let me tell you that most of the spiritual men in the pulpits of Great Britain are firm in this faith. Spurgeon preaches it. I have heard Newman Hall say that he knew no reason why Christ might not come before he got through with his sermon. But in certain wealthy and fashionable Churches, where they have the form of godliness but deny the power thereof—just the state of things which Paul declares shall be in the last days—this doctrine is not preached or believed. They don't want sinners to cry out in their meeting, "What must I do to be saved?" They want intellectual preachers, who will cultivate their taste; brilliant preachers, who will please their imagination; but they don't want the preaching that has in it the power of the

Holy Ghost. We live in the day of shams in religion. The Church is cold and formal; may God wake us up! And I know of no better way to do it than to set the Church to looking for the return of our Lord.

Some people say, "O, you will discourage the young converts if you preach that doctrine." Well, my friends, that hasn't been my experience. I have felt like working three times as hard ever since I came to understand that my Lord was coming back again. I look on this world as a wrecked vessel. God has given me a life-boat, and said to me, "Moody, save all you can." God will come in judgment and burn up this world, but the children of God don't belong to this world; they are in it, but not of it, like a ship in the water. This world is getting darker and darker; its ruin is coming nearer and nearer; if you have any friends on this wreck unsaved you had better lose no time in getting them off. But someone will say, "Do you, then, make the grace of God a failure?" No; grace is not a failure, but man is. The antediluvian world was a failure; the Jewish world was a failure; man has been a failure every-where, when he has had his own way and been left to himself. Christ will save his Church, but he will save them finally by taking them out of the world. Now, don't take my word for it; look this doctrine up in your Bibles, and, if you find it there, bow down to it and receive it as the word of God. . . .

Now let the question go round, "Am I ready to meet the Lord if he comes to-night?" "Be ye also ready, for in such an hour as ye think not the Son of man cometh. . . ."

11.

Samuel P. Jones

"Personal Consecration: 'Quit Your Meanness'"
(1887)

Evangelicalism differed less between North and South than it did between rural and urban or among the various social classes. On the whole Southern Evangelicalism was more similar to the frontier earnestness of Cartwright and Finney than to the suburban romanticism of Beecher and Bushnell. After the war "the New South" produced cities of its own and the Rev. Samuel P. Jones, a Southern Methodist circuit-rider who turned professional evangelist in 1880, conducted campaigns in these cities which differed little from those of Moody in the Northeast. Like Moody, he had no use for Populists, Grangers, Greenbackers, labor union agitators, and other radicals who wanted to reform society without converting men's hearts. Like most Southern Evangelicals Jones expected the Negro to stay in his place. Moody himself considered Jones somewhat uncouth because the Southerner saw no harm in introducing humor, ridicule, and sarcasm into his sermons and often attacked the preaching of "high-toned, learned ministers." "We have been clamoring for forty years for a learned ministry," he said, "and we have got it today and the church is deader than it ever has been in history. Half of the literary preachers in this town are A.B.'s, Ph.D.'s, D.D's, LL.D.'s, and A.S.S.'s." From the freely given individual contributions for his revivalism and from his lecture fees on the Lyceum circuit, Jones claimed to be "the best paid preacher on the continent" in the 1890's. The selection here is one of Jones's most popular sermons. It is typical of the Evangelical concern for moral reform and of the extreme Arminian emphasis upon freedom of the will which often seemed to reduce religion to a decision of the sinner to "quit his meanness." After Jones died in 1906, the Rev. William A. (Billy) Sunday carried on in his folksy, rural style rather than in the more businesslike, matter-of-fact style of Moody.

[This sermon, given here in its entirety is from *Sam Jones' Own Book* (Cincinnati, 1887).]

SERMON I

Personal Consecration: "Quit your Meanness"

"Rejoice evermore; pray without ceasing; in every thing give thanks. For this is the will of God in Christ Jesus concerning you."—1 Thess. v. 16–18.

A man who understands practically what those three verses teach is not only a Christian, but a philosopher. There's a great deal of philosophy in Christianity, and the best philosophers make the best Christians. This term "rejoice" is a very different word from "happy," or "happiness." Our word "happy" comes from the same word that "happening" comes from, and my happiness depends largely on my happenings; but joy is very different in its meaning, and different in its effects on the human heart. Joy, when we analyze it, is a sort of trinity in unity: 1. I am satisfied with the past. 2. I am contented with the present. 3. I am hopeful for the future. If you will combine these three elements in a human life, I will show you a man who rejoices evermore.

"I am satisfied, first, with the past." How many persons can look back over the past and say: "I have done my best since the day I started in on a religious life?" Let me say right here, brethren, that heaven is just the other side of where a man has done his best; and sanctification, when you bring it down to where you can get hold of it, is nothing more nor less than doing the best you can under the circumstances.[1] That's practical sanctification, and, really, I don't care much about any other sort. I want a practical religion.

"I am satisfied with the past." That's the grandest thing a man ever said—"I have done my best." I was talking some time ago with a grand old man in our State—one of the noblest men I ever knew—and he said, "Jones, I don't know what people talk so much about a second blessing for. I got all that was necessary in the first place." "Well," said I, "what do you mean?" The old man replied, "Jones, when I got religion I told the truth, and I have stuck to it

[1] Mr. Jones would insist that divine grace is a circumstance not to be left out.

ever since. When I told God I was going to quit my meanness, I quit it; I meant what I said." I asked him, "Do you mean to say you never repeated a sin you repented of?" and he said to me, "Certainly not, sir; never." Right here, brethren, I bring in this point: I have said that if we would only quit our lying we would get nine-tenths of our difficulties out of the road. Mr. Finney relates an incident that occurred at one of his revival services. One of the elders in the Presbyterian Church received an overwhelming baptism of the Holy Spirit, and that day there came in from an adjoining town an elder from another Church. At the dinner-table this elder discovered the traces and movements of divine power in the very face of his host. Finney says he himself was sitting at the table. This visiting elder looked at his host and said: "Tell me how you have received such heavenly baptism? How did you get it?" The host looked at him and answered: "I fell down on my knees and said to God, 'I have told my last lie. I will never tell thee another while I live', and the Holy Ghost descended on me, and I have been so gloriously filled since that time I scarcely know whether I am in the body or out." This elder to whom the host was speaking then jumped up from the table, and ran into a sitting-room near by, and fell down on his knees and prayed: "My God, I have told my last lie. I will never tell another on my knees or off my knees in my life," and when they arose and walked from the dinner-table the holy blessing fairly beamed. He had received the baptism, and went on his way rejoicing.

Brethren, that's our trouble. We have been promising God all our life that we would quit our meanness and get to doing right, but we never have done it. If I were to stop at this point and ask every Christian in the house who never told God a lie to stand up, how many do you suppose could stand up and say: "I told God the truth at the beginning, and have stuck to it to this hour. I said I would quit my meanness, and I did it. I said I would do right, and I have done it."

I want to tell you that every man's condemnation is bottomed on this one word, neglect. Take the best citizen in this town, and let him be everything else you want him to be, and yet let him neglect to pay his debts, and there isn't a tramp on your streets who would have any respect for him. Isn't that a fact? My duty is my debt to

God, and if I neglect to pay my debts to God, there isn't an angel in heaven who would respect me, even if I had sneaked in there unnoticed.

Duty! "I am satisfied with the past, with myself as a father. I have set a good example, and have led a Christian life before my children." "I am satisfied with myself as a mother; I have done my duty to my children." "I am satisfied with myself as a member of the Church. I have kept my vows to it." Brethren, here's a source of joy—"I have done my best from the time I started until this hour." Can you say that? Brethren, did you ever, when your innocent children played about in your lap, say: "I am the purest father God ever blessed with children?" Did you ever say that? Mother, have you looked at your innocent children, as they threw their soft, white arms around your neck, and said: "I am the purest mother God ever blessed with children?" What is your home life? "I am satisfied. I have done my duty." Sister, you may be satisfied with some things in your home to-night, but you'll be very much dissatisfied later along. You card-playing fathers and mothers! Playing cards with your children! You may think that's very nice now, but when you turn out on the streets of this city three more gamblers from your so-called Christian home, you are going to get very much dissatisfied with the way you have made things at your house.

I think statistics will bear me out when I assert that nine out of every ten gamblers in this country were raised in Christian—so-called Christian—homes. They are refined, educated, and well raised men—many of them—and they come from the homes where mother and father have dedicated them to God, and, it may be, had them baptized in the name of the Trinity.

I want to say another thing. People say, "Jones, you hit a little thing as hard as you hit a big thing." Yes, I do, brethren. The Church is paralyzed in this country. It hasn't the power, and we may just as well acknowledge it. Hear me! It is not lying that is hurting the Church, nor stealing, nor drink. It is not this kind of meanness that is hurting the Church. Every body knows that Church members who do these things are vagabonds, and pays no attention to them. Hear me. If you want to know what is demoralizing the Church, and paralyzing the Church, I'll tell you. It is this tide of worldliness that is sweeping over the Christian homes of this country. That's it! O, my sister, the day you entered society you laid down your piety, and you know it as well as I do, and you have learned that when a woman gives up her consecrated life to enter society, she begins a life of misery that hardly a damned spirit can exceed in bitterness.

Now, when you can say, "I am satisfied with the past, with the way I have lived before my family, my church, my community, satisfied with my example in all respects," you are laying the foundation for Spiritual joy.

Then the next point is, "I am contented with the present." When a man looks back with the consciousness that he has done his best, and is contented with the present, he is rich, and rich enough. St. Paul said: "I have learned, in whatsoever state I am, therewith to be content." He said another thing on that line: "Godliness with contentment is a great gain." Brother, contentment is one of the elements of real Scriptural joy in this life. When a man builds on God's pattern, and is contented with his lot, and is hopeful for the future, that man is happy anywhere and everywhere.

Hear me, brethren. Hope, as it shines out of a consecrated past and a contented present, is like the mile-posts on the way to God, telling us how far we have come, and how much further we have to go. Thank God for hope in the Christian life, and we sing:

> "O, what a blessed hope is ours
> While here on earth we stay!"

Satisfied with the past, contented with the present, hopeful for the future—a joyous Christian—you will find the secret right along in there.

Now, brethren, what are you going to do? Thank God, you can do something; thank God, there is only one thing necessary to be done. Quit your meanness. Go to God in honest penitence and tell him: "My Lord, this night I burn up the cards; this night I turn out the wines and entertainments; this night I draw the line, and I come over to God's side. Good Lord, forgive me for the way I have lived as a professor of religion." Then comes in the pardon.

O, mothers, fathers, let's call a halt; let us bring these matters to an understanding at our homes, and say, "We are done." Let us call a halt, and, on our knees before God, repent of these things.

I want to live before God and my family, so that when I come to die I can say to my children, "Go and live just as your father has lived, and do just as he has done, and as certain as Christ died for sinners, some of these days we will all meet in heaven."

Satisfied with the past, content with the present, and hopeful for the future! This gives me the attitude and the altitude where I can rejoice evermore.

Then we take the next verse, "Pray without ceasing." You say, "I can see how a fellow can act when he can rejoice evermore, but to talk about praying without ceasing—that is all foolishness. A man has got to work; he has got to do other things. A man can't pray all the time. That won't do at all." I heard of a fellow once who had so much work to do on a certain day that he had to lay all down and stop and pray three hours in order to get through with it. Well, you say, "That is the biggest foolishness I ever heard of in my life." Do you see that engine stopping yonder? The schedule of that passenger train is forty-five miles an hour, and that train has stopped still. I look at it and I say: "What does this all mean? The engineer has stopped, and he is on schedule time. Why doesn't he go on? What has he stopped for? He has stopped one minute, two minutes, three minutes, five minutes. O, why doesn't he go on?" I look a little closer, and I see he is taking on coal and letting water into the tender. He has spent six minutes at the station, and has secured a supply of coal and water, and now he says to himself: "I have lost six minutes, but I have got steam power enough to carry me along sixty miles an hour if I want to go that fast; but if I had run by that coal station I would have got stalled on the first grade. But now I have power enough to carry me through." I will tell you, brethren, when you run up to God Almighty's coal and water station, you must take on enough for your needs. That is it. That is the way to get steam to make the trip. That is the meaning of prayer.

I will say a thing now, and I would say it loud enough for all the earth to hear me. We have got men that won't pray in public and won't pray in their families. Do you want to know why that is? It is because they don't pray anywhere. Hear me. I want to be understood now, if you don't understand anything else to-night. The man who really prays anywhere, will pray everywhere. The man who maintains secret prayer will pray everywhere in God's world that you call on him. You say the reason you don't pray in your family is just because you are timid. That is a lie. It is because you are mean, and you know it. Talk about a great big fellow, with whiskers six inches long, who will go downtown on 'Change and talk bigger than any man in the pit, and he won't go home and pray with his children. "You know I would do it," he says, "if I were not so timid." Look here. If a man doesn't pray in his family there is but one reason for it, and that is because he doesn't live right before his family. I know what I am talking about. I recollect once since I was converted I got up one morning out of humor, and I said some things I had no business to say. I had the dyspepsia they said. It was meanness. Every time a fellow gets his meanness off, it is dyspepsia. Do you hear that, wife? As I said, I was talking right smart around that morning, and directly, just before the break-fast bell rang, wife got down the Bible. I looked at it, and I would have given fifty dollars that morning if I had some preacher there to have prayer in the family for me. O, how I hated to get down after talking that way. Brother, when you get to living right before your family, it is just as easy to pray before them as it is to sit down and eat before them. If I didn't have sense enough to pray in my family, I'll tell you what I would do. I would go and hire me an old colored man that wife and children had confidence in, and I would pay him by the month to come and hold family prayer for me. I would.

Talk about a man being religious who does not pray in his family! Ridiculous! I found out long ago that religion is a good thing to have, and a father who becomes religious wants his wife and children to have all the good things in the world; and the next thing you hear from him he will be leading in prayer and demon-strating his religion in his family, and they will fall into line with him. Brother, if you don't pray in your family, go home and begin to-night. Do you hear that? Begin to-night.

"Pray without ceasing." How many people in this house hold family prayer and go to the theater? How many people in this house that pray in their families, play cards in their families? How many people in this house who give wine suppers pray at night and morning with the children? Ah, brother, those things won't mix, and you needn't tell me they will. They won't. Pray in your families. I like family prayer, and I can't get along without it at my house.

I want to get God's old family prayer elevator down into my house every night, and let wife and children get into it and all go to heaven for a few minutes, and then come back and go to bed. And then in the morning before the breakfast bell rings, down comes God's old family prayer elevator, and we will all get into it for a few minutes and go to heaven, and come back and get our breakfast and go to work. If I can just get wife and children to heaven that way a few years, they will be such children that when they come to die, they will go to heaven as naturally as they breathe. The Lord save my home. If there is one thought that my mind dwells upon in restful, peaceful moments, it is when I am looking ahead to that happy time when I shall dwell with my wife and loved ones in heaven. Mother, children, all of us at home in heaven forever! Then will I have received pay for every lick I have ever struck for God and right on this side of the grave. God bless and save you, brethren.

12.

Josiah Strong

Our Country
(1886)

Josiah Strong's best-selling volume, *Our Country*, captured many aspects of the Evangelical temper of its day: the fear of the urban proletariat, the dangers of the increasing concentration of wealth, and the perils of intemperance, "Popery," Mormonism, and socialism. But while its purpose was to raise funds for home missions by alarming churchgoers, it also struck an essentially hopeful, even militant note in its assertion of the inevitable destiny of the white, Anglo-Saxon Protestant mission of the Americans to save the world. Strong's book captures the patriotic nationalism which was to propel America into its belated efforts at imperialism following the Spanish-American War. But the book is also important for its reassertion of the old Puritan doctrine of stewardship or "the law of sacrifice." America was now a wealthy nation, as Strong's statistics demonstrated. It professed to be a Christian nation. Its obligation therefore was to give to "the Lord's work" or "to the advancement of the Kingdom of God on Earth" an increasng proportion of that wealth. This selection from Strong's final chapter emphasizes that buoyant optimism which Evangelicalism continued to display despite the doubts of men like Moody about the future. There is no doubt that statistically Americans give more money to religion and charity per capita than any other people in the world and they also donate large parts of their taxes (with some grumbling at the lack of thanks) to programs like the Marshall Plan, Foreign Aid, and the Peace Corps. Strong's book straddles two eras: his emphasis upon stewardship and upon "cooperative production" in this chapter mark the changing mood of Evangelicalism as it veered from an *individualistic* to a *social* gospel. The advancement of the Kingdom of God on Earth became the theme of the Social Gospel movement at the turn of the century and Strong eventually was swept up in this new reorientation in American religious thought. Unlike Moody's Evangelicalism which feared that the world was growing "worse and worse," Strong's Evangelical message looked forward to the new era of Liberal Protestantism with its emphasis upon the social teachings of Jesus and its desire to keep the doctrines and intellectual work of the churches in rapport with the latest findings of science and biblical scholarship. [This selection is from the second edition of 1891.]

CHAPTER XV. MONEY AND THE KINGDOM

Average Annual Increase of Wealth of Church-Members in the United States from 1880 to 1890, $434,790,000.

Contributions to Home and Foreign Missions in 1890, $10,695,259.

Property is one of the cardinal facts of our civilization. It is the great object of endeavor, the great spring of power, the great occasion of discontent, and one of the great sources of danger. For Christians to apprehend their true relations to money, and the relations of money to the kingdom of Christ and its progress in the world, is to find the key to many of the great problems now pressing for solution.

Money is power in the concrete. It commands learning, skill, experience, wisdom, talent, influence, numbers. It represents the school, the college, the church, the printing-press, and all evangelizing machinery. It confers on the wise man a sort of omnipresence. By means of it, the same man may, at the same moment, be founding an academy among the Mormons, teaching the New Mexicans, building a home missionary church in Dakota, translating the Scriptures in Africa, preaching the gospel in China, and uttering the precepts of ten thousand Bibles in India. It is the modern miracle worker; it has a wonderful multiplying and transforming power. Sarah Hosmer, of Lowell, though a poor woman, supported a student in the Nestorian Seminary, who became a preacher of Christ. Five times she gave fifty dollars, earning the money in a factory, and sent out five native pastors to Christian work. When more than sixty years old, she longed to furnish Nestoria with one more preacher of Christ; and, living in an attic, she took in sewing until she had accomplished her cherished purpose. In the hands of this consecrated woman, money transformed the factory girl and the seamstress into a missionary of the Cross, and then multiplied her six-fold. God forbid that I should attribute to money power which belongs only to faith, love, and the Holy Spirit. In the problem of Christian work, money is like the cipher, worthless alone, but multiplying many fold the value and effectiveness of other factors.

In the preceding chapter has been set forth the wonderful opportunity enjoyed by this generation in the United States. It lays on us a commensurate obligation. We have also seen (Chap. X.) that our wealth is stupendous. If our responsibility is without a precedent, the plenitude of our power is likewise without a parallel. Is not the lesson which God would have us learn so plain that he who runs may read it? Has not God given us this matchless power that it may be applied to doing this matchless work?

The kingdoms of this world will not have become the kingdoms of our Lord until the money power has been Christianized. "Talent has been Christianized already on a large scale. The political power of states and kingdoms has been long assumed to be, and now at least really is, as far as it becomes their accepted office to maintain personal security and liberty. Architecture, arts, constitutions, schools, and learning have been largely Christianized. But the money power, which is one of the most operative and grandest of all, is only beginning to be; though with promising tokens of a finally complete reduction to Christ and the uses of His Kingdom. . . . That day, when it comes, is the morning, so to speak, of the new creation.[1] Is it not time for that day to dawn? If we would Christianize our Anglo-Saxon civilization, which is to spread itself over the earth, has not the hour come for the Church to teach and live the doctrines of God's Word touching possessions? Their general acceptance on the part of the church would involve a reformation scarcely less important in its results than the great Reformation of the sixteenth century. What is needed is not simply an increased giving, an enlarged estimate of the "Lord's share," but a *radically different conception* of our relations to our possessions. Most Christian men need to discover that they are not proprietors, apportioning their own, but simply trustees or managers of God's property. All Chris-

[1] Horace Bushnell, *Sermons on Living Subjects* (New York, 1872), pp. 264–265.

tians would admit that there is a sense in which their all belongs
to God, but deem it a very poetical sense, wholly unpractical and
practically unreal. The great majority treat their possessions exactly
as they would treat property, use their substance exactly as if it
were their own.

Christians generally hold that God has a thoroughly real claim
on some portion of their income, possibly a tenth, more likely no
definite proportion; but some small part, they acknowledge, belongs
to him, and they hold themselves in duty bound to use it for him.
This low and unchristian view has sprung apparently from a mis-
conception of the Old Testament doctrine of tithes. God did not,
for the surrender of a part, renounce all claim to the remainder....
Tithes were devoted to certain uses, specified by God, in recognition
of the fact that all belonged to him.

The Principle Stated

God's claim to the whole rests on exactly the same ground as
his claim to a part. As the Creator, he must have an absolute ownership in all his creatures; and, if an absolute claim could be strengthened, it would be by the fact that he who gave us life sustains it,
and with his own life redeemed it. "Ye are not your own; for ye
are bought with a price" (I Cor. vi, 19, 20). Manifestly, if God
has absolute ownership in us, we can have absolute ownership in
nothing whatever. If we cannot lay claim to our own selves, how
much less to that which we find in our hands. . . . Here, then, is
the principle always applicable, that *of our entire possessions, every
dollar, every cent, is to be employed in the way that will best
honor God.*

The Principle Applied

The statement of this principle at once suggests difficulties in its
application. Let us glance at some of them. . . .

If every man did his duty, gave according to ability, there would
be abundant provision for all Christian and philanthropic work,
and substance left for the patronage of art. But not one man in a
hundred is doing his duty; hence those who appreciate the necessities of Christian work must fill the breach, are not at liberty to
make expenditures which would otherwise be wholly justifiable....

God has laid upon Christian nations the work of evangelizing the heathen world. He has laid on us the duty of Christianizing our own heathen, and under such conditions that the obligation presses with an overwhelming urgency. If this duty were accepted by all Christians, the burden would rest lightly upon each; but great multitudes in the church are shirking all responsibility. . . .

The general acceptance, by the Church, of the Christian principle that every penny is to be used in the way that will best honor God, would cause every channel of benevolence to overflow its banks, and occasion a blessed freshet of salvation throughout the world. "But," says some one, "that principle demands daily self-denial." Undoubtedly; and that fact is the Master's seal set to its truth. "If any man will come after me, let him deny himself, and take up his cross DAILY, and follow me" (Luke ix, 23).

And there are no exceptions to this law of sacrifice; it binds all alike. Christian people will agree that missionaries are called to make great sacrifices for Christ; but why does the obligation rest on them any more than on all? Does the missionary belong absolutely to God? No less do we. Do the love and sacrifice of Christ lay him under boundless obligation? Christ died for every man. Why is not the rich man in America under as great obligation to practice self-sacrifice for the salvation of the heathen as the missionary in Central Africa, provided his sacrifice can be made fruitful of their good? And that is exactly the provision which is made by missionary boards to-day. They establish channels of inter-communication which bring us into contact with all heathendom, and make Africa, which, centuries ago, fell among thieves, and has ever since been robbed and sore wounded, our neighbor. To live in luxury, and then leave a legacy for missions, does not fulfill the law of sacrifice. Every steward is responsible for the disposition of his trust made by will. The obligation still rests upon him to bestow his possessions where, after his death, they will do most for God. Legacies to benevolent societies ought to be greatly multiplied, and would be, if the principle of Christian stewardship were accepted; but such a legacy cannot compound for an unconsecrated life. If the priest or Levite, who passed by on the other side, wrote a codicil to his will, providing for wounded wayfarers, I fear it was hardly counted unto him for righteousness, was hardly a proof that he loved his neighbor as himself. Christ said: "Go ye into all the world, and preach the gospel;" and he did not say it to the twelve, but to the whole body of believers. If we cannot go in person, we are under obligations to go by proxy. The rich man has more power to send than the missionary has to go; he can, perhaps, send a dozen. And why is he not called to make as great sacrifices in *sending* as the missionary in *going*?[2] The obligations of all men rest on the same grounds. The law of sacrifice is universal. Bishop Butler said to his secretary: "I should be ashamed of myself, if I could leave ten thousand pounds behind me." Many professed Christians die disgracefully and "wickedly rich." The shame and sin, however, lie not in the fact that the power was gathered, but that it was unwielded.

It is the duty of some men to make a great deal of money. God has given to them the money-making talent; and it is as wrong to bury that talent as to bury a talent for preaching. It is every man's duty to wield the widest possible power for righteousness: and the power in money must be gained before it can be used. But let a man beware! This power in money is something awful. It is more dangerous than dynamite. The victims of "saint-seducing

[2]Glance at some of the sacrifices of missionaries who go to the frontier. Writing to the *Congregational Union* for aid to build a parsonage, one says:

"Am sleeping in a shack three miles from town, and taking my meals at the hotel. Not a house or building of any kind to be had to live in. My family are in Ohio, awaiting arrangements for a home. Can you help us?"

Another writes: "During the first two years' service here, was obliged to live in Seattle, seven miles away, going to and fro on foot. For one year since, have occupied such a building as I could erect in thirty days, with my own hands."

Another: "My wife and myself, with our daughter of six years, have been doing our best to live (if it can be called living) in an attic of a store. It is all unfinished inside. By putting up a board partition we have two rooms. To reach our rooms we have to go around to the rear of the store, and make our way among boxes, barrels, tin cans, etc., to the foot of the outside stairway that leads to our attic. We are doing our best to keep warm; but with mercury twenty degrees below zero we do not find it easy. Then for these accommodations, which are the best and all we can get, we have to pay $10 a month. Our salary is only $500. Cannot the Union loan us $250 to help us build?"

Another, writing for a loan, says, "My family of seven lived all summer in a house twelve by sixteen, having only two rooms."

Many are heroically enduring hardship for the Kingdom, at the front, whose sacrifices would be less if ours were greater, whose sufferings could be relieved if our luxuries were curtailed.

gold" are numberless. If a Christian grows rich, it should be with
fear and trembling, lest the "deceitfulness of riches" undo him; for
Christ spoke of the salvation of a rich man as something miraculous
(Luke xviii, 24–27).

Let no man deceive himself by saying: "I will give when I have
amassed wealth. I desire money that I may do good with it; but
I will not give now, that I may give the more largely in the future."
That is the pit in which many have perished. If a man is growing
large in wealth, nothing but constant and generous giving can save
him from growing small in soul. In determining the amount of
his gifts and the question whether he should impair his capital, or
to what extent, a man should never lose sight of a distinct and
intelligent aim to do the greatest possible good in a life-time. Each
must decide for himself what is the wisest, the highest, use of money;
and we need often to remind ourselves of the constant tendency
of human nature to selfishness and self-deception. . . .

There were, in 1890, 13,411,000[3] members of Evangelical Protestant churches in the United States. The accompanying table gives
their contributions to home missions[4] for the fiscal year closing
in 1890.

Of course a great deal of money was given to various benevolences of which there could be no record, but $6,717,000 repre-
sents approximately what was given through the regular denomina-

[3]*New York Independent* (July 31, 1890.) [The figure quoted by Strong is not
given in the July 31 issue.] The religious statistics of the Eleventh Census are
not yet available, but as those of the *Independent* and of the Census were
compiled by the authority, Rev. H. K. Carroll, D.D., the former, which are
used in this division, are presumably reliable.

[4]In "home missions" are included in this instance the ordinary domestic
missions, mission church building, work among the Mormons, New Mexicans,
colored people, Indians and Chinese in the United States and the work of the
missionary department of the denominational publishing societies. Of course
city missions are "home missions," but the city missionary work of local
churches is not included because it is impossible to get anything more than
fragmentary statistics concerning it.

The accompanying table includes only 11,889,427 of the evangelical church
membership in the United States in 1890. But the remainder is made up of
colored people (600,000) and foreigners who give very little to missions, and
of small denominations which, so far as I can learn, have no regular denominational channels through which they give to home missionary objects. If the
gift of these denominations to missions could be ascertained, they would not
very materially change our total.

Contributions to Home Missions in 1890

	Membership	Contribution	Average per caput
Congregational	491,985	$1,365,507.55	$2.77
Presbyterian—North	753,749	1,137,205.80	1.50
Protestant Episcopal	470,076	657,018.31	1.39
Moravian	11,358	15,594.15	1.37
Evangelical Association	145,703	183,330.38	1.25
United Presbyterian	101,858	111,644.40	1.09
Primitive Methodist	5,502	5,453.01	.99
Baptist—North	780,000	633,267.74	.81
Reformed (Dutch)	88,812	66,128.66	.78
Wesleyan Methodist	18,000	12,000.00*	.66
Reformed Presbyterian	6,800	3,786.78	.55
Seventh-Day Baptist	9,000	4,857.29	.53
Presbyterian—South	161,742	74,003.96	.45
Methodist Epis.—North	2,236,463	891,850.00	.39
Disciple	750,000	216,279.44	.28
Reformed (German)	194,044	45,000.00*	.23
Lutheran	1,188,876	268,358.62	.22
Baptist—South	1,100,000	244,334.26	.22
Methodist Epis.—South	1,161,666	245,836.37	.21
United Brethren	199,709	38,653.29	.19
Cumberland Presbyterian	160,185	27,216.39	.16
Free-Will Baptist	86,297	13,073.88	.15
Methodist Protestant	147,604	11,842.00	.08
Free Methodist	19,998	1,525.70	.07
Baptist—Colored	1,200,000	40,432.47	.03
African Meth. Epis.	400,000	9,000.00*	.02
American Bible Soc.		173,640.00*	
American S.S. Union		86,326.94*	
American Tract Soc.		93,673.90	
Massachusetts Bible Soc.		24,316.74	
Am. Seamen's Friend Soc.		15,500.00*	
Western Tract Soc.		9,000.00*	
	11,889,427	$6,717,558.03	.56

*Estimated.

tional channels for home missions, which is an average of fifty-six cents per member. If, however, we include the several hundred thousand church members whose denominations report no home missionary contributions, and bear in mind that a considerable portion of the above sum was given by church-goers who were not church-members and that another large portion was made up of legacies—the gifts of the dead—we may fairly say that the home missionary contributions of the evangelical church-membership in 1890 did not average more than fifty cents per caput.[5] . . . The great majority of church-members give only a trifle or nothing at all for the work of missions.

During the year 1889–1890 contributions in the United States for foreign missions were $3,977,701.[6] A total of $10,695,259 for home and foreign missions sounds like a large sum. But great and small are relative terms. Compared with the need of the world and the ability of the church it is pitiable indeed. Look at that ability. The Christian religion, by rendering men temperate, industrious, and moral, makes them prosperous. There are but few of the very poor in our churches. The great question has come to be: "How can we reach the masses?" Church-membership is made up chiefly of the well-to-do and the rich.[7] On the other hand, a majority of the membership is composed of women, who control less money than men. It is, therefore, fair to say that the church-member is at least as well off as the average citizen. In 1890, one in every 4.7 of the population was a member of some evangelical church, that is, 21.92 per cent of all the people. We may reasonably infer, then, that this percentage of the wealth of the United States, or $13,076,-300,000 was in the hands of evangelical church-members at that time; and this takes no account of the immense capital in brains and muscles. Of this great wealth *one thirty-second part of one per cent* or one dollar out of 3,287, was given in 1890 to foreign

[5]This is a decided advance on ten years before, when home and foreign missions together received only about fifty cents for each church-member.

[6]*Almanac for 1891 issued by the American Board of Commissioners for Foreign Missions* (Boston), p. 35.

[7]*The Century* says that, of the fifty leading business men of Columbus, Ohio, and Springfield, Mass. (if we are not mistaken in the unnamed cities), four-fifths are attendants upon the churches and supporters of them, while three-fifths are communicants.

missions for the salvation of seven or eight hundred million heathen.
We do not know what the income of our church-members is, but
if in 1890 they had spent every cent of wages, salary and other
income on themselves and had given to home and foreign missions
only *one-hundredth part* of their real and personal property (which
would have been unspeakably mean and unchristian) their contribution would have been $130,763,000 instead of $10,695,259. For
the one item of uncut jewels, largely consisting of diamonds, the
people of the United States in 1888 paid $10,000,000; and in 1880,
church-members paid out nearly six times as much for sugar and
molasses as for the world's salvation, seven times as much for boots
and shoes, sixteen times as much for cotton and woolen goods,
eleven times as much for meat, and eighteen times as much for
bread. From 1880 to 1890 the average annual increase of the
wealth of church-members was $434,790,000. And this, remember,
was over and above all expense of living and all benevolences!
That is, the average annual increase of wealth in the hands of professed Christians was forty times greater than their offering to missions, home and foreign. How that offering looks, when compared
with their wealth and its annual increase, may be seen on the
opposite page.

If the members of our Sunday-schools in America, gave, each,
one cent a Sabbath to missions, it would aggregate about one-half
as much as is now secured, with endless writing and pleading and
praying, from our entire church-membership. If each of these professed Christians gave five cents—the price of one cigar—once a
week, it would amount in a year to $35,000,000. If each gave one
cent every day to that which he professes is the object of his life—
the building of the Kingdom—it would amount to $49,202,000.

Immense sums are invested freely if there is only a chance of
large dividends. The *Times of India* says that "nearly $25,000,000
have been invested in search for gold in India, and that not $2,500
worth of the precious metal has been obtained after three years
of labor." Christians have opportunities to invest, and with perfect
security, where they will realize thirty, sixty, a hundred-fold—that
is three thousand, six thousand, ten thousand per cent—yet how
few and small the investments!

Seventy businessmen of New York subscribed $1,400,000, or

$20,000 each, toward the Metropolitan Opera House in that city, which was completed a few years ago; and this without receiving or expecting pecuniary return. Where are the seventy men who will give one-half that amount to home missions? Is the love of Italian opera a more powerful motive than love of country, love of souls, and love of Christ?

It is estimated[8] that in 1889 the liquor bill of the nation was $1,000,000,000. As comparatively few women and children use intoxicating drinks, and many men do not, it is safe to say that this bill was paid by one quarter or one-fifth of the population. That is, in 1890, about 13,000,000 people paid $1,000,000,000 for liquors, and a like number of professed Christians gave $10,-695,000 for missions. Any one that did not know better might naturally infer that the one class loves beer and whiskey better than the other loves souls.

A while ago a brutal prize-fighter got a purse of $12,000 for pounding an opponent into pulp. Money can be had in abundance for illegitimate uses, but a thousand interests, dear to the Master as the apple of his eye, must languish for the lack of funds. We have seen that there is no lack of wealth; there is money enough in the hands of church-members to sow every acre of the earth with the seed of truth; but the average Christian deems himself a despot over his purse. God has intrusted to his children power enough to give the gospel to every creature by the close of this century; but it is being misapplied. Indeed, the world would have been evangelized long ago, if Christians had perceived the relations of money to the Kingdom, and had accepted their stewardship. . . . Christ's refusal to be made a king, and his rejection of Satan's offer of the world's scepter, ought to teach those who seek to save the world that moral means are necessary to moral ends. Christ saw that the world could not be saved by legislation, that only by his being "lifted up" could all men be drawn unto him. He saw that he could not save the world without sacrificing for it; no more can we. The saving power of the Church is its sacrificing power.

The gospel is the radical cure of the world's great evils, and its promulgation, like its spirit, requires sacrifice. Money is the sinews of spiritual warfare as well as carnal, and a sufficient

[8]*The Cyclopedia of Temperance and Prohibition* (New York, 1891), p. 137.

amount of it would enable us to meet these perils with the gospel. Christianize the immigrant and he will be easily Americanized. Christianity is the solvent of all race antipathies. Give the Romanist a pure gospel and he will cease to be a Romanist. It has already been shown that Christian education will solve the Mormon problem. The temperance reform, like all others which depend on popular agitation, must have money, and is being retarded by the lack of it. Concerning the remedy for socialism, accept the opinion of an economist who has made it a subject of special study. Says Prof. Ely: "It is an undoubted fact that modern socialism of the worst type is spreading to an alarming extent among our laboring classes, both foreign and native. I think the danger is of such a character as should arouse the Christian people of this country to most earnest efforts for the evangelization of the poorer classes, particularly in large cities. What is needed is Christianity, and the Christian Church can do far more than political economists toward a reconciliation of social classes. The Church's remedy for social discontent and dynamite bombs is Christianity as taught in the New Testament. Now in all this you will find nothing new. It is only significant in this regard: others have come to these conclusions from the study of the Bible; from a totally different starting point, from the study of political economy, I have come to the same goal."*

But the acceptance of the Christian doctrine concerning property would have a direct, as well as indirect, influence on socialism. Let us therefore dwell a moment on the subject. In the popular ferment, a hundred years ago, which culminated in the French Revolution, the demand was for equal rights and the watchword was *Liberty*. There is a popular ferment throughout Europe to-day which is more universal and extends to the United States. The popular demand now is equality of condition, and the watch word is *Property* —a cry the meaning of which the dullest and most earthly can understand. This movement, which is steadily gathering force, results from the two most striking facts of the nineteenth century:

*From a letter by Prof. R. T. Ely to Rev. H. A. Schauffler, D.D. I regret that lack of space forbids my quoting the entire letter, which may be found in *Home Missionary*, 58 (October 1884), 227–229 [Ely's letter is dated May 26, 1884, and is addressed to Samuel H. Virgin.]

first, the general diffusion of knowledge through the press, which has wonderfully multiplied wants up and down the entire social scale; and, second, the creation of immense wealth by means of the steam engine. But this wealth, which is necessary to the satisfaction of these wants, has been massed. In a word, the difficulty is *knowledge multiplied and popularized, and wealth multiplied and centralized.*

The right distribution of property, which is the kernel of the social question, is the great problem of our civilization; and it may well be doubted whether the true solution will be found until the Church accepts, both in doctrine and practice, the teachings of God's Word touching possessions. For the Church is responsible for public opinion on all moral questions, and no great question of rights can be settled for the world until Christian men come into right relations with it.

The inexorable law of our present industrial system is that the cost of subsistence determines the rate of wages. This makes no provision for the higher wants of increasing intelligence, and therefore insures an increasing popular discontent. It would seem that the solution of the great difficulties between capital and labor must be found in some form of co-operation by which the workman will be admitted to a just share in the profits of his labor. Professor Cairns, who is considered one of the greatest economists England has produced, believes that co-operative production affords the laboring classes "the sole means of escape from a harsh and hopeless destiny" (*Leading Principles*, p. 338). Referring to several thousand co-operative societies in England, having some millions of capital, Thomas Hughes says: "I still look to this movement as the best hope for England and other lands." The eminent statistician, Carroll D. Wright," Commissioner of the Department of Labor, Washington, referring to the duty of the rich manufacturer to regard himself as "an instrument of God for the upbuilding of the race," and the promotion of the highest welfare of those in his employ, says: "This may sound like sentiment. I am willing to call it sentiment; but I know it means the best material prosperity, and that every

⁹[Carroll Davidson Wright (1840–1909), statistician, economist, lawyer, served as first Chief of the Massachusetts Bureau of Labor Statistics and as U.S. Commissioner of Labor.]

employer who has been guided by such sentiments has been rewarded twofold: first, in witnessing the wonderful improvement of
his people, and, second, in seeing his dividends increase, and the
wages of his operatives increase with his dividends. The factory
system of the future will be run on this basis. The instances of such
are multiplying rapidly now."[10] Manifestly, the acceptance on the
part of Christian capitalists of the scriptural doctrine of possessions
would greatly facilitate the introduction of co-operation or any other
plan which promised justice to the workman.

The Christian man who is not willing to make the largest profits
which an honest regard for the laws of trade permits is a rare
man. But the laws of trade permit much that the laws of God do
not permit. Many transactions are commercially honest which are
not righteous. If, now, a man accepts the truth that his possessions
are a trust to be administered for God's glory, he will not consent
to increase them by any unrighteous means. And since justice and
righteousness, like honesty, will prove to be the best *policy*, the
acceptance on the part of Christian men of a thoroughly righteous
plan of co-operation between capital and labor would eventually
compel its general acceptance. Let Christian men gain a correct
conception of their relations to their possessions, let them accept
the duty of Christian stewardship, and it would command their
getting as well as their spending. There would be no motive to drive
a sharp bargain. It would purify trade. It would mediate between
capital and labor. It would destroy the foundation on which the
rising structure of socialism rests. It would cut one of the principal
roots of popular unbelief; for extended inquiry in Cincinnati elicited
the almost unanimous response that the reason workingmen neglect
the churches is that there are on the church rolls the names of
employers who wrong their employees.

The acceptance of the true principle of Christian giving is urged
upon us by the fact that money is power, which is needed everywhere for elevating and saving men. It is further urged upon us by
the fact that only such a view of possessions will save us from the
great and imminent perils of wealth. God might have sent his
angels to sing his gospel through the world, or he might have

[10]For a history of profit-sharing see Nicholas Paine Gilman, *Profit-Sharing
Between Employer and Employee* (Boston, 1889).

written it on the sky, and made the clouds his messengers; but we
need to bear the responsibility of publishing that gospel. He might
make the safe of every benevolent society a gold mine as unfailing
as the widow's cruse of oil; but we need to give that gold. The
tendency of human nature, intensified by our commercial activity,
is to make the life a whirlpool—a great maelstrom which draws
everything into itself. What is needed to-day is a grand reversal
of the movement, a transformation of the life into a fountain. And
in an exceptional degree is this the need of Anglo-Saxons. Their
strong love of liberty, and their acquisitiveness, afford a powerful
temptation to offer some substitute for self-abnegation. We would
call no man master; we must take Christ as master. We would
possess all things; we must surrender all things.

One of the grave problems before us is how to make great
material prosperity conduce to individual advancement. The severest
poverty is unfavorable to morality. Up to a certain point increase
of property serves to elevate man morally and intellectually, while
it improves him physically. But, as nations grow rich, they are prone
to become self-indulgent, effeminate, immoral. The physical nature
becomes less robust, the intellectual nature less vigorous, the moral
less pure. The pampered civilizations of old had to be reinvigorated,
from time to time, with fresh infusions of barbaric blood—a remedy
no longer available. If we cannot find in Christianity a remedy or
preventive, our Christian civilization and the world itself is a failure;
and our rapidly increasing wealth, like the "cankered heaps of
strange-achieved gold," will curse us unto destruction.

But the recognition of God's ownership in all our substance is a
perfect antidote for the debilitating and corrupting influence of
wealth. It prevents self-indulgence, and the apprehension of religious truth implied in such recognition affords the strongest possible motives to sacrifice and active effort of which men are capable.
A hundred years ago poverty compelled men to endure hardness,
and so served to make the nation great. Now that we are exposed
to the pampering influence of riches, Christian principle must inspire
the spirit of self-denial for Christ's sake, and the world's sake, and
so make the nation greater.

Where that spirit obtains, Mammonism and materialism, as well
as luxuriousness, lose their power, and wealth, instead of being

centralized, is distributed. So that Christian stewardship, so far as it is accepted, affords perfect protection against all the perils of wealth.

Our cities, which are gathering together the most dangerous elements of our civilization, will, in due time, unless Christianized, prove the destruction of our free institutions. During the last hundred years, the instruments of destruction have been wonderfully multiplied. Offensive weapons have become immeasurably more effective. Not so the means of defense. Your life is in the hand of every man you meet. Society is safe to-day only so far as every man becomes a law unto himself. The lawless classes are growing much more rapidly than the whole population; and nothing but the gospel can transform lawless men and women into good citizens.

The number of missionaries in our cities ought to be increased ten- or twenty-fold; and their work is expensive. It is usually the densest populations which are most neglected, and in such quarters mission chapels cannot be built without large expenditures. If our cities are to be evangelized, laymen must greatly enlarge their ideas of the demands of the work, and of their pecuniary responsibility for it.

The perils which have been discussed (Chaps. IV.-XI.) have, all of them with the single exception of Mormonism, continued to grow more rapidly during the past five years than the whole population. It is also true that the membership of the evangelical churches has increased more rapidly than the population. The Church of Christ has aroused herself in some measure, but, so far as I can judge, the dangerous and destructive elements of society are still making greater progress than the conservative.

Has not the time fully come when the Church must make a new departure of some sort? And is it not evident that one of the first needs is a true view of the relations of money to the Kingdom, and such a spirit of consecration as will lay it and all else on the altar?

We have seen, in the preceding chapters, that a mighty emergency is upon us. Our country's future, and much of the world's future, depend on the way in which Christian men meet the crisis. Do you say: "I trust in God, and therefore have no fear; I believe what some one has said, 'If God intends to save the world, he cannot afford to make an exception of America.' This country is his chosen instrument of blessing to mankind; and God's plans never fail"? The difference between a true and a false faith is that one inspires action while the other paralyzes it. God saved the nation during the War of the Rebellion; but it was not by a false faith, which, with folded arms, rehearsed its confidence in the divine decrees. It was by a faith which inspired sacrifice. At the time of Paul's shipwreck, it was revealed to him that they were all to be saved; but, nevertheless, there were conditions with which they must comply, or be lost. Their salvation was *certain*, but not *necessary*; it was conditioned. I believe our country will be saved. Its salvation may be certain in the counsels of God; but it is not necessary. I believe it to be conditioned on the Church's rising to a higher spirit of sacrifice.

When the drum beat the nation to battle, a generation ago, no sacrifice was too great; wives gave their husbands, parents gave their sons. A Christian mother had sent seven sons into the Union army. Near the close of the war, the eighth, and only remaining son, paid a visit to his mother, and, speaking of the war said: "Mother, what would you do if one of the boys should fall in the struggle?" Turning her deep eyes upon him, she said: "God has given me nine noble sons; one he has taken to himself, seven are in the army, and I want you to understand, my son, that I *only hold you as a reserve* for your country's defense; and the first breach that you hear of as being made in our number, go quickly, and fill it; and may God take care of you, and I will take care of your children." Is it easier to give one's flesh and blood than to give silver and gold? We are engaged in what Lord Bacon called the "heroic work of making a nation," for which heroic sacrifices are demanded.

And our plea is not America for America's sake; but America for the world's sake. For, if this generation is faithful to its trust, America is to become God's right arm in his battle with the world's ignorance and oppression and sin. If I were a Christian African or Arab, I should look into the immediate future of the United States with intense and thrilling interest; for as Professor Hoppin of Yale has said: "America Christianized means the *world* Christianized." And, "If America fail," says Professor Park, "the *world* will fail." During this crisis, Christian work is unspeakably more important in the United States than anywhere else in the world. "The nations whose conversion is the most pressing necessity of the world to-day," says Professor Phelps, "are the Occidental nations. Those whose *speedy* conversion is most vital to the conversion of the rest are the nations of the Occident. The pioneer stock of mind must be the Occidental stock. The pioneer races must be the Western races. And of all the Western races, who that can read skillfully the providence of God, or can read it at all, can hesitate in affirming that the signs of divine decree point to this land of ours as the one which is fast gathering to itself the races which must take the lead in the final conflicts of Christianity for possession of the world? Ours is the elect nation for the age to come. We are the chosen people. We cannot afford to wait. The plans of God will not wait. Those plans seem to have brought us to one of the closing stages in the world's career, in which we can no longer *drift* with safety to our destiny. We are shut up to a perilous alternative. Immeasurable opportunities surround and overshadow us. Such, as I read it, is the central fact in the philosophy of American Home Missions."[11]

The emergency created by the settlement of the states and territories of the West—a grand constellation of empires—is to be met by placing in the hand of every Christian agency there at work all the power that money can wield. There is scarcely a church, or society, or institution of any kind doing God service there which is not embarrassed, or sadly crippled for lack of funds. Missionaries should be multiplied, parsonages and churches built, and colleges generously endowed. The nation's salt, with which the whole land and pre-eminently the tainted civilization of the frontier, must be sweetened, is *Christian* education. The tendency, which is so marked in many of our older and larger colleges, to develop and furnish simply the intellect, is full of peril. Divorce religion and education, and we shall fall a prey either to blundering goodness or well-schooled villainy. The young colleges of the West, like Drury,

[11]From letter read at the Home Missionary Anniversary in Chicago, June 9th, 1881. [Austin Phelps, "The Present Exigency in Home Missions," *Home Missionary,* 54 (December 1881), 227.]

Doane, Carleton, Colorado, Yankton, Fargo, and others, founded
by broad-minded and far-seeing men are characterized by a strong
religious influence, and send a surprising proportion of their gradu-
ates into the ministry. In view of their almost boundless possibilities
for usefulness in their relations to the future of the West and of
the nation, and in view of their urgent needs, it is a wonder that
those who, like Boaz, are mighty men of wealth, can deny themselves the deep and lasting pleasure of liberally endowing such
institutions. Said one who had just given fifty thousand dollars to
a Western college: "I cannot tell you what I have enjoyed. It is
like being born into the Kingdom again."

This emergency demands the acceptance of Christian stewardship,
that our great benevolent societies may be adequately furnished for
their work. They are kept constantly on their knees before the
public, and with pleas so pitiful, so moving, the marvel to me is
that, when Christian men hold their peace and their purse, the
very stones do not cry out. And, notwithstanding all their efforts
to secure means, they must, every one, scrimp at every point, decline providential calls to enlarge their work, and even retrench, in
order to close the fiscal year without a debt.

The door of opportunity is open in all the earth; organizations
have been completed, languages learned, the Scriptures translated,
and now the triumph of the Kingdom awaits only the exercise of the
power committed to the Church, but which she refuses to put forth.
If she is to keep step with the majestic march of the divine Providence, the Church must consecrate the power which is in money.

Oh! that men would accept the testimony of Christ touching
the blessedness of giving! He who sacrifices most, loves most; and
he who loves most, is most blessed. Love and sacrifice are related
to each other like seed and fruit; each produces the other. The seed
of sacrifice brings forth the fragrant fruit of love, and love always
has in its heart the seeds of new sacrifice. He who gives but a part
is not made perfect in love. Love rejoices to give all; it does not
measure its sacrifice. It was Judas, not Mary, who calculated the
value of the alabaster box of ointment. He who is infinitely blessed
is the Infinite Giver; and man, made in his likeness, was intended
to find his highest blessedness in the completest self-giving. He
who receives, but does not give, is like the Dead Sea. All the fresh

floods of Jordan cannot sweeten its dead, salt depths. So all the
streams of God's bounty cannot sweeten a heart that has no outlet;
that is ever receiving, yet never full and overflowing.

If those whose horizon is as narrow as the bushel under which
they hide their light could be induced to come out into a large
place, and take a worthy view of the Kingdom of Christ and of
their relations to it, if they could be persuaded to make the principle
of Christian giving regnant in all their life, their *happiness* would
be as much increased as their usefulness.